RADICAL ATHEISM

MERIDIAN

Crossing Aesthetics

Werner Hamacher

Editor

*Stanford
University
Press*

———————

*Stanford
California*

RADICAL ATHEISM

Derrida and the Time of Life

Martin Hägglund

Stanford University Press
Stanford, California

Printed in the United States of America
on acid-free, archival-quality paper

Library of Congress Cataloging-in-Publication Data

Hägglund, Martin.
Radical atheism : Derrida and the time of life /
Martin Hägglund.
p.   cm.—(Meridian, crossing aesthetics)
Includes bibliographical references and index.
ISBN 978-0-8047-0077-1 (cloth : alk. paper)
ISBN 978-0-8047-0078-8 (pbk. : alk. paper)
1. Derrida, Jacques—Religion.   2. Atheism.
3. Deconstruction.   4. Philosophy and religion.
I. Title.   II. Series: Meridian (Stanford, Calif.)
B2430.D484H33   2008
211'.8092—dc22
2008016110

Contents

Acknowledgments   *ix*

Introduction   1

§ 1   Autoimmunity of Time: Derrida and Kant   13

§ 2   Arche-Writing: Derrida and Husserl   50

§ 3   Arche-Violence: Derrida and Levinas   76

§ 4   Autoimmunity of Life:
       Derrida's Radical Atheism   107

§ 5   Autoimmunity of Democracy:
       Derrida and Laclau   164

Notes   *207*

Works Cited   *237*

Index   *249*

Acknowledgments

First of all, I want to thank Jonathan Culler and Richard Klein for their generous support and their insightful comments on the manuscript. I also want to thank Rodolphe Gasché and Ernesto Laclau for their responses to my work and their inspiring philosophical vigilance. My personal and intellectual friendship with David E. Johnson has been vital throughout the writing of this book. I also want to extend my profound gratitude to William Egginton and to all the other participants in our Philosophical Reading Group, for the singular intellectual energy that was channeled during our meetings.

I owe a special debt to the Swedish essayist Horace Engdahl, not only for the encouragement he has provided over the years but also for the integrity of style he has displayed as a writer. Reading Engdahl's essays taught me to always strive for clarity and to philosophize with the hammer. At various stages of the manuscript, I received valuable comments from Philip Adamek, Peter Gilgen, Anders Lundberg, Douglas McQueen-Thomson, and Jessica Smith. I am also grateful to Alberto Moreiras and Dan W. Smith for productive disagreements, and to Samir Haddad for stimulating discussions of the notion of 'lesser violence' in Derrida's thought. At the last stages of writing, I benefited from the personal generosity and intellectual inspiration of my friends in the Theory Reading Group at Cornell. A particular gratitude is due to my friend Niklas Brismar Pålsson, with whom I have shared matters of life and philosophy for more than ten years. Finally, I want to thank my parents and my sisters for always being there and for giving me more than I can comprehend.

At Stanford University Press, Norris Pope, Emily-Jane Cohen, Joe Abbott, and Tim Roberts have been exemplary in shepherding the manuscript through the publication process. An earlier version of Chapter 3 appeared in *Diacritics* 34, no. 1 (spring 2004) under the title "The Necessity of Discrimination: Disjoining Derrida and Levinas." I am grateful to the Johns Hopkins University Press for permission to reprint.

Introduction

This book presents a sustained attempt to reassess the entire trajectory of Derrida's work. Refuting the notion that there was an ethical or religious "turn" in Derrida's thinking, I demonstrate that a radical atheism informs his writing from beginning to end. Atheism has traditionally limited itself to denying the existence of God and immortality, without questioning the desire for God and immortality. Thus, in traditional atheism mortal being is still conceived as a lack of being that we desire to transcend. In contrast, by developing the logic of radical atheism, I argue that the so-called desire for immortality dissimulates a desire for survival that precedes it and contradicts it from within.

The notion of survival that I develop is incompatible with immortality, since it defines life as essentially mortal and as inherently divided by time. To survive is never to be absolutely present; it is to remain after a past that is no longer and to keep the memory of this past for a future that is not yet. I argue that every moment of life is a matter of survival, since it depends on what Derrida calls the structure of the trace. The structure of the trace follows from the constitution of time, which makes it impossible for anything to be present *in itself*. Every now passes away as soon as it comes to be and must therefore be inscribed as a trace in order to be at all. The trace enables the past to be retained, since it is characterized by the ability to remain in spite of temporal succession. The trace is thus the minimal condition for life to resist death in a movement of survival. The trace can only live on, however, by being left for a future that may erase it. This radical finitude of survival is not a lack of being that is desirable to overcome. Rather, the finitude of survival opens the chance for everything that is desired and the threat of everything that is feared.

The key to radical atheism is what I analyze as the unconditional affirmation of survival. This affirmation is not a matter of a choice that some people make and others do not: it is unconditional because everyone is engaged by it *without exception.* Whatever one may want or whatever one may do, one has to affirm the time of survival, since it opens the possibility to live on—and thus to want something or to do something—in the first place. This unconditional affirmation of survival allows us to read the purported desire for immortality against itself. The desire to *live on* after death is not a desire for immortality, since to live on is to remain subjected to temporal finitude. The desire for survival cannot aim at transcending time, since the given time is the only chance for survival. There is thus an internal contradiction in the so-called desire for immortality. If one were not attached to mortal life, there would be no fear of death and no desire to live on. But for the same reason, the idea of immortality cannot even hypothetically appease the fear of death or satisfy the desire to live on. On the contrary, the state of immortality would annihilate every form of survival, since it would annihilate the time of mortal life.[1]

To establish the logic of radical atheism, I proceed from Derrida's notion of spacing (*espacement*). As he points out in his late work *On Touching,* spacing is "the first word of any deconstruction, valid for space as well as time" (181/207).[2] More precisely, spacing is shorthand for the becoming-space of time and the becoming-time of space. Although this coimplication of space and time defines all of Derrida's key terms (such as *trace, arche-writing,* and *différance*), it has received little attention in studies of his work. Derrida himself does not undertake a detailed elaboration of how the becoming-space of time and the becoming-time of space should be understood, while maintaining that it is the minimal operation of deconstruction that is at work in everything that happens. My aim with regard to this matter is threefold. I seek to develop the philosophical significance of Derrida's argument by accounting for *why* spacing is irreducible, *how* it should be understood, and *what* implications follow from thinking it as a constitutive condition. All these issues will be addressed at length in the chapters that follow, so I will here limit myself to emphasizing the aspect that is most crucial for radical atheism. This aspect concerns the ontological status of spacing. Derrida repeatedly argues that *différance* (as a name for the spacing of time) not only applies to language or experience or any other delimited region of being. Rather, it is an *absolutely general condition*, which means that there cannot even in principle be anything that is exempt from temporal finitude.

It is here instructive to consider the relation between negative theology and deconstruction, which has been an issue since Derrida's earliest writings. Derrida describes *différance* as the condition for everything that can be, while emphasizing that it "is" nothing in itself: it is neither sensible nor intelligible, neither present nor absent, neither active nor passive, and so on. This account of *différance* is formally similar to the account of God in negative theology. Negative theology describes God as the condition for everything that can be, while emphasizing that God himself "is" not a being. The respective reasons why God and *différance* are described as without being are, however, diametrically opposite. The God of negative theology is described as without being insofar as being is understood as a category of finitude. To predicate God is deemed to be inadequate since God transcends the determinations of time and space that all predication entails. God is a positive infinity that is absolutely in itself and must be described in negative terms when one speaks the language of finitude. In contrast, *différance* articulates the negative infinity of time. No moment is given in itself but is superseded by another moment in its very event and can never be consummated in a positive infinity.[3] The negative infinity of time is an *infinite finitude*, since it entails that finitude cannot ever be eliminated or overcome. The infinite finitude of *différance* is at work before, within, and beyond anything one may circumscribe as being. *Différance* is thus without being but not because it is something ineffable that transcends time and space. On the contrary, *différance* is nothing in itself because it designates the spacing of time that makes it impossible for anything to be in itself. Consequently, Derrida emphasizes that even though the syntax of his argument resembles that of negative theology, it is *not* theological:

> not even in the order of the most negative of all negative theologies, which are always concerned with disengaging a superessentiality beyond the finite categories of essence and existence, that is, of presence, and always hastening to recall that God is refused the predicate of existence, only in order to acknowledge his superior, inconceivable, and ineffable mode of being. Such a development is not in question here. (*Margins of Philosophy*, 6/6)

Derrida repeats the same argument in his two main texts on negative theology: "How to Avoid Speaking" and *Sauf le nom*.[4] There is nothing radical about saying that God is nothing as long as one means that God is nothing that can be apprehended by a finite being, but is infinitely superior to anything that can be described in language. Negative theology adheres to the most traditional metaphysical logic by positing an instance that is exempt from temporal finitude.

Nevertheless, there have been numerous attempts to assimilate deconstruction to negative theology. In *The Trespass of the Sign*, Kevin Hart claims that Derrida underestimates the radicality of negative theology and in particular the writings of Pseudo-Dionysius. According to Hart, negative theology is a "non-metaphysical theology" because it does not make positive statements about God as a supreme being or a foundational presence. Rather, negative theology "deconstructs" positive theology by showing that God is neither being nor nonbeing, neither present nor absent. For Hart such negative statements are necessary to ensure that "our discourse about God is, in fact, about *God* and not just about human images of God."[5] To construe this elevation of God as a deconstructive move, one must completely misunderstand Derrida's thinking. Hart's argument only makes sense if one presupposes that there are two realms: on the one hand the finitude of being, with its "human images," and on the other hand the infinity of God, which is beyond all such improper images. Hart argues that God is not a being because "being is finite" (xxv) and thus incompatible with the transcendence of God: "God comes only from God, certainly not from being. For without God there could be neither being nor beings" (xxii). Nothing could be further from Derrida's thinking than this division between two realms. For Derrida, there is only one realm—the infinite finitude of *différance*—since everything is constituted by the trace structure of time. Hence, deconstruction has nothing to do with showing that the signifiers of language are inadequate to a transcendent signified such as God. As Derrida maintains in *Of Grammatology*, the trace structure does not only apply to the chain of signifiers but also to the signified itself. Indeed, "the signified is essentially and originally (and not only for a finite and created spirit) trace" (73/108).

Since Hart fails to assess the logic of deconstruction, he ends up showing the opposite of what he claims to show. As proof of how Pseudo-Dionysius "deconstructs" positive theology, Hart quotes a passage from *The Mystical Theology* where Pseudo-Dionysius refuses to apply either affirmations or negations to the Cause inasmuch as "It transcends all affirmation by being the perfect and unique Cause of all things, and transcends all negation by the pre-eminence of Its simple and absolute nature—free from every limitation and beyond them all" (quoted in Hart, *The Trespass of the Sign*, 201). The notion of a perfect Cause with a simple and absolute nature, regardless of whether one places it beyond all possible predication, is a metaphysical notion par excellence. This does not trouble Hart, who himself promotes "the deity's sovereign freedom of self-determination" (xxii) as the cornerstone for a supposedly nonmetaphysical theology. So when Hart sets out to demonstrate that negative theology does not adhere to the metaphysics that Derrida deconstructs, he in fact demonstrates that negative theology adheres to the most classic metaphysical axiom of a sovereign instance.

In a recent essay on Derrida and religion, Hart employs the same argumentative structure in claiming that Pseudo-Dionysius offers an alternative to the metaphysics of presence: "that Pseudo-Dionysius affirms a deity whose hyper-essentiality is a blazing moment of self-presence is not supported by his writings. The God evoked in the *Corpus Areopagiticum* is neither present nor absent, neither being nor non-being, neither one nor many, and is entirely free to determine itself."[6] The logic of this passage is quite self-contradictory. To say that one does not affirm absolute self-presence and then affirm an instance that is "entirely free to determine itself" is untenable, since only an absolute self-presence could be entirely free to determine itself. Hart's argument, however, is not simply based on a logical oversight that could be corrected by him or any other negative theologian. Rather, the logic of negative theology and the logic of deconstruction are diametrically opposite.

Let me specify the above claim by considering the most prominent modern negative theologian, the French philosopher Jean-Luc Marion, who has also engaged extensively with Derrida's thinking. Marion explicitly takes issue with Derrida's assertion that negative theology is a metaphysics of presence, but he can do so only by misconstruing what Derrida means by the term. Marion reduces the metaphysics of presence to the notion that God can be conceptually comprehended and named as an essence or being. Given Marion's understanding of the metaphysics of presence, he can oppose it to a *theology of absence* that renounces all names because they are inadequate to the divine Name.[7] As Marion writes, "the Name does not name God as an essence; it designates what passes beyond every name" (38), namely, "He who surpasses all nomination" (27). The aim is not "to find a name for God, but to make us receive our own from the unsayable Name" (38). Because of this deference before an unnameable God, negative theology is, according to Marion, "at least as much" (38) opposed to the metaphysics of presence as is deconstruction.

Like Hart, Marion displays a profound inability to assess what is at stake in deconstruction. For Derrida, the metaphysics of presence is by no means limited to the notion that the absolute can be conceptually comprehended and named as an essence or being. Rather, *every* notion of an absolute that is exempt from the spacing of time is a version of the metaphysics of presence. It does not make any essential difference if one says that the absolute is absent and impossible to grasp for the finite human understanding. For Marion, as for every other negative theologian, it is not a question of renouncing God; it is only a matter of denouncing "idolatrous" concepts of God that reduce him to human measures.[8] To make God unnameable and unthinkable is not a deconstructive move. On the contrary, it is the most traditional metaphysical move since it posits God as absolutely absolute by making him independent from anything other than himself. Marion explicitly asserts that the absolute of God is "undone from any relation, and therefore also from any thinkable relation, which would tie it to an absurd 'other than it.'"[9]

Marion's defense of negative theology against Derrida's critique repeats the very move that Derrida criticizes. Derrida's persistent demarcation of deconstruction from negative theology is motivated by the latter's aim to preserve a God beyond being. To negate all predicates when speaking of God is for negative theology a way of saving God from the contamination of finitude. The apparent negation of God is thus in fact an affirmation of God. Or as Derrida puts it in *Writing and Difference*: "The negative moment of the discourse on God is only a phase of positive ontotheology," since it serves to affirm God as a "superessentiality" beyond everything that is destructible.[10] Marion's response to Derrida's critique is to argue that negative theology offers a "third way" beyond affirmation and negation. According to Marion, Derrida is wrong to assert that negative theology operates in the service of a metaphysical affirmation, since the God of negative theology is explicitly posited as beyond both affirmation and negation. In Marion's formulation, "the third way does not hide an affirmation beneath a negation, because it means to overcome their duel" (26). Like Hart, Marion here cites Pseudo-Dionysius, who asserts that

God is above every negation and affirmation, as well as beyond even the most elevated names we may use to describe him. "Neither one nor one-ness, neither divinity nor goodness, nor spirit in the sense we understand it; neither sonship nor fatherhood, nor anything else that is known by us or by any of the other beings" (quoted in Marion, "In the Name," 26). Marion's argument, however, does not in any way counter Derrida's critique of negative theology. There is nothing radical about Pseudo-Di-onysius's claim that God is beyond affirmation and negation, positivity and negativity, since what he means is that God is beyond everything that can be predicated by a finite being. When Pseudo-Dionysius places God above all names, above everything that can be affirmed or negated, it is explicitly in order to place God "above every privation" (quoted in ibid.). In short, it is a matter of positing God as absolutely indestructible.

The same move is evident in Marion's own theology, which is committed to enforcing what he calls "the dividing line between creator and creature" (39). On the one hand there is the mortality of the world, on the other hand the immortality of God. Marion is thus as far as one can get from the deconstructive thinking of a general mortality. A telling example is Marion's reading of the dictum "God is dead," which opens his book *The Idol and Distance*. Marion argues that the death of God only affects the false, idolatrous God, since a proper God could never die in the first place:

> A "God" who can die harbors already, even when he is not dying, such a weakness that from the outset he falls short of the idea that we cannot not form of a "God." And is it not the least of courtesies that he should satisfy a propaedeutic concept, even if it is only our own? A "God" who decides to die dies from the beginning, since he undoubtedly needs a beginning—which means that the "death of God" sets forth a contradiction: that which dies does not have any right to claim, even when it is alive, to be "God." What is it that dies in the "death of God" if not that which could not in any case merit the name of "God"? And therefore "the death of God" expresses, beyond the death of "God," the death of that which announces it: the death of the "death of God" itself. The contradiction of the terms of the proposition comes to completion in the self-erasure of the proposition: it renders null and void that which it states by annulling the object of the statement. . . . "God" is dead only if "God" can die, that is, if in the first place it was not a question, in the demonstration, of God. (1, 3/17–18, 20)

For Marion the true life of God is immortal. If God were not immortal, he would not be God. Marion employs this definition of God in order to make God immune from any possible refutation. If God is immortal, he cannot ever die and is consequently safe from the atheist proclamation that God is dead.

I am not concerned here with the circularity of Marion's argument, but only with how his assessment of mortality is the opposite of Derrida's. For Derrida life is essentially mortal, which means that there can be no instance (such as God in Marion's account) that is immortal. Even the supposedly divine declaration "I am that I am" is in Derrida's reading "the confession of a mortal," since "*I am* originally means *I am mortal*."[11] Proceeding from Derrida's premise, we can pursue a reading of the death of God that goes in the opposite direction from Marion. If to be alive is to be mortal, it follows that to *not* be mortal—to be immortal—is to be dead. If one cannot die, one is dead. Hence, Derrida does not limit himself to the atheist claim that God is dead; he repeatedly makes the radically atheist claim that *God is death*.[12] That God is death does not mean that we reach God through death or that God rules over death. On the contrary, it means that the idea of immortality—which according to Marion is "the idea that we cannot not form of a 'God'"—is inseparable from the idea of absolute death.

That God is death does not only mean that God does not exist but also that the immortality of God is not desirable in the first place.[13] This radically atheist argument emerges forcefully through the notion of "autoimmunity," which is at the center of Derrida's main text on religion: the essay "Faith and Knowledge." Derrida here maintains that all religions are founded on the value of "the unscathed" (*l'indemne*), which he glosses as the pure and the untouched, the sacred and the holy, the safe and sound. According to Derrida, "every religion" holds out such a "horizon of redemption, of the restoration of the unscathed, of indemnification" (84n30/75n25). The common denominator for religions is thus that they promote *absolute immunity* as the supremely desirable. This ideal of absolute immunity is succinctly formulated by Augustine in the seventh book of his *Confessions*. Augustine asserts that the immutable is better than the mutable, the inviolable better than the violable, and the incorruptible better than the corruptible. All religious conceptions of the highest good (whether it is called God or something else) hold out such an absolute immunity, since the highest good must be safe from the corruption of evil.

Derrida's argument is, on the contrary, that nothing can be unscathed. His notion of autoimmunity spells out that everything is threatened from within itself, since the possibility of living is inseparable from the peril of dying.

The logic of autoimmunity is radically atheist, since it undermines the religious conception of what is desirable. Mutability, corruptibility, and violability do not testify to a lack of being that we desire to overcome. On the contrary, these features are essential to everything that is desired and cannot be removed. Inversely, the absolute immunity that religions hold out as "the best" (the immutable, the incorruptible, and the inviolable) is on Derrida's account "the worst," since it would eliminate everything that can be desired. If one removes what threatens the object of desire—the evil that threatens the good, the death that threatens life—one removes the object of desire itself. Consequently, Derrida maintains that "a heart would not be good unless it could be other, bad, radically, *unforgivably* bad, ready for any infidelity, any treachery and any perjury" (*On Touching*, 283/319). We will see how the same logic of desire recurs in different variations throughout Derrida's thinking. Whatever is desired as good is autoimmune, since it bears within itself the possibility of becoming unbearably bad.

I develop the logic of autoimmunity throughout this book, but I want to point out that I am not concerned with the relation between how Derrida uses the term "autoimmunity" and how it is employed in biological science. Autoimmunity is for me the name of a deconstructive logic that should be measured against the standards of philosophical logic. This does not mean that the biological connotations of the term are not important, but they do not make the argument dependent on its correspondence with discoveries in contemporary science. The biological connotations of the term "autoimmunity" remind us that Derrida pursues a logic of life (or, rather, life-death), but I seek to establish the power of this logic on philosophical rather than scientific grounds. I argue that the reason why autoimmunity is inscribed at the heart of life is because there cannot be anything without the tracing of time. The tracing of time is the minimal protection of life, but it also attacks life from the first inception, since it breaches the integrity of any moment and makes everything susceptible to annihilation.

Taking Derrida's insight into the trace structure of time as my point of departure, I demonstrate how he rethinks the condition of identity, ethics, religion, and political emancipation in accordance with the logic of radical atheism. Chapter 1 addresses the relation between Derrida's deconstruction and Kant's critical philosophy. While Kant restricted time to a "transcendental" condition for the experience of a finite consciousness, I maintain that for Derrida the spacing of time is an "ultratranscendental" condition from which nothing can be exempt. The spacing of time is the condition not only for everything that can be cognized and experienced, but also for everything that can be thought and desired. The radicality of this argument emerges through Derrida's notion of the "unconditional," which must be strictly distinguished from Kant's. For Kant, the unconditional is the Idea of a sovereign instance that is not subjected to time and space (e.g., God). For Derrida, on the contrary, the unconditional is the spacing of time that undermines the very Idea of a sovereign instance. Thus, Chapter 1 develops a deconstructive logic of identity that allows one to think time as an unconditional condition, without renouncing the exigencies of philosophical reason to which Kant responded in the first Critique. More precisely, I demonstrate how Derrida can be said to write a new transcendental aesthetic (which accounts for the synthesis of temporality without positing a formal unity of apperception that subordinates the division of time) and a new transcendental dialectic (which deconstructs the Idea that the consummation of time is thinkable and desirable).

Chapter 2 develops the deconstructive notion of the synthesis of time through an analysis of what Derrida calls "arche-writing." In particular I seek to consolidate Derrida's reading of Husserl's phenomenology of internal time-consciousness. I engage with prominent phenomenologists, such as Paul Ricoeur, Rudolf Bernet, and Dan Zahavi, who have raised a number of questions that a deconstructive reading of Husserl must answer. The difficulty, however, is that Derrida's own analysis of Husserl is not as thorough as it could be. Consequently, my reading aims at deepening Derrida's analysis of Husserl's theory of time, as well as at elucidating how the question of time is central for deconstructing the logic of identity.

Chapter 3 articulates the link between arche-writing and what Derrida calls "arche-violence." I pursue the notion of arche-violence through a critical reading of Emmanuel Levinas's ethical metaphysics, and take issue with the influential Levinasian readings of Derrida by Robert Bernasconi, Simon Critchley, and Drucilla Cornell. Refuting the prevalent idea that Derrida subscribed to Levinas's conception of alterity, I argue that Derrida pursued a consistent thinking of time and violence throughout his career. The argument is sustained by detailed analyses of Derrida's late work on questions of justice, hospitality, and responsibility.

Chapter 4 elaborates the significance of Derrida's radical atheism at length. The proliferation of apparently religious terms in Derrida's later work—which engages with notions such as messianicity, faith, and God—has given rise to numerous theological accounts of deconstruction. In contrast to these theological accounts (including those of John Caputo, Hent de Vries, and Richard Kearney), I argue that Derrida relies on the desire for mortal life in order to read even the most religious ideas against themselves. Messianic hope is for Derrida a hope for temporal survival, faith is always faith in the finite, and the desire for God is a desire for the mortal, like every other desire. I conclude the chapter with an in-depth analysis of Derrida's *Circumfession*, which demonstrates how he stages the radically atheist desire for survival in his own confessional writing.

Chapter 5 links the logic of radical atheism to Derrida's conception of democracy. I here further develop the notion of autoimmunity, which Derrida brings to the fore in his discussion of democracy. Specifically, I demonstrate how the radically atheist logic of autoimmunity opens a new perspective on the challenges of democratic politics and on the desire that drives political emancipation. The argument is pursued in dialogue with Ernesto Laclau's theory of hegemony and democracy. On the one hand, I demonstrate how Laclau offers important resources for a deconstructive thinking of the political. On the other hand, I take issue with the Lacanian notion of desire on which Laclau relies. Specifically, I argue that the possibility of democracy hinges on a constitutive desire for temporal survival rather than a constitutive desire for atemporal fullness, as in Lacan. This argument allows me to tie together all the threads of the book and press home the stakes of Derrida's radical atheism, not only for our thinking of politics but also for our basic conceptions of life and desire.

Finally, I would like to offer a remark on the strategy that informs my reading. As will become clear, my main approach is analytical rather than exegetical. I not only seek to explicate what Derrida is saying; I seek to develop his arguments, fortify his logic, and pursue its implications. An instructive example is my treatment of the notion of "survival." Derrida repeatedly indicates that it is of central importance for his entire oeuvre, but he never provides an explicit account of the logic of survival and its ramifications for our thinking of identity, desire, ethics, and politics.

By providing such an account, I seek to "inherit" Derrida in the precise sense he has given to the word. To inherit is not simply to accept what is handed down from the master; it is to reaffirm the legacy in order to make it live on in a different way.[14]

Such inheritance cannot be accomplished through pious conservation but only through critical discrimination. One question that is bound to arise, then, is whether there are aspects of Derrida's work that do not adhere to the radically atheist logic I develop, especially since it stands in sharp contrast to the readings proposed by many other major interpreters. My response is that even if one is able to find passages in Derrida that cannot be salvaged by the logic of radical atheism, it is far from enough to refute the reading I propose here. Like everyone else, Derrida was certainly liable to be inconsistent. However, in order to turn these inconsistencies into an argument against the logic of radical atheism that I establish, one has to show that they are not in fact inconsistencies but rather testify to the operation in Derrida of a different logic altogether.

§ 1   Autoimmunity of Time:
Derrida and Kant

In Jacques Derrida's major book on democracy, *Rogues*, there is a short but crucial discussion of the elections in Algeria in 1992. The elections were projected to give power to a majority that wanted to change the constitution and undercut the process of democratization in Algeria. To avoid such a result, the state and the leading party decided to suspend the elections. They thus suspended democracy in the name of democracy, abolishing the very principle of what they claimed to protect.

Derrida's discussion is not concerned with judging whether it was right or wrong to suspend the elections in Algeria. Rather, Derrida dwells on the Algerian elections as an example of what he calls the "autoimmunity" of democracy. Democracy is autoimmune because it is threatened not only by *external* enemies but also by *internal* forces that can corrupt its principles. For example, it is always possible that a democratic election will give power to a nondemocratic regime. Derrida reminds us that "fascist and Nazi totalitarianisms came into power or ascended to power through formally normal and formally democratic electoral processes."[1] The immune-system of democracy—the strategies it employs to protect itself—may thus be forced to attack itself in order to survive. The effects of such autoimmunity may be positive or negative, but in either case they reinforce that democracy is necessarily divided within itself. The principles that protect democracy may protect those who attack the principles of democracy. Inversely, the attack on the principles of democracy may be a way of protecting the principles of democracy. There is no way to finally decide whether it is legitimate for democracy to attack or to refrain from attacking itself, since either one of these strategies may turn against it at any moment.

In Derrida's analysis the autoimmunity of democracy is not a deplorable fact that we could or should seek to overcome. Rather, Derrida emphasizes that there can be no democratic ideal that is exempt from autoimmunity, since the very concept of democracy is autoimmune. In order to be democratic, democracy must be open to critique and to the outcome of unpredictable elections. But for the same reason, democracy is essentially open to what may alter or destroy it. There is thus a double bind at the core of democracy. It must both protect itself against its own threat and be threatened by its own protection.

Derrida does not limit autoimmunity to the problem of democracy. On the contrary, he underscores that autoimmunity is a condition for *life in general*.[2] As Derrida puts it in *Specters of Marx*, "life does not go without death, and that death is not beyond, outside of life, unless one inscribes the beyond in the inside, in the essence of the living" (141/224). The coimplication of life and death spells out an autoimmunity at the heart of life as such. Even if all external threats are evaded, life still bears the cause of its own destruction within itself. The vulnerability of life is thus *without limit*, since the source of attack is also located within what is to be defended.

If autoimmunity remains difficult to think, it is because it violates the principle of noncontradiction. This principle is the foundation of what I will call the philosophical logic of identity. Its canonical formulation is found in Aristotle's *Metaphysics*, where Aristotle asserts that "the same attribute cannot at the same time belong and not belong to the same subject" (1005b).[3] The temporal qualification is important here. Aristotle does not exclude that the same subject can have contradictory attributes at different times (e.g., a body can be in motion at one juncture and in repose at another), but it cannot have contradictory attributes *at the same time*. The principle of noncontradiction thus prescribes that what is must be identical to itself—that its originary form must be an indivisible unity.

If we follow the philosophical logic of identity, autoimmunity is inconceivable. What is indivisibly identical to itself has no need to immunize itself against itself. It may be threatened by what is other than itself, but it cannot turn against itself. Accordingly, an immune reaction is supposed to defend the body against foreign antigens. The identity of the body is necessary in order to distinguish between what is "good" and what is "bad" for the organism, what will kill it and what will enable it to survive. Thus, if there is no indivisible identity, every immune system runs the risk of being autoimmune, since there can be no guarantee that it will be in the service of maintaining health. What is attacked as an enemy of the body may turn out to be an essential part of the body, and what is welcomed as beneficial to the body may turn out to destroy the body from within.

A first question, then, is how we can revise the philosophical logic of identity in order to defend what Derrida calls the "illogical logic" of autoimmunity. In the second part of *Rogues* Derrida points out that the ultimate cause of autoimmunity "is located in the very structure of the present and of life, in the temporalization of what Husserl called the Living Present (*die lebendige Gegenwart*). The Living Present is produced only by altering and dissimulating itself. I do not have the *time*, precisely, to pursue this path here, but I would like to note its necessity" (127/179). While Derrida did not have the time to develop this argument in what was to become one of his last lectures, I have sought to provide considerable space for it in this book. The link between time and autoimmunity is at the center of my exposition, since I believe that autoimmunity brings out the most provocative implications of deconstructive logic and that the problem of time opens the most consistent way to defend the rigor of that logic.

I will argue that Derrida's deconstruction of the logic of identity proceeds from a notion of temporality that informs his work from beginning to end. As Derrida points out in *Speech and Phenomena*, "what is ultimately at stake, what is at bottom decisive [is] the concept of time" (63/70). The concept of time plays a dual role in the history of metaphysics, which is why it is so decisive for Derrida's deconstruction. On the one hand, time is thought *on the basis of* the present and in conformity with the philosophical logic of identity. The presence of the present is thus the principle of identity from which all modifications of time are derived. The past is understood as what has been present, and the future as what will be present. On the other hand, time is incompatible with presence in itself. The temporal can never be in itself but is always divided between being no longer and being not yet. Thus, although "the present is that from which we believe we are able to think time," this understanding of time in fact effaces "the inverse necessity: to think the present from time as *différance*."[4] It is the proposition that time is *différance* that I wish to develop. Such a deconstruction cannot consist in constructing *another* concept of time. Rather, the traditional concept of time as succession provides the resources to deconstruct the logic of identity.[5]

In "Ousia and Grammè," Derrida pursues the link between the problem of temporality and the logic of identity by analyzing the treatment of time in the fourth book of Aristotle's *Physics*. Aristotle points out that there would be no time if there were only one single now (218b). Rather, there must be at least *two* nows—"an earlier one before and a later one after" (219a)—in order for there to be time. Time is thus defined as succession, where each now is always superseded by another now. In thinking succession, however, Aristotle realizes that it contradicts his concept of identity as *presence in itself*. A self-present, indivisible now could never even begin to give way to another now, since what is indivisible cannot be altered. This observation leads Aristotle to an impasse, since his logic of identity cannot account for the succession that constitutes time. Derrida articulates the problem as follows:

> Let us consider the sequence of nows. The preceding now, it is said, must be destroyed by the following now. But, Aristotle then points out, it cannot be destroyed "in itself" (*en heautōi*), that is, at the moment when it is (now, in act). No more can it be destroyed in an other now (*en allōi*): for then it would not be destroyed as now, itself; and, as a now which has been, it is . . . inaccessible to the action of the following now. (57/65)

Hence, as long as one holds on to the idea of an indivisible now—or more succinctly: as long as one holds on to the concept of identity as presence in itself—it is impossible to think succession. The now cannot *first* be present in itself and *then* be affected by its own disappearance, since this would require that the now began to pass away after it had ceased to be. Rather, the now must disappear *in its very event*. The succession of time requires not only that each now is superseded by another now, but also that this alteration is at work from the beginning. The purportedly single now is always already divided by the movement of temporalization in which "the dyad [is] the minimum," as Derrida contends (56/65).

The pivotal question is what conclusion to draw from the antinomy between divisible time and indivisible presence. Faced with the relentless division of temporality, one must subsume time under a nontemporal presence in order to secure the philosophical logic of identity. The challenge of Derrida's thinking stems from his refusal of this move. Deconstruction insists on a primordial division and thereby enables us to think the radical irreducibility of time as constitutive of any identity. I will thus argue that the apparent paradoxes in Derrida's writings follow a deconstructive "logic," which thinks the condition of identity without positing an instance that is exempt from time. An important clue is Derrida's essay on *différance*, where he describes how the present necessarily is divided within itself:

> An interval must separate the present from what it is in order for the present to be itself, but this interval that constitutes it as present must, by the same token, divide the present in and of itself, thereby also dividing, along with the present, everything that is thought on the basis of the present. (*Margins of Philosophy*, 13/13)

Derrida's description of how "an interval must separate the present from what it is in order for the present to be itself" answers to a conundrum that surfaces in all philosophical accounts of time. The crux is that even the slightest temporal moment must be divided in its becoming: separating before from after, past from future. Without the interval there would be no time, only a presence forever remaining the same.

Thus, the movement of temporalization cannot be understood in terms of a presence that emerges from a past presence and that is overtaken by a future presence. The "past" cannot refer to what *has been* present, since any past was itself divided from its beginning. Likewise the "future" cannot refer to what *will be* present but designates a relentless displacement inherent in everything that happens. Any so-called presence is divided in its very event and not only in relation to what precedes or succeeds it.

The difficult question is how identity is possible in spite of such division. Certainly, the difference of time could not even be marked without a synthesis that relates the past to the future and thus posits an identity over time. Philosophies of time-consciousness have usually solved the problem by anchoring the synthesis in a self-present subject, who relates the past to the future through memories and expectations that are given in the form of the present. This solution to the problem, however, must assume that the consciousness that experiences time in itself is present and thereby exempt from the division of time. Hence, if Derrida is right to insist that the self-identity of presence is impossible a priori, then it is all the more urgent to account for how the synthesis of time is possible without being grounded in the form of presence.

Derrida's notion of "the trace" can be seen to account for such a synthesis. Derrida describes the trace as an originary synthesis, while insisting that this synthesis must be understood as "irreducibly non-simple," since it marks the interval of time as the precondition of any identity:

> In constituting itself, in dividing itself dynamically, this interval is what might be called *spacing,* the becoming-space of time or the becoming-time of space (*temporization*). And it is this constitution of the present, as an 'originary' and irreducibly nonsimple (and therefore, *stricto sensu* nonoriginary) synthesis of marks . . . that I propose to call arche-writing, arche-trace, or *différance.* (*Margins of Philosophy,* 13/13–14)

Derrida here defines the trace in terms of "spacing." Spacing is shorthand for the becoming-space of time and the becoming-time of space, which is also the definition of arche-writing and *différance.* My argument is that an elaboration of Derrida's definition allows for the most rigorous thinking of temporality by accounting for an originary synthesis *without* grounding it in an indivisible presence.[6]

The synthesis of the trace follows from the constitution of time we have considered. Given that the now can appear only by disappearing—that it passes away as soon as it comes to be—it must be inscribed as a trace in order to be at all. This is the *becoming-space of time.* The trace is necessarily spatial, since spatiality is characterized by the ability to remain in spite of temporal succession. Spatiality is thus the condition for synthesis, since it enables the tracing of relations between past and future. Spatiality, however, can never be in itself; it can never be pure simultaneity. Simultaneity is unthinkable without a temporalization that relates one spatial juncture to another.[7] This *becoming-time of space* is necessary not only for the trace to be related to other traces, but also for it to be a trace in the first place. A trace can only be read after its inscription and is thus marked by a relation to the future that temporalizes space. This is crucial for Derrida's deconstruction of the logic of identity. If the spatialization of time makes the synthesis *possible,* the temporalization of space makes it *impossible* for the synthesis to be grounded in an indivisible presence. The synthesis is always a trace of the past that is left *for the future.* Thus, it can never be in itself but is essentially exposed to that which may erase it.

In the next chapter I further develop the deconstructive notion of synthesis, in particular through a close study of Edmund Husserl's phenomenology of internal time-consciousness. What I want to emphasize here is that Derrida describes the trace and *différance* as conditions for life in general. They should not be understood as "transcendental" conditions of possibility in Kant's or Husserl's sense, because such conditions only apply to the experience of a finite consciousness. For Derrida, the spacing of time is an "ultratranscendental" condition from which nothing can be exempt. The present chapter is concerned with elaborating what it means that the spacing of time has such an ultratranscendental status. On the one hand, the spacing of time has an ultratranscendental status because it is the condition for everything *all the way up* to and including the ideal it-self. The spacing of time is the condition not only for everything that can be cognized and experienced, but also for everything that can be thought and desired. On the other hand, the spacing of time has an ultratranscen-dental status because it is the condition for everything *all the way down* to the minimal forms of life. As Derrida maintains, there is no limit to the generality of *différance* and the structure of the trace applies to all fields of the living.[8]

The spacing of time and the concomitant structure of the trace is the deepest source of autoimmunity. Already in *Writing and Difference*, Derr-ida spoke of the trace as a "mortal germ" (230/339) that is inseparable from the seed of life. To think the trace as an ultratranscendental condition is thus to think a constitutive finitude that is absolutely without exception. From within its very constitution life is threatened by death, memory is threatened by forgetting, identity is threatened by alterity, and so on.

Derrida's later works reiterate the ultratranscendental argument by de-scribing the structure of the event and the coming of the future as *un-conditional.* The unconditional coming of the future is further linked to terms such as *justice, hospitality,* and *democracy.* Derrida's use of these terms has led many readers to believe that he subscribes to an Idea in the Kantian sense. The unconditional justice, hospitality, or democracy would then designate an ideal that we can think and toward which we should aspire, even though it remains inaccessible for us as finite beings.[9] Derrida himself has repeatedly denied that he adheres to such a Kantian schema, but the specific reasons why the unconditional in Derrida's sense must be dissociated from the unconditional in Kant's sense need to be developed. I will argue that the two notions are quite incompatible. This is crucial for assessing the radicality of Derrida's thinking. For Kant, the unconditional is the Idea of a sovereign instance that is not subjected to time and space (e.g., God). For Derrida, on the contrary, the unconditional is the spacing of time that undermines the very Idea of a sovereign instance.

A closer comparison of Kant and Derrida is instructive for assessing how the constitution of time challenges the philosophical logic of identity. Kant's *Critique of Pure Reason* can be seen to proceed from his discriminating use of the principle of noncontradiction, and it clearly brings out what is at stake in deconstructing this principle. As Derrida points out in *Writing and Difference*, the principle of noncontradiction is "the cornerstone of all metaphysics of presence" (217/321), since it provides the definition of being as presence in itself. The past is no longer and the future is not yet; hence everything that *is* identical to itself must be in the present. If one follows this logic of identity, then time must be defined as nonbeing. Being is presence in itself, whereas time can never be present in itself. In "Ousia and Grammè" Derrida rehearses the argument as follows:

> If it appears that one may demonstrate that time is no-thing (nonbeing), it is because one already has determined the origin and essence of no-thing as time, as nonpresent under the heading of the "not yet" or the "already no longer". . . . Being is nontime, time is nonbeing insofar as being already, secretly has been determined as present, and beingness (*ousia*) as presence. As soon as being and present are synonymous, to say nothingness and to say time are the same thing. (50–51/57–58)

The logical inference that Derrida describes has often been employed to denounce time as an illusion or as a corruption of the essential, since it undermines the ideal of absolute presence. Derrida points to "the massively evident fact that, until Kant, metaphysics held time to be the nothingness or the accident foreign to essence or to truth" (47–48/53). Derrida goes on to say, however, that the metaphysical subordination of time "is *still* to be seen in Kant. Not only in Kant's linking of the possibility of time to the *intuitus derivativus* and to the concept of a *derived* finitude or passivity, but above all in that which is most revolutionary and least metaphysical in his thought of time" (48/53).

Derrida consolidates his claim by pointing to a double move in Kant's treatment of time in the *Critique of Pure Reason*. On the one hand, Kant maintains that time is a condition for appearances in general, a pure form of sensibility without which there could be no experience in the first place. Kant thus asserts that time is *empirically real*, since "no object can ever be given to us in experience that would not belong under the condition of time" (B 52). On the other hand, Kant emphasizes that time only applies to the subjective conditions of sensible intuition. Time is thus *transcendentally ideal*; it does not apply to things in themselves but is only a condition of possibility for the appearance of things in finite experience. As Kant puts it: "Time is therefore merely a subjective condition of our (human) intuition (which is always sensible, i.e., insofar as we are affected by objects) and in itself, outside the subject, is nothing. Nonetheless it is necessarily objective in regard to all appearances, thus also in regard to all things that can come before us in experience" (B 51).

Kant's argument that time cannot have the status of transcendental reality—namely, that it cannot be a condition for things in themselves—follows strictly from the principle of noncontradiction. If one defines being as presence in itself, then time must be defined as nonbeing since it can never be in itself. Kant, however, dissociates himself from the dogmatic metaphysics that would deny the reality of time on purely logical grounds. Rather, Kant seeks to account for the constitutive limitations of human finitude by granting time empirical reality, while safeguarding the Idea of an infinite being by denying time transcendental reality.

Kant's task in *Critique of Pure Reason* is thus to separate legitimate from illegitimate uses of the principle of noncontradiction. He recognizes the principle of noncontradiction as "inviolable" but is careful to restrict it to a "negative criterion of all truth" (B 191). The principle of noncontradiction provides a necessary but not sufficient criterion to judge the truth of something. What contradicts itself is always false, but what does not contradict itself is not necessarily true. For Kant, it is especially important to maintain this distinction with regard to the finitude of human cognition. Previous metaphysical systems had failed to distinguish strictly between what can be thought in accordance with the principle of noncontradiction and what can be posited as an object of possible experience. Thus, one had sought to prove the existence of God or the immortality of the soul on the basis that these concepts were thinkable without contradiction. Such arguments are for Kant "transcendental illusions" because they disregard that all human knowledge is restricted by space and time, which are the conditions of every possible experience. For Kant, it is out of the question to prove the existence of something that transcends time and space, since we can only cognize what is temporal and spatial.

Kant scrutinizes the transcendental illusions in his sections on the paralogisms, antinomies, and ideals of pure reason. I will not go into a detailed exposition of Kant's examples, but only point to their underlying argumentative structure. Kant shows that reason becomes trapped in irresolvable contradictions when it proceeds from the *logical* possibility of thinking a metaphysical notion such as God to the inference of its *real* existence in the world. All metaphysical theses (e.g., that there must be a simple substance, an uncaused cause, or a necessary being that is the ground of all contingent beings) can be countered by an antithesis that demonstrates that these theses are incompatible with the constitution of time and space. The antinomies are thus structured around the conflict between a thesis that asserts that there must be an indivisible instance and an antithesis that asserts that there cannot be an indivisible instance since everything is divided by time and space.

In exposing the antinomies of pure reason, Kant does not discredit the notion that there is something beyond the restrictions of time and space; he merely denies that we can experience it as such. Kant's crucial distinction here is between cognition and thinking, which parallels his distinction between the phenomenal and the noumenal. We can only cognize the phenomenal (what is bound by time and space), but we can think the noumenal (what transcends time and space) as an Idea. The principle of noncontradiction is ultimately what grounds this distinction between the phenomenal and the noumenal. Even though everything that can be experienced is subjected to time, the principle of noncontradiction ensures Kant that it is possible and legitimate to think an indivisible identity that is exempt from time.

The principle of noncontradiction not only consolidates Kant's Idea of the noumenal; it also determines his understanding of identity within the phenomenal realm that is subjected to time as an a priori condition. Kant here encounters the problem of the relation between succession and synthesis that I delineated above. Although the temporal is relentlessly divided into past and future phases, there could be no experience of time if these phases were not related to each other. A synthesis of successive moments is thus necessary for the awareness of any temporal extension. For example, if I listen to a sequence of tones, I can only apprehend them *as* a melody by retaining what has passed away and joining it to what follows. The question that all theories of time-consciousness must answer is how such a synthesis of succession is possible. Kant writes:

> Now it is obvious that if I draw a line in thought, or think of the time from one noon to the next, or even want to represent a certain number to myself, I

must necessarily first grasp one of these manifold representations after another in my thoughts. But if I were always to lose the preceding representations (the first part of the line, the preceding parts of time, or the successively represented units) from my thoughts and not reproduce them when I proceed to the following ones, then no whole representation and none of the previously mentioned thoughts, not even the purest and most fundamental representations of space and time, could ever arise. (A 102)

On the one hand, the manifold of intuition is not only a multiplicity but a temporal succession. On the other hand, the succession of time could never be experienced if the discrete moments were not related to each other and thus synthesized. The problem for Kant is how to conceive of such a synthesis and how to reconcile the prevalence of temporality with the formal demand for a fundamental unity of consciousness.

Kant's solution to the problem is to contrast the ever-changing empirical consciousness with the unity of transcendental apperception: "the pure, original, unchanging consciousness" (A 107). This unity is necessarily bound up with time, but it cannot be temporal in itself. If it were, the very ground for the synthetic unity of consciousness would itself be subjected to succession and thus in need of being synthesized by an instance other than itself, and so on. To avoid such an infinite regress, Kant distinguishes between the empirical self that is subjected to time and the pure apperception of the transcendental subject: the "I think" that according to Kant "must be capable of accompanying all my representations" (B 131). The "I think" is a spontaneous source of synthesis, which connects the manifold of intuition in one self-identical consciousness. Such apperception closes the infinite regress by being "that self-consciousness which, because it produces the representation *I think* . . . cannot be accompanied by any further representation" (B 132).

Kant is careful, however, to distinguish his notion of the transcendental I of apperception from the subject conceived as substance. The synthetic unity of apperception only provides the fundamental awareness "*that* I am" (B 157), whereas there can be "*no cognition* of myself *as I am*, but only as *I appear* to myself" (B 158) because any cognition of ourselves must take place in accordance with the form of inner sense (i.e., time). Thus, Kant emphasizes that pure apperception is "only the formal condition, namely the logical unity of every thought, in which I abstract from every object" (A 398). Beyond this conception of the transcendental I as a formal necessity, Kant maintains that there cannot be any knowledge of the subject in itself.

The argument concerning the constitution of the subject is a clear example of Kant's discriminating use of the principle of noncontradiction. The principle of noncontradiction prescribes that there must be a unity of consciousness that subordinates the division of time. Following the same logic, Kant argues that the form of a self-identical object (designated by his formula object = X) is necessary in order to synthesize successive appearances as the appearance of one and the same thing. To thus posit a formal unity as the condition for the experience of time is for Kant a legitimate use of the principle of noncontradiction. The metaphysical mistake that Kant criticizes is the move from the "I think" as a formal unity to a supposed proof of the soul as an indestructible substance, or the move from the self-identical form object = X to a supposed proof of the thing-in-itself. Such illegitimate use of the principle of noncontradiction gives rise to the "transcendental illusion" that one can cognize or experience what is exempt from time and space.

We can see how Kant's employment of the principle of noncontradiction informs all of the major divisions in *Critique of Pure Reason*. In the "Transcendental Aesthetic" and the "Transcendental Analytic" Kant analyzes the conditions for an a priori synthesis of experience as given in time and space. The principle of noncontradiction here allows him to posit a pure apperception, which secures the unity of consciousness despite the endless divisibility of spatiotemporal experience. In the "Transcendental Dialectic" Kant analyzes the paralogisms, antinomies, and ideals of pure reason. The principle of noncontradiction here allows him to save the Idea of a sovereign instance, even though such an instance is shown to be impossible under the condition of time and space.

Kant's purpose is to make reason consistent with itself and prevent it from being put to shame by false inferences and unsustainable proofs. Throughout the first *Critique* he maintains an admirable rigor in his use of the principle of noncontradiction. Kant does not assert anything that cannot be asserted on the basis of this principle, which is the supreme principle of reason.

The only way to deconstruct Kant is thus to deconstruct the principle of noncontradiction and to develop a new conception of reason. In the second part of *Rogues* Derrida makes the latter task explicit. With reference to a phrase found in Kant, he sets out to "save the honor of reason" in the name of deconstruction. Indeed, Derrida describes deconstruction as an "unconditional rationalism," which is also a "hyperrationalism."[10] These assertions are all the more remarkable since Derrida openly challenges the sovereignty of reason and the concept of indivisible identity that serves as its foundation. Sovereignty defines an instance that is absolutely *in itself.* As such, it conforms to the logic of identity that follows from the principle of noncontradiction. Derrida deconstructs this logic by dissociating sovereignty from "unconditionality," which is unthinkable within the traditional paradigms of reason. Sovereignty is by definition unconditional in the sense that it is not dependent on anything other than itself. In contrast, Derrida argues that the unconditional is the spacing of time that divides every instance in advance and makes it essentially dependent on what is other than itself. What makes X *possible* is at the same time what makes it *impossible* for X to be in itself. Such is the minimal formula for the illogical logic of identity that deconstructive reason employs.

Deconstructive reason can helpfully be compared to the philosophical reason employed by Kant in the "Transcendental Aesthetic" and the "Transcendental Dialectic." In the subsequent chapter on Husserl I will demonstrate how Derrida addresses the problem concerning the relation between time and subjectivity that Kant broaches in the "Transcendental Aesthetic." What troubles Kant is that human intuition does not possess the characteristics of a divine intuition, which would allow the subject to create its object and posit itself as an immediate unity. Such a divine intuition is what Kant calls an original intuition (*intuitus originarius*), whereas human intuition is a derived intuition (*intuitus derivativus*) that can never give access to the subject as a being in itself. Even when I merely posit myself *as* myself, the act of positing takes time and cannot grant a simultaneous identity of I = I. If I am only given to myself through time, I am thus always already divided.

For Kant, as well as for Husserl, such divisibility must be subordinate, since it gives rise to an infinite regress that is deemed unacceptable. Derrida, however, insists on nothing less than endless divisibility. As he recalls in *Resistances*, if deconstruction were reduced to one single thesis, "it would pose divisibility: *différance* as divisibility" (33/48). For philosophical reason, to advocate endless divisibility is tantamount to an irresponsible empiricism that cannot account for how identity is possible. Consequently, if one wants to defend deconstruction as "reasonable," one must demonstrate how it can provide such an account. Derrida does not seek to abolish the subject or to simply debunk the transcendental analysis with reference to the empirical. Rather, I will show that deconstructive notions such as "arche-writing" operate on an ultratranscendental level, which allows us to think the necessary synthesis of time without grounding it in a nontemporal unity.

Derrida obliquely relates such a project to Kant in *Of Grammatology*, when he writes that "a new transcendental aesthetic must let itself be guided not only by mathematical idealities but by the possibility of inscriptions in general, not befalling an already constituted space but producing the spatiality of space" (290/410). While Derrida goes on to say that such an account of spatiality must be dissociated from Kant's, it is instructive to compare the two in order to assess in what sense Derrida can be said to write a new transcendental aesthetic.

In the "Transcendental Aesthetic" Kant establishes his distinction between time and space. Time is the immediate form of interiority (inner sense) because all experience, including one's experience of oneself, necessarily is successive. Space is the mediate form of exteriority (outer sense) because it presupposes the form of succession while introducing an additional dimension: all things that appear in space appear as exterior to the one that apprehends them and as exterior from one another. Kant himself, however, shows that time as the form of interiority is always already penetrated by space as the form of exteriority. Consider the following passage, which elucidates the example of drawing a line to which Kant often returns:

> In order to make even inner alterations thinkable, we must be able to grasp time, as the form of inner sense, figuratively through a line, and grasp the inner alteration through the drawing of this line (motion), and thus grasp the successive existence of ourselves in different states through outer intuition; the real ground of which is that all alteration presupposes something that persists in intuition, even in order merely to be perceived as alteration, but there is no persistent intuition to be found in inner sense. (B 292)

Kant here rehearses the problem that haunts his transcendental aesthetic, namely, that time as the form of inner sense cannot provide a ground for the subject. Since the temporal can never be in itself, it must be synthesized by something other than itself in order to appear as such. No alteration—and hence no passage of time—can be marked without something that persists as a measure of the change. Kant usually anchors the synthesis in the persistence of a transcendental apperception, but here he opens the way for a different solution. The synthesis is not effectuated by a spontaneous "I think" beyond the intuition of time, but by the act of spatial inscription that is the drawing of the line. The persistence of such spatial inscription is quite different from the persistence of a self-identical consciousness. The spatial inscription can archive time and thus make it possible to grasp alteration, but it is itself exposed to alteration at every juncture. Both the act of inscription and the reading of inscription necessarily take time. Thus, the drawing of the line marks not only the becoming-space of time but also the becoming-time of space as the condition for synthesis.[11]

Derrida can be said to radicalize the above account of time and space. For Derrida, time and space are not transcendental forms of human intuition, which would be given in the same way regardless of their empirical conditions. Rather, the ultratranscendental status of spacing deconstructs the traditional divide between the transcendental and the empirical. If time must be spatially inscribed, then the experience of time is essentially dependent on which material supports and technologies are available to inscribe time. That is why Derrida maintains that inscriptions do not befall an already constituted space but produce the spatiality of space. Derrida can thus think the experience of space and time as constituted by historical and technological conditions, without reducing spacing to an effect of a certain historical or technological epoch. If spacing were merely an effect of historical conditions, it would supervene on something that precedes it and thus adhere to the metaphysical notion of spacing as a Fall. Spacing is rather an ultratranscendental condition because there has never been and will never be a self-presence that grounds the passage between past and future. That is why any moment *always* must be recorded in order to be. The ultratranscendental movement of spacing thus accounts for why there is neither a beginning nor an end to historicity and technicity. The inscriptions that trace time are susceptible to all sorts of transformations, manipulations, and erasures, but the general condition of spacing cannot be eliminated.

Moreover, the ultratranscendental condition of spacing precedes and exceeds any delimitation of "the human." As Derrida remarks in *Of Grammatology*, the history of life in general is the history of *différance*. The evolution of life has always been a matter of different types of inscription,

from the "'genetic inscription' and 'the short programmatic chains' regu-
lating the behavior of the amoeba and the annelid up to the passage beyond alphabetic writing to the orders of the logos and of a certain *homo
sapiens*" (84/125). Spacing is not a property of the human but marks "an
exteriorization always already begun . . . from the elementary programs of
so called 'instinctive' behavior up to the constitution of electronic card-
indexes and reading machines" (84/125).[12]

If Derrida writes a new transcendental aesthetic, he thus profoundly
displaces the Kantian schema by writing an ultratranscendental aesthetic.
For Kant, time and space are merely forms of human intuition and do
not answer to anything outside such intuition. For Derrida, the tracing
of time is the condition for life in general. As he maintains in *Of Grammatology*, the trace "must be thought before the opposition of nature and
culture, animality and humanity" since it designates "the opening of the
first exteriority in general, the enigmatic relation of the living to its other
and of an inside to an outside: spacing" (70/103).

Furthermore, Derrida does not only claim that spacing is the condition
for the living as such. He also claims that spacing is the condition for
everything that can be thought and desired. The latter move has the most
radical consequences, which Derrida also outlines in *Of Grammatology*:

> All dualisms, all theories of the immortality of the soul or of the spirit, as
> well as all monisms, spiritualist or materialist, dialectical or vulgar, are the
> unique theme of a metaphysics whose entire history was compelled to strive
> toward the reduction of the trace . . . [which is] required by an onto-theology
> determining the archeological and eschatological meaning of being as pres-
> ence, as *parousia*, as life without *différance*: another name for death, historical
> metonymy where God's name holds death in check. That is why, if this move-
> ment begins its era in the form of Platonism, it ends in infinitist metaphysics.
> Only infinite being can reduce the difference in presence. In that sense, the
> name of God . . . is the name of indifference itself. (71/104)

What traditionally has been figured as the most desirable—the absolute
being of God or the immortality of the soul—is here figured as the most
undesirable: as the pure indifference of death that would annihilate the
impure difference of life. We will see how this argument recurs in different versions throughout Derrida's writings. If there can be nothing without the spacing of time, then all metaphysical ideas of something that
would eliminate the spacing of time are ideas of something that would

extinguish everything. The ideal of pure life is the ideal of pure death, according to a formula that informs Derrida's deconstruction of metaphysics from beginning to end. Further on in *Of Grammatology* he emphasizes that the "pure presence of the pure present, which one may either call purity of life or purity of death," is the "determination of being that has always superintended not only theological and metaphysical but also transcendental questions, whether conceived in terms of scholastic theology or in a Kantian or post-Kantian sense" (291/411).

The ultratranscendental aesthetic of deconstruction can thus be seen to lead to an ultratranscendental dialectic as well. Like Kant in his transcendental dialectic, Derrida scrutinizes metaphysical concepts of the unconditional as an instance of absolute sovereignty: an origin or end that would be completely *in itself*. But whereas Kant employs the philosophical logic of identity in order to save absolute sovereignty as an Idea, Derrida employs the deconstructive logic of identity in order to refute the very Idea of absolute sovereignty.

We can here return to the dissociation between unconditionality and sovereignty that Derrida proposes in *Rogues*. Derrida pursues his argument by aligning the unconditional with the structure of the event and the coming of the future. The key word in his exposition is the French verb *arriver*, which can mean to come, to happen, and to arrive. Derrida plays on these multiple meanings in order to reinforce that what happens cannot be given in the form of presence but is divided by the spacing of time. Every event is both superseded (*no longer*) and to come (*not yet*) in its very event. Whatever happens is therefore transgressed by the future and becomes past.

Derrida's crucial move is to mobilize the unconditional exposure to *what happens*—to whatever or whoever comes—in order to deconstruct the concept of sovereignty.[13] If there were a sovereign instance, nothing could ever happen to it since it would be completely given *in itself*. The concept of sovereignty is thus predicated on the exclusion of time. As Derrida puts it in *Rogues*, "sovereignty neither gives nor gives itself time; it does not take time" (109/154). While the indivisible presence of sovereignty traditionally has been hailed as absolute life, Derrida underscores that it is inseparable from absolute death. Without the exposition to time, nothing could ever happen and nothing could emerge. Or as Derrida writes in *Of Grammatology*: "pure presence itself, if such a thing were possible, would be only another name for death" (155/223). Absolute sovereignty is thus not a desirable consummation that is unattainable because of our human limitations. Absolute sovereignty is unattainable, unthinkable, and undesirable because it would extinguish every trace of life.

The deconstruction of sovereignty is fatal for the Idea in the Kantian sense. The three regulative Ideas that Kant defends in the "Transcendental Dialectic" (the soul, the world as totality, and God) are all Ideas of something to which nothing could happen. If the immortality of the soul were essentially exposed to the coming of time, it would not be immortal since it could perish at any juncture. If the totality of the world were essentially exposed to the coming of time, it would not be a totality since it could never be given as a complete unity. If the perfection of God were essentially exposed to the coming of time, it would not be perfect since it could be altered at any juncture.

Kant elides the problem by positing absolute sovereignty as an Idea that is impossible to cognize for a mind that is bound by time, but nevertheless is possible to think and desire as an ideal. Given the philosophical logic of identity, this argument is irrefutable. If the essence of X is to be identical to itself, then the consummation of X must be thinkable as an Idea even though it is inaccessible for our temporal cognition. Finitude is thus a negative limitation that prevents us from having access to the fullness of being. But given the deconstructive logic of identity, a completely different argument emerges. If the essence of X is to *not* be identical to itself, then the consummation of X cannot even be posited as an Idea since it would cancel out X. Finitude is thus not a negative limitation that prevents us from having access to the fullness of being. On the contrary, finitude is an unconditional condition that makes the fullness of being unthinkable as such.

The relation between the conditional and the unconditional in Derrida's thinking can thus be described as an autoimmune relation. Inscribed within the condition for X is the unconditional coming of time that attacks the integrity of X a priori. Accordingly, Derrida maintains that there can be nothing without autoimmunity:

> If an event worthy of this name is to arrive or happen, it must, beyond all mastery, affect a passivity. It must touch an exposed vulnerability, one without absolute immunity, without indemnity; it must touch this vulnerability in its finitude and in a nonhorizontal fashion, there where it is not yet or is already

no longer possible to face or face up to the unforeseeability of the other. In this regard, autoimmunity is not an absolute ill or evil. It enables an exposure to the other, to *what* and to *who* comes—which means that it must remain incalculable. Without autoimmunity, with absolute immunity, nothing would ever happen or arrive; we would no longer wait, await, or expect, no longer expect one another, or expect any event. (*Rogues*, 152/210)

This passage reiterates one of the most persistent claims in Derrida's writings, namely, that there *must* be exposition to an unpredictable future, there *must* be finitude and vulnerability, there *must* be openness to whatever or whoever comes. The failure to understand the status of this "must" has given rise to a number of influential misreadings that I will scrutinize in the course of this book. Their common denominator is that they ascribe a normative dimension to Derrida's argument.[14] The ultratranscendental *description* of why we must be open to the other is conflated with an ethical *prescription* that we ought to be open to the other. However, Derrida always maintains that one cannot derive any norms, rules, or prescriptions from the constitutive exposition to the other. The other can be anything whatsoever or anyone whosoever and one cannot know in advance how one should act in relation to him, her, or it. On the contrary, the relation to the other is inseparable from the coming of time, which means that it may alter its character at every moment. One cannot *face up to* or even *face* the other, as Derrida emphasizes in the passage above, since the other is no longer or not yet. What I welcome as a vital chance may turn out to be a lethal threat, since it can never be given in itself.

Autoimmunity entails that the same temporal alterity constitutes my self-relation. Whenever I open myself to myself—which is to say, at every moment—I open myself to someone who exceeds my given identity and always may violate me to the point of death. This autoimmune openness to the other is not something one can choose, and it cannot be posited as good in itself, since it opens the possibility of existence at the same time that it opens the peril of destruction. When Derrida writes that there *must* be autoimmune openness to the other—or even, as he does in other passages, that there *should* be or *ought* to be such openness—he is thus not making a normative statement concerning how we should act in relation to the other. Rather, he is indicating the ultratranscendental status of his argument. The autoimmunity of finitude is not merely an empirical condition that we *cannot* avoid because of the limitations imposed by our historical situation, nor is it merely a transcendental condition that we *cannot* avoid because of our human constitution; it is an ultratranscendental condition that even ideally speaking *must not* and *ought not* to be avoided, because if it were avoided, there would only be absolute death. Autoimmunity opens the space and time for all kinds of violence, but without autoimmunity there would be nothing: "Without autoimmunity, with absolute immunity, nothing would ever happen."

The same formal argument recurs with a remarkable frequency in Derrida's writings. Derrida first asserts that for something to happen, there must be both a chance and a threat. He then asserts that this double bind cannot even in principle be eliminated, since if nothing happened there would be nothing at all. What I want to stress is that this argument presupposes that being is essentially temporal (to be = to happen) and that it is inherently valuable that something happens (the worst = that nothing happens). In other words, it presupposes that *temporal finitude is the condition for everything that is desirable.* Metaphysical and religious traditions have readily admitted that nothing can happen in the ideal realm of eternity, but they have been able to dismiss this problem by not ascribing any inherent value to the temporal. On the contrary, the most desirable has explicitly been posited as the immutable and the inviolable—in short, as that to which nothing can happen. When Derrida argues that the most undesirable would be that nothing happened, he is thus presupposing a quite different conception of desire, which needs to be developed in order to consolidate his argument.

Derrida himself did not provide a systematic account of his notion of desire, and it has remained unexplored by his commentators, but I will argue that it is altogether crucial for his thinking. For example, the innumerable sentences in Derrida's work that refer to "the chance and the threat" or to "the best and the worst" demand that one understands what Derrida regards as a chance and a threat or what he regards as the best and the worst. In short, they demand that one understands his assessment of what is desirable.

The decisive issue concerns the status of mortality. Mortality has traditionally been determined as a negative predicament, but Derrida reinscribes it as the condition for everything positive and everything negative. Mortality is thus not a lack of being that it is desirable to overcome. Rather, mortality is the possibility for both the desirable *and* the undesirable, since it opens the chance of life and the threat of death in the same stroke. Conversely, the immortality that is generally posited as the most desirable ("the best") is for Derrida the most undesirable ("the worst") because immortality would annihilate the time of mortal life.

Hence, we must distinguish between what Derrida calls "the chance and the threat" and what he calls "the best and the worst." Derrida never supplies a formal definition of the respective phrases, and they may appear to be interchangeable in his writing. I will demonstrate, however, that they must be ascribed quite different meanings, in accordance with the logic that can be traced in Derrida's texts. On the one hand, *the chance is the threat* since the chance is always a chance of mortal life that is intrinsically threatened by death. On the other hand, *the best is the worst* since the best can never become better or worse and thus abolishes the chance and threat of mortal life.

My argument does not necessarily imply that Derrida never uses the two phrases interchangeably. One must always analyze the syntax in question, since only a sentence and not a word has meaning (as Austin said and Derrida liked to repeat). Depending on the syntax, the phrase "the best and the worst" can perform the same function as the phrase "the chance and the threat." Thus, when Derrida invokes the necessary opening toward "the best and the worst," this phrase can function as a synonym for the necessary opening toward the chance and the threat of temporal finitude (which is "the best" in the sense that there cannot be anything better than finitude, and "the worst" in the sense that it will destroy itself, destroy the best). My argument, then, does not aim at an a priori determination of how the respective phrases operate in Derrida's texts. Rather, it aims at demonstrating that the logic of Derrida's thinking hinges on the radical incompatibility between "the chance" in the deconstructive sense and "the best" in the sense of a metaphysical absolute. On the one hand, the chance in the deconstructive sense is inseparable from the threat of its own destruction and thus always a matter of mortal life. On the other hand, the best in the metaphysical sense is inseparable from the worst, since it is predicated on the elimination of mortal life.

An important clue to Derrida's revaluation of mortality is offered in his last interview. Derrida here emphasizes that his thinking proceeds from an unconditional affirmation of *life*, which in his vocabulary is synonymous with mortality. The deconstructive notion of life entails that living is always a matter of *living on*, of surviving. As I emphasized in my introduction, this notion of survival is incompatible with immortality, since it defines life as essentially mortal and as inherently divided by time. The unconditional "yes" to such finitude does not oblige one to accept whatever happens; it only marks the exposure to what happens as an unconditional condition of life. Whatever we do, we have always already said "yes" to the coming of the future, since without it nothing could happen. But for the same reason, every affirmation is essentially compromised and haunted by negation, since the coming of the future also entails all the threats to which one may want to say "no." Thus, the precarious time of survival is neither something to be lamented nor something to be celebrated as such. It is rather the condition for everything one wants and everything one does not want. As Derrida points out in his last interview:

> Everything I say about survival as a complication of the opposition life/death proceeds in me from an unconditional affirmation of life. . . . It is the affirmation of a living being who prefers living, and thus surviving, to death, because survival is not simply that which remains but the most intense life possible. I am never more haunted by the necessity of dying than in moments of happiness and joy. To feel joy and to weep over the death that awaits are for me the same thing.[15]

This apparently confessional statement epitomizes the double bind of desire that is central to Derrida's thinking. The finitude of survival is not a lack of being that it is desirable to overcome. Rather, Derrida makes clear that whatever is desired is finite in its essence. Even the most intense enjoyment is haunted by the imminence of death, but without such finitude there would be nothing to enjoy in the first place. There is thus an incurable autoimmunity at the heart of every experience, since whatever one wants to affirm is constituted by the fact that it will be negated. There is no way out of this double bind because the threat of loss is not extrinsic to what is desired; it is intrinsic to its being as such.

When Derrida in the same interview points out that "deconstruction is always on the side of the *yes*, on the side of the affirmation of life" (51/54), he is not advocating that we should become healthy, affirmative beings. The unconditional affirmation of life is not something that can cure us of the fear of death or the pain of loss. On the contrary, it makes us susceptible to fear and pain from the first inception. Before any act of will one has necessarily affirmed the coming of the unpredictable, but the response *to* the coming and the response *of* the coming are never given in advance. One may come to negate what one wanted to affirm, and what comes may negate the coming that one affirmed.[16]

Derrida inscribes the possibility of negation at the core of affirmation by analyzing it as essentially temporal. On the one hand, to say "yes" is to turn toward the past, since it responds to something that precedes it, if only a moment before. On the other hand, to say "yes" is to turn toward the future, since one has to confirm the affirmation by repeating it, if only a moment after. The moment I say "yes" is immediately succeeded by another moment and has to record itself as a memory for the future in order to have been stated.[17] Derrida unpacks the implications as follows:

> There is a time and a spacing of the "yes" as "yes-yes": it takes time to say "yes." A single "yes" is, therefore, immediately double, it immediately announces a "yes" to come and already recalls that the "yes" implies another "yes." So, the "yes" is immediately double, immediately "yes-yes."
>
> This immediate duplication is the source of all possible contamination. . . . The second "yes" can eventually be one of laughter or derision at the first "yes," it can be the forgetting of the first "yes." . . . With this duplicity we are at the heart of the "logic" of contamination. One should not simply consider contamination as a threat, however. To do so continues to ignore this very logic. Possible contamination must be assumed, because it is also opening or chance, our chance. Without contamination we would have no opening or chance. Contamination is not only to be assumed or affirmed: it is the very possibility of affirmation in the first place. For affirmation to be possible, there must always be at least two "yes's." If the contamination of the first "yes" by the second is refused—for whatever reasons—one is denying the very possibility of the first "yes." Hence all the contradictions and confusion that this denial can fall into. Threat is chance, chance is threat—this law is absolutely undeniable and irreducible. If one does not accept it, there is no risk, and, if there is no risk, there is only death. If one refuses to take a risk, one is left with nothing but death.[18]

The interval that divides the moment of the "yes"—the spacing of time that is intrinsic to affirmation as such—opens it to being forgotten, derided, or otherwise negated. In spite of Derrida's recourse to voluntary metaphors, such contamination cannot be "accepted" or "refused" in the sense of a personal resolution, since one cannot do anything without being contaminated. The necessity of "accepting" contamination precedes any act of will and is concomitant with the advent of life as such. For the same reason, deconstruction cannot teach us how to deal with contamination. Rather, deconstruction spells out that there can be no final cure against contamination and that all ideals of purity are untenable, since their "refusal" of contamination equals nothing but death.

Thus, the passage above accounts for why the chance is the threat and why the best is the worst. The chance is the threat because every chance is the chance of a temporal finitude that has to be contaminated in order to be what it is and always runs the risk of being extinguished. Derrida emphasizes that "this law is absolutely undeniable and irreducible," since without contamination there would be nothing at all. Inversely, the best is the worst, since it would have to be absolutely purified of anything that could make it better or worse and consequently extinguish the contamination that is inherent to life.

Given the law of contamination, we must ask how Derrida can appeal to a "pure" gift or a "pure" hospitality, as he regularly does in his later writings. The appeal to purity may seem to contradict the deconstructive insight concerning the necessity of contamination. I will argue, however, that Derrida analyzes the ideal purity of a given concept to show that the necessity of contamination is inscribed in the ideal purity of the concept itself. Thus, Derrida's analysis of "pure" hospitality demonstrates that even the most ideal hospitality must be open to the contamination of others that may corrupt it. Moreover, Derrida maintains that the same "deconstructive law of hospitality" applies to all concepts: "each concept opens itself to its opposite, reproducing or producing in advance, in the rapport of one concept to the other, the contradictory and deconstructive law of hospitality."[19] I address the concept of hospitality at length in Chapter 3, so I will focus here on how the same conceptual logic informs Derrida's analysis of the "pure" gift. As we will see, contamination is not something that happens to the pure gift because it has to realize itself in the world. On the contrary, the very concept of the gift requires that it be contaminated by what is other than itself.

For a gift to be pure, it would have to absolve itself from every form of economic exchange, but in so doing it would cancel itself out. Whenever a gift is given or received, there is an economic relation, which contaminates the purported purity of the gift. Even if I give with the greatest generosity, the mere desire to give makes me profit from the act of giving. Inversely, even if I receive the most generous gift, I become indebted to the donor. Already the most elementary reception of the gift—the recognition of the gift *as* a gift—puts me in debt and opens an economic relation, even if the gift is given without any demands of repayment.[20]

Hence, Derrida argues that the *possibility* of the gift is the *impossibility* of a pure gift. The standard misreading of this argument is to understand the impossibility as a negative limitation that prevents us from having access to the pure gift.[21] The pure gift would then be a regulative Idea of pure goodness, which cannot be experienced as such but is thinkable and desirable as an ideal beyond the contaminating calculations of self-interest. Such a model for reading Derrida has been largely assumed, but it is quite untenable. Derrida persistently maintains that the impossibility of purity is *not* a negative limitation.[22] Contamination is not a privation or a lack of purity—it is the originary possibility for anything to be. Thus, a pure gift is not impossible because it is contaminated by our selfish intentions or by the constraints of economic exchange; it is impossible because a gift *must* be contaminated in order to be a gift. If the gift were not contaminated, it could neither be given nor received. Moreover, the very desire for a gift is a desire for contamination. If I desire to give or to receive a gift, I desire to contaminate and to be contaminated by the gift. When Derrida analyzes the conditions for a "pure" gift, he is thus not promoting purity as an ideal. On the contrary, he demonstrates why the gift *even in its ideal purity* must be contaminated and why a pure gift is neither thinkable nor desirable as such.

The relation between gift and economy should thus not be understood as an opposition, where the former is good and the latter is bad. Rather, Derrida analyzes why neither of these concepts can be pure and why they must be contaminated by each other. A pure economy would be a closed circle where everything that is given returns to the origin that gave it away. Such a pure economy is strictly impossible, however, since the circulation of economy only can be set in motion by a gift that may always break the circle. If nothing were given, there would be nothing to capitalize on and no economy in the first place. But by the same token, an economy cannot ever be closed against the risk of irremediable loss, since what is given can always be wasted or destroyed, either in the process of being dispatched or by the one who receives it.

The deepest reason why there cannot be a closed circle is the constitution of time. The interval of time divides everything in advance and makes it impossible for anything to be closed in itself. Without the interval of time there would be neither gift nor economy, since there would be nothing separating the moment of giving from the moment of receiving. Consequently, the interval of time is the condition for anything to be given. Time is unconditionally given, since nothing can be given without being temporal. The given time is what makes economy *possible*, since it immediately separates the gift from itself and gives it over to calculation. But the given time is also what makes it *impossible* for economy to be a closed system, since the temporality of the gift cannot be mastered by calculation. Rather, it exposes every calculation to the incalculable coming of time and opens the economy to irretrievable loss, since time cannot be recuperated. The necessary interval of time entails that what is given *never* can return as the same. Even if I return the same thing I received, it is already different, since it is no longer the same time.

Hence, the unconditional gift is the gift of time and cannot be assimilated to the regulative Idea of a transcendent gift. Derrida himself invites such a misreading when he compares the structure of his argument to Kant's transcendental dialectic without clearly explaining the difference.[23] If we scrutinize his argument, however, we can see that it answers to what I have called an ultratranscendental dialectic. There is an apparent formal similarity between Kant's and Derrida's respective arguments, but they support radically different conclusions. Kant argues that the object of an Idea exceeds the order of knowledge and cannot be experienced as such, whereas Derrida argues that the gift exceeds the order of knowledge and cannot be experienced as such. However, the respective reasons why the Idea and the gift cannot be experienced as such are diametrically opposite. The object of an Idea cannot be experienced as such because it is beyond time. The gift, on the contrary, cannot be experienced as such because it is temporal in itself.[24] The very idea of the gift spells out that there is no gift as such, since the gift can be what it is only by becoming other than itself. Thus, while the Kantian Idea refers to a thing in itself beyond the restrictions of time and space, the deconstructive analysis maintains the ultratranscendental status of the becoming-space of time and the becoming-time of space. As Derrida reinforces in a striking passage, *the thing itself is différance*, which is to say that the spacing of time is inscribed in the thing itself.[25]

Accordingly, when Derrida asserts that the gift we desire exceeds the order of knowledge, it is not because the gift we desire belongs to a noumenal beyond. On the contrary, the gift we desire exceeds the order of knowledge because it is a gift of time, which is unpredictable and cannot be reduced to a given presence. For the same reason, the gift we desire exceeds the order of economy without answering to the regulative Idea of a gift that would be good or generous in itself. Rather, the gift of time that we desire exceeds the order of economy because its effects cannot be completely calculated. This gift of time is quite incompatible with the regulative Idea of a gift that is good or generous in itself. If the gift is essentially temporal, it cannot have a given value, since it can never be given in itself. Every apparently "positive" value of the gift is haunted by its "negative" counterpart. When Derrida describes the gift of time as the condition for anything to be given, he thus points out that it opens an "undecidability that allows all the values to be inverted."[26] The purportedly good gift must run the risk of being a poison (*Gift* in German), and the purportedly generous gift must run the risk of dealing with counterfeit money. The point is not only that the gift *cannot* be secured against these risks but also that it *ought not* to be secured against them, since such security would cancel out the gift. If the gift were secured against being corrupted it could never be given, since nothing could happen to it.

Moreover, the gift of time undercuts the opposition between giving and taking. Everything that happens *gives* time by *taking* time. As Derrida writes, "Only a 'life' can give, but a life in which this economy of death presents itself and lets itself be exceeded. Neither death nor immortal life can ever give anything, only a singular *survivance* can give" (*Given Time*, 102/132).[27] The gift is thus always a gift of mortal life that is haunted by death. Nothing can be given without the time of survival, which gives the chance of living and the threat of dying at every juncture.

If the gift is essentially a gift of time, there cannot even in principle be a gift that is good or generous in itself. If the gift were good or generous in itself, it would be quite calculable, since one would be able to count on it as being good or generous. Derrida's argument is, on the contrary, that the incalculable coming of time is the unconditional condition of the gift. In the course of this book I will demonstrate how the same logic informs Derrida's treatment of all the concepts he links to the unconditional, which in addition to the gift include justice, hospitality, and democracy. Far from subscribing to a regulative Idea of absolute justice, hospitality, or democracy, Derrida spells out why the coming of time is the unconditional condition for there to be justice, hospitality, democracy, and everything else.

I will here address the example of *justice,* which is the term in Derrida that most persistently has been misread in accordance with the structure of the Kantian Idea. The source of misreading is Derrida's distinction between law (*droit*) and justice. Derrida describes law as deconstructible, whereas justice is said to be the "undeconstructible" condition of deconstruction. Law is thus aligned with the conditional and justice with the unconditional that exceeds law. This has led many readers to believe that Derrida invokes an Idea of absolute justice, but such a reading is untenable. As we will see, the unconditional that exceeds law is not an Idea of absolute justice; it is the coming of time that undercuts the very Idea of absolute justice.

A key term is what Derrida calls *undecidability.* With this term he designates the necessary opening toward the coming of the future. The coming of the future is strictly speaking "undecidable," since it is a relentless displacement that unsettles any definitive assurance or given meaning. One can never know what *will have happened.* Promises may always be turned into threats, friendships into enmities, fidelities into betrayals, and so on.

There is no opposition between undecidability and the making of decisions. On the contrary, it is *because* the future cannot be decided in advance that one has to make decisions. If the future could be predicted, there would be nothing to decide on and no reason to act in the first place. Derrida reiterates this line of thought in his description of the relation between law (*droit*) and justice. The former term designates how we establish rights and lay down laws in order to reckon with unpredictable and potentially violent events. Derrida does not deny the necessity of such defensive measures, but he maintains that every law and right is deconstructible. The established laws may always turn out to be inadequate and are fundamentally exposed to the undecidable coming of time, which can challenge or overturn what has been prescribed.

The second step in Derrida's argument is the one that is usually misunderstood.[28] Derrida describes the undecidable future as the very possibility of justice or quite simply as a "justice" beyond law. The point is that decisions concerning justice cannot be reduced to a rule for how the law should be applied. Rather, the demand for justice is always raised in relation to singular events, which there is no guarantee that the law will have anticipated. The condition of justice is thus an essential contingency. The specific applications of the law cannot be given in the law itself but require decisions in relation to events that exceed the generality of the law.

Derrida's argument is that there can be no justice without such decisions, which are precipitated by the undecidable coming of time. Justice is thus essentially a matter of temporal finitude, since it is ultimately because of temporal finitude that one has to make decisions. Derrida writes:

> The moment of *decision as such*, what must be just, *must* always remain a finite moment of urgency and precipitation. . . . Even if time and prudence, the patience of knowledge and the mastery of conditions were hypothetically unlimited, the decision would be structurally finite, however late it came—a decision of urgency and precipitation, acting in the night of non-knowledge and non-rule. Not of the absence of rules and knowledge but of a reinstitution of rules that by definition is not preceded by any knowledge or by any guarantee as such.[29]

It is this necessity of making finite decisions—of calculating with the incalculable coming of time—that Derrida calls "justice." As he writes, justice requires an incalculable temporality in which "the *decision* between just and unjust is never insured by a rule" (244/38).[30] This may appear paradoxical, since it means that justice is nothing but the predicament that decisions only can be made from time to time, without any assurance concerning what is just or unjust. But it is exactly this condition on which Derrida insists. If laws and rights cannot encompass everyone and everything, if they cannot be grounded in a totalizing instance, then it is inevitably necessary to negotiate what exceeds them. This exigency of "justice" is not something positive in itself but designates that every decision is haunted by the undecidable coming of time, which opens the risk that one has made or will have made unjust decisions. Without such risk, there would be no question of justice in the first place, since the execution of law would be nothing but a faultless application of rules.

Accordingly, Derrida emphasizes that the relation between law and justice cannot be understood as an *opposition*: "Everything would still be simple if this distinction between justice and law were a true distinction, an opposition the functioning of which was logically regulated and masterable. But it turns out that law claims to exercise itself in the name of justice and that justice demands for itself that it be established in the name of a law that must be put to work [*mis en oeuvre*] (constituted and applied) by force *enforced*" ("Force of Law," 250–51/49–50). This relation between law and justice can helpfully be understood as an autoimmune relation. The system of law functions as an immune protection for justice. It maintains the principles for what is just and makes it possible to identify what is considered harmful for the political body. Without such a system of law there would be nothing that could determine or safeguard justice, since there would be no rules for evaluating a given decision. At the same time, decisions of justice have to suspend or attack the law that protects them, since they are made in relation to events that may question the laws or transform the rules. Thus, in the essay on justice from which I have been quoting ("Force of Law") Derrida can be seen to describe the autoimmunity of justice, even though the term "autoimmunity" had not yet entered his vocabulary when the essay was written. Consider, for example, the following formulation:

> For a decision to be just and responsible, it must [*il faut*], in its proper moment, if there is one, be both regulated and without regulation, it must preserve the law [*loi*] and also destroy or suspend it enough to have [*pour devoir*] to reinvent it in each case, rejustify it, reinvent it at least in the reaffirmation and the new and free confirmation of its principle. Each case is other, each decision is different and requires an absolutely unique interpretation, which no existing, coded rule can or ought to guarantee absolutely. (251/51)

It is always possible that the law is more unjust than the injustice against which it asserts itself. The attack on the law may thus be a defense of justice, and the defense of the law may be an attack on justice. But for the same reason, one may attack justice when one thinks that one is defending it, since there is no absolute rule for distinguishing between what is just and unjust. Neither law nor justice, neither the general nor the singular, can be ascribed a positive value in itself. Indeed, these poles do not have any meaning at all if they are not played out against each other, in a process where it cannot be known which instance will be more violent than the other.

If law is essentially deconstructible, the undecidable coming of time is thus the undeconstructible condition of justice. Far from promoting an Idea of absolute justice, this undeconstructible condition of justice opens it to injustice from the first instance.[31] For justice to be absolute, it would have to preclude the coming of time, which may always jeopardize or question the given justice. For Derrida, on the contrary, the coming of time is unconditional and inscribed in the concept of justice as such. The *possibility* of justice is thus the *impossibility* of absolute justice. Justice is and *must be* more or less unjust, since it must demarcate itself against a future that exceeds it and may call it into question.

To assess the radicality of the deconstructive argument, it is important to see how the structure of the Kantian Idea is endemic in our established ways of thinking. Even if we know that there is no absolute immunity, we assume that the most desirable would be a state of absolute immunity (e.g., an absolute justice that is immune to injustice). We thus assume that absolute justice is possible to think as an Idea, even though it is impossible to cognize for us as finite beings. In contrast, deconstructive reason demonstrates that the Idea of absolute justice is neither thinkable nor desirable as such. The risk of injustice is inscribed in the very possibility of justice, which means that it cannot be a question of eliminating injustice once and for all. On the contrary, an absolute justice that was immune to injustice would eliminate justice itself.

The logic in question is operative throughout Derrida's work. By thinking the exposure to what happens as *unconditional*—namely, as a condition for everything, including everything that can be thought and desired—Derrida transforms the most fundamental assumptions about what is desirable. Regardless of which concept he analyzes, Derrida maintains that it must be open to "the other," which is to say that it must be open to what contaminates and may undermine it. Hence, Derrida asserts that life must be open to death, that good must be open to evil, that peace must be open to violence, and so on. Inversely, an absolute life that is immune to death, an absolute goodness that is immune to evil, or an absolute peace that is immune to violence is for Derrida the same as an absolute death, an absolute evil, or an absolute violence. As he puts it in *Specters of Marx*, "absolute life, fully present life, the one that does not know death," would be "absolute evil" (175/278). This is because an absolute immunity would have to close all openness to the other, all openness to the unpredictable coming of time, and thereby close the opening of life itself.

The logic of deconstruction thus allows us to read the Kantian Idea against itself. The reason why there cannot be an absolute instance is not because it is an inaccessible Idea but because it is self-refuting as such. I here want to exemplify this claim by relating it to Kant's remarkable essay "The End of All Things." Written in 1794, after the publication of the three *Critiques*, this essay addresses the Idea of immortality, which is inseparable from the Idea of something that is good in itself. If everything is subjected to time—that is, if everything is mortal—it may be altered at any juncture and is structurally open to becoming evil and becoming corrupted. Consequently, there has to be an *end of time* for there to be something that is good in itself. Kant's essay, however, is haunted by the insight that such an end of time is the same as death. These are the opening lines of the essay:

> It is a common expression, used chiefly in pious language, to speak of a person who is dying as going *out of time into eternity*.
>
> This expression would in fact say nothing if *eternity* is understood here to mean a time proceeding to infinity; for then the person would indeed never get outside time but would always progress only from one time to another. Thus what must be meant is an *end of all time*, along with the person's uninterrupted duration . . . as a magnitude (*duratio Noumenon*), wholly incomparable with time, of which we are obviously able to form no concept (except a merely negative one). (221)

This distinction between two types of infinity is crucial for understanding how we can deconstruct the Idea of immortality. Immortality requires a *positive infinity* that reposes wholly in itself and grants the person an "uninterrupted duration." Every form of duration, however, requires the *negative infinity* of time that does not allow anything to repose in itself, since it consists in a relentless succession from one time to another. Without succession duration would be the same as absolute immobility, since there would be no passage of time that marked it *as* duration. But by the same token, duration is necessarily divided within itself, since the succession of time entails that each moment is succeeded by another moment in its very event. The concept of an "uninterrupted duration" is thus self-refuting, as Kant himself concedes when he designates it as "merely negative." If there is duration, there is always susceptibility to interruption, since duration presupposes a temporal process of alteration.

Accordingly, immortality cannot admit any form of duration. But for the same reason, immortality cannot be dissociated from the petrification of death. Kant himself acknowledges this problem in "The End of All Things":

> But that at some point a time will arrive in which all alteration (and with it, time itself) ceases—this is a representation that outrages the imagination. For then the whole of nature will be rigid and as it were petrified: the last thought,

the last feeling in the thinking subject will then stop and remain forever the same without any change. For a being which can become conscious of its existence and the magnitude of this existence (as duration) only in time, such a life—if it can even be called life—appears equivalent to annihilation, because in order to think itself into such a state it still has to think something in general, but *thinking* contains a reflecting, which can occur only in time. (227)

This passage summarizes the problem that keeps returning in Kant's essay. On the one hand, Kant argues that we have to posit an end of time, since otherwise there cannot be a highest good. On the other hand, the end of time cannot be separated from the end of everything—from complete annihilation. As Kant himself notes, *nothing can happen* in eternity because it does not allow for the temporality of events.[32]

Kant's solution to the problem is to posit the end of time as an Idea, which only *appears* to be the same as annihilation for us as time-bound creatures. In "The End of All Things" Kant pursues this argument via a discussion of religious writings on the apocalypse. The word *apocalypse* derives from the Greek word for "revelation." Typically, it designates an end of the world when the timeless truth will be revealed and everything that is mere temporal appearance will be destroyed. Following the basic move in his critical philosophy, Kant reinforces that such apocalyptic consummation should not be made into an object of cognition, since reason is then caught in irresolvable contradictions. For example, if we describe the end of the mortal world as the beginning of the immortal world "the former is brought into the same temporal series with the latter, which contradicts itself" (226). Kant can thus criticize the religious dogmas that claim to have knowledge of the apocalypse and the last judgment, since they disregard the limitations of all cognition. At the same time, Kant maintains that the Idea of apocalyptic consummation has a legitimate source in the Idea of the highest good, which requires an end of time. If everything always will be subjected to time, there cannot ever be anything that is "the best," since it may always become better or worse. The postulate Kant shares with religious traditions of revelation is thus that *there ought to be an end to finitude*, which is to say: there ought to be an end to the negative infinity of time.

The logic of deconstruction is the inverse of such apocalyptic logic. As I will elaborate in Chapter 3, Derrida articulates the negative infinity of time as an irreducible condition for being in general. We can describe it

as an *infinite finitude* in order to spell out that finitude never can be consummated in a positive infinity.[33] Each finitude is always transcended by
another finitude, which in turn is transcended by another finitude, and so
on. Such temporal finitude entails all sorts of extermination and erasure,
but it cannot come to a final apocalyptic end. Or rather: the end of finitude would be "the worst," since it would destroy everything.

It is instructive here to consider the two texts that Derrida himself has
devoted to the question of apocalypse. In the first of these texts—"On
a Newly Arisen Apocalyptic Tone in Philosophy"—Derrida mobilizes
the single word *Come* (*Viens*) against the idea of apocalypse.[34] *Come* articulates the coming of time as the ultratranscendental condition for all
events; it is that "starting from which there is any event" (164/91) because an event only can take place by being succeeded by what is other
than itself. The "Come" is thus "at once absolute and absolutely divisible"
(165/92). It is absolute because it is the condition for everything, and it is
absolutely divisible because it spells out that nothing can be in itself.[35] As
Derrida puts it with a striking phrase, "Come" announces "the apocalypse
of apocalypse," since the coming of time opens a negative infinity that
cannot be closed. Ironically mimicking an apocalyptic prophet, Derrida
can thus declare: "I tell you this, I have come to tell you this, there is not,
there has never been, there will never be apocalypse" (167/96).

The ramifications of Derrida's argument can be traced in his second
text on apocalypse—"No Apocalypse, Not Now." This text was written
for a conference on "nuclear criticism" in 1983 and proceeds from the cold
war hypothesis of a total nuclear holocaust, which Derrida links to his
deconstruction of apocalypse. As we have seen, the event of apocalypse
would have to be the last event that ever took place. If it were not the last
event, if it were succeeded by other events, time would still remain and
there would be no consummation. Consequently, the event of apocalypse
must be an absolute referent that eliminates every reference to what has
been and what will come. But by the same token it must eliminate every
trace of survival, since what survives is always a trace of the past that is
left for the future. The absolute referent of apocalypse is thus indissociable from an absolute nuclear holocaust that would not allow anything
to survive:

> The only referent that is absolutely real is thus of the scope or the dimension
> of an absolute nuclear catastrophe that would irreversibly destroy the entire
> archive and all symbolic capacity, would destroy the 'movement of survival,'

what I call *survivance*, at the very heart of life. This absolute referent . . . is on a par with the absolute effacement of any possible trace. (28/379)

Derrida's argument undermines the very Idea of apocalypse, which hinges on the distinction between temporal appearance and thing in itself. For there to be apocalypse, the destruction of time and space must not entail the destruction of everything but rather reveal a thing in itself that is indestructible. Following Kant's schema, the apocalypse would appear to be the same as complete destruction for a *derived* intuition that is bound by time, but for an *original* intuition it would reveal the thing in itself that cannot be destroyed. In contrast, Derrida is concerned with thinking an *absolute destructibility* that does not exempt anything. As Derrida points out, Kant's critical opposition between derived and original intuition "forecloses a finitude so radical that it would annul the basis of the opposition and would make it possible to think the very limit of criticism. This limit comes into view in the groundlessness of a remainderless self-destruction of the self, auto-destruction of the *autos* itself" ("No Apocalypse, Not Now," 30/383).

The hypothesis of a total nuclear holocaust offers a powerful way to think such destructibility, since it is dreaded as "the possibility of an irreversible destruction, leaving no traces" (26/376) and opens "the historical and a-historical horizon of an absolute self-destructibility without apocalypse, without revelation of its own truth" (27/377). However, Derrida's reflections on absolute destructibility do not only pertain to a certain epoch in history, such as the nuclear age of the cold war. Rather, the hypothesis of a total nuclear holocaust reinforces the radical finitude that deconstruction articulates as the condition for life in general. As a finite being I am always living in relation to the threat of absolute destruction, since with my death the entire world that opens through me and that lives in me will be extinguished. As Derrida puts it: "I live this anticipation [of my own death] in anguish, terror, despair, as a catastrophe that I have no reason not to equate with the annihilation of humanity as a whole: this catastrophe occurs with every individual death. There is no common measure adequate to persuade me that a personal mourning is less serious than a nuclear war" (28/379).[36]

Absolute destructibility entails that deferral, detour, and delay is *internal* to life as such, since the final destination is nothing but death. From the first inception, life has to protect itself against the force of destruction that it bears within itself and without which it could not be. Life can thus only be given through the movement of survival, which takes the time to live by postponing death. As Derrida underscores in *Writing and Difference*, "there is no life present *at first* which would *then* come to protect, postpone, or reserve itself" (203/302). Rather, "life can defend itself against death only through an *economy* of death, through deferment, repetition, reserve" (202/300–301). These formulations point to the notion of autoimmunity that Derrida was to articulate thirty years later and that offers the most powerful way to think the movement of survival. Derrida proposes neither a philosophy of life nor a philosophy of death but insists on the stricture of "life-death." This necessary intertwinement of life and death spells out the autoimmunity of mortality as a general condition and undercuts the Idea of immortality. On the one hand, *life is opposed to death* because to live is to be mortal, to resist and defer death. On the other hand, life is *internally bound to what it opposes* because mortality is inextricably linked to death. The defense of life is thus attacked from within. There can be no cure for such autoimmunity since life is *essentially* mortal. From the definition of life as essentially mortal, it follows that immortality is death. To live is to be mortal, which means that the opposite of being mortal—to be immortal—is to be dead. If one can no longer die, one is already dead.[37]

The above argument is at the center of what I analyze as the radical atheism of deconstruction. As I pointed out in my introduction, atheism has traditionally limited itself to denying the existence of God and immortality, without questioning the desire for God and immortality. Thus, in traditional atheism mortal being is still conceived as a *lack* of being that we desire to transcend, even though the transcendent state of being is denied or deemed to be unattainable. Such a conception of desire clearly adheres to the structure of the Kantian Idea. The consummation of immortality is figured as an Idea that propels the desire for life but remains forever out of reach. In contrast, what I call radical atheism not only denies the existence of God and immortality but also takes issue with the assumption that God and immortality are desirable. Rather, I argue that the time of survival is the unconditional condition for everything that can be desired.

The reason why life does not ever reach the consummation of immortality is thus not because it is an unattainable Idea, but because life is not oriented toward consummation in the first place. If life and the desire for life is essentially a matter of temporal survival, it cannot be oriented toward immortality. The consummation of immortality is incompatible with the unconditional affirmation of survival because it would not allow anything to live on in the negative infinity of time.

Hence, the first challenge for a radical atheism is to demonstrate that every moment of life is indeed a matter of survival. In his early work Derrida developed this argument by analyzing how the minimal condition for life in general is an "arche-writing." Such writing testifies that nothing can be given in itself but is always already passing away. If what happened were given in itself and did not pass away, there would be no reason to inscribe anything for the future. If writing is originary, then it is because there is no life without the movement of survival, which can persist only by leaving destructible traces for an unpredictable time to come. It is consequently with arche-writing that life itself will have begun.

§ 2   Arche-Writing:
Derrida and Husserl

Memory projects itself toward the future, and it constitutes the presence of
the present.

—Derrida, *Mémoires* (57/69)

To inscribe something is first of all an act of memory. Regardless of
what, to whom, or why I write, my words become traces of the past at the
very moment when they are imprinted. Accordingly, writing has a capac-
ity to store historical data, to document and record what has taken place.
By inscribing what happens on a particular occasion, I provide myself
with a supplement that can retain details even if I forget them. Thereby
I increase my chances of recalling past events—of holding on to my own
life—but by the same token I mark a precarious temporality. Without
the thought of a reader to come (whether myself or someone else), there
would be no reason for me to write. The addressed future, however, is essentially perilous. When someone reads my text, I may already be dead,
or the significance of my words may no longer be the same. Moreover, the
inscriptions themselves always risk being erased.

Thus, if writing can counter oblivion, it simultaneously reveals a latent
threat. Writing would be superfluous for an immortal being, who could
never experience the fear of forgetting. Conversely, the need to write (if
only a memo or a mental note) stems from the temporal finitude of everything that happens. My act of inscribing something already indicates that
I may forget it. Writing thus testifies to my dependence on that which
is "exterior" to me. In his essay "Plato's Pharmacy," Derrida unpacks the
argument in the following way:

The "outside" does not begin where what we now call the psychic and the
physical meet, but at the point where the *mnēmē*, instead of being present to
itself in its life as a movement of truth, is supplanted by the archive, evicted

by a sign of re-memoration or of com-memoration. The space of writing, space *as* writing, is opened up in the violent movement of this surrogation, in the difference between *mnēmē* and *hypomnēsis*. The outside is already *within* the work of memory. The evil slips in within the relation of memory to itself, in the general organization of the mnesic activity. Memory is finite by nature. Plato recognizes this in attributing life to it. As in the case of all living organisms, he assigns it, as we have seen, certain limits. A limitless memory would in any event not be memory but infinite self-presence. Memory always therefore already needs signs in order to recall the non-present, with which it is necessarily in relation. (*Dissemination*, 109/135)

This passage is crucial for understanding Derrida's notion of "arche-writing." Arche-writing should not be confused with the empirical concept of writing or be placed in opposition to speech. Rather, Derrida's argument is that a number of traits associated with empirical writing—such as the structure of representation, intrinsic finitude, and the relation to an irreducible exteriority—reinforce the conditions of possibility for experience and life in general, which is thus characterized by an arche-writing. Prior to any actual system of notation, whose application and use would be a matter of empirical need, there is an "ultratranscendental" necessity that experience be inscribed in order to be what it is.

In the case of memory, the tradition of philosophy has indeed admitted an intimate link between experience and inscription. As Derrida reminds us in the passage quoted above, Plato realized that memory "needs signs in order to recall the non-present." The reason for this is straightforward enough. Precisely because the past is no longer present, no longer accessible as a presence in itself, it must have been inscribed as a mark that can be repeated from one time to another.

If philosophy from Plato onward has recognized writing as the condition of mnemotechnics, it has nonetheless attempted to *derive* it from a primordial presence that is given to itself without mediation. The past is then understood as something that once was present and only subsequently had to be replaced by a trace. Furthermore, the trace is conceived in relation to a present consciousness that reactivates the past and ensures that we remember it in the present. This may seem irrefutable. The content of memory is certainly past, but how can we deny that the act of memory takes place *in the present?* Indeed, how can we speak of any experience without presupposing the form of presence? The past is no longer and the future is not yet; hence everything that happens—everything that *is*—must be in the present.

Such, at least, is the fundamental premise of the philosophical logic of identity. This logic prescribes that *what is* must be identical to itself—that its originary form must be an indivisible unity. To question the logic of identity is to encounter the most difficult problems and to risk sounding nonsensical. Nevertheless, it is precisely these problems and this risk we must face, since Derrida's deconstruction aims at nothing less than a revision of the logic of identity. To be sure, one can be content to simply rehearse Derrida's claims about a primordial division and a past that has never been present, as is evidenced by the ease with which many of Derrida's commentators have reiterated his formulas. Such an approach, however, does little to consolidate the philosophical importance of deconstruction. Rather, it confirms the suspicion that deconstruction indulges in paradoxes that deliberately scorn the rigor of argumentation. What is needed is thus an argument addressing *why* the self-identity of presence is impossible and *why* writing in Derrida's sense is originary, as well as an elaboration of *how* this arche-writing should be understood.

In this chapter I will attempt to answer these questions through a reading of Edmund Husserl's phenomenology of internal time-consciousness. My focus on Husserl's phenomenology of time has three motivations. First, Derrida developed his notion of arche-writing, along with his other key notions of *trace* and *différance*, largely through a reading of Husserl's phenomenology.[1] Second, the necessity of elaborating Derrida's reading is underscored by the critique that has been directed against his interpretation of Husserl by such prominent phenomenologists as Paul Ricoeur, Rudolf Bernet, and Dan Zahavi. Their studies have raised a number of questions that a deconstructive reading of Husserl must answer. So while I will take issue with their arguments, I want to acknowledge that they provide a valuable opportunity for an informed and advanced philosophical discussion of deconstruction. Third, we will see how the arguments in this debate hinge on the question of internal time-consciousness. Certainly, Derrida's analysis of the subject is not as thorough as it could be, so my reading aims at further developing Derrida's analysis of Husserl's theory of time, as well as at elucidating how the question of time is central for deconstructing the logic of identity.

Husserl's phenomenology arguably offers the most sophisticated account of the form of presence as the form of time. Thus, it also poses the greatest challenge for Derrida's attempt to deconstruct the form of presence. *If* there is an originary presence, writing is a derivative phenomenon, since an originary presence needs no inscription in order to constitute its own identity. To consolidate Derrida's notion of arche-writing, then, one must demonstrate how the structural features of writing—the division between past and future, the spacing of time, the simultaneous opening of possibility and risk—are constitutive of presence as such. Or to put it in the terms of my epigraph: one must demonstrate how the inscription of memory constitutes the presence of the present.

It is this argument that is at stake in Derrida's reading of Husserl's phenomenology of time. To approach it, we should first consider the main traits of Husserl's chief methodological operation, the so-called *epoché* or phenomenological reduction, which provides the framework for his explorations into the temporality of consciousness. To perform the phenomenological reduction is to bracket the question of whether objects actually exist, in order to examine the acts of consciousness through which they are made to appear. This operation is important for several reasons. Husserl does not seek to *prove* that anything exists but to analyze the conditions for appearance in general. The method of phenomenological reduction serves to distinguish this project from the skeptical approach, as well as from the assumptions entertained in everyday life. By bracketing the question of existence, Husserl can both evade the epistemological doubts concerning our knowledge of the external world *and* go beyond what he calls "the natural attitude," which takes our experience of the world for granted. Rather, Husserl's ambition is to disclose the subjective acts through which objectivity is constituted. His philosophical writings are largely an ever more refined system of descriptions that attempt to live up to this task.

A decisive question for Husserl's project concerns how we apprehend that which does not belong to ourselves. Husserl's answer consists in an investigation of what he calls the *intentionality* of consciousness, namely, its characteristic of being directed toward something other than itself. Intentionality is the common denominator for all experience and exhibits two main poles, which Husserl calls *noesis* and *noema*. The first term designates subjective acts through which I experience something, while the latter term designates objects as they are given in my experience. Importantly, the *noema* should not be equated with a real object but belongs to an intrinsic structure of the intentional consciousness. For example, when

I speak of a table, I may very well refer to it as an actual object but I only have access to the table through my experience of it: as a *noema* correlated with the noetic process that presents it for me. Whether the table exists is not relevant for the description of the two-sided structure, which characterizes the experience even if it concerns a fantasy or a mistaken perception. In other words, the *epoché* reduces objects to their sense *as* objects appearing for an intentional consciousness, in order to thematize the acts through which sense is constituted.

The founding ambition in Husserl's philosophy is thus to account for the conditions of meaning on the basis of subjective intentionality. Husserl, however, does not advocate any form of solipsism. On the contrary, he emphatically maintains a relation to objectivity within subjectivity. As he puts it in his *Cartesian Meditations*, analyzing the *eidos* of the ego necessarily implies analyzing "how the ego, by virtue of this proper essence, likewise constitutes in itself something 'other,' something 'objective,' and thus constitutes everything that within the ego has the status of being non-ego" (§ 41). One should not be misled by the terminology here. That the subject "constitutes" the exterior does *not* mean that it creates the world. From a phenomenological perspective it only makes sense to speak of objects or other people if one understands what it means to experience them.

Phenomenology is thus a "transcendental" philosophy, which seeks to elucidate the fundamental—structural as well as genetic—constitution of experience. It is important to understand that Derrida begins by following this transcendental approach. Deconstruction is not a traditional critique of phenomenology, since it does not question the legitimacy of its philosophical claims with reference to other principles or methods. Rather, Derrida sets out to read Husserl against himself on the deepest level of transcendental phenomenology itself. To be sure, such a strategy is a general trait of Derrida's readings. But Husserl cannot simply be regarded as one metaphysician among others. Followers of Derrida have often all too easily tagged Husserl's thinking as a "metaphysics of presence," without a proper assessment of the transcendental phenomenology of time. As we will see, Husserl was very attentive to the problem of temporality and his analyses take us to the heart of Derrida's concerns with the logic of identity.[2]

Exactly how Husserl's radicality should be understood is, however, a difficult question. A number of phenomenologists have recently emphasized the importance of *prereflexive* subjectivity in Husserl and on the basis of this developed a critique of Derrida's reading. The most forceful examples of such critique are in studies by Rudolf Bernet and Dan Zahavi.[3] Both Bernet and Zahavi argue that Husserl's concept of subjectivity does not presuppose a closed sphere or a self-sufficient monad but proceeds from a constitutive openness toward other subjects, as well as toward the past and the future. This argument is central in Derrida's reading as well, which paved the way for a more profound understanding of precisely these issues in Husserl's phenomenology. Neither Bernet nor Zahavi, however, follow Derrida in their conclusions. In particular, they defend Husserl's theory of a "living presence" (*lebendige Gegenwart*) as pointing toward a nonmetaphysical theory of time. Underlying their arguments is the assumption that the metaphysical tendencies in Husserl's thinking stem from his adherence to a *reflexive* model of consciousness. In contrast, Husserl's notion of a living presence is based on a prereflexive model, which Bernet and Zahavi posit as an alternative to the metaphysics of presence that Derrida targets.

As I will attempt to demonstrate, however, Bernet's and Zahavi's perspective is misleading. Certainly, there are good reasons to develop a more sophisticated understanding of intentionality than the simple correlation of subject and object. But Husserl's potential radicality is not to be found in his notion of prereflexivity. If one follows the course of argument in Husserl's writings on the phenomenology of time, it turns out that the problems inherent to *reflexivity* question Husserl's metaphysical postulates, whereas the concept of a prereflexive subjectivity is introduced in order to save the idea of a fundamental presence. It is therefore misleading to promote a phenomenology "beyond" the metaphysics of presence with reference to Husserl's notion of prereflexivity—a notion that rather aims to explain away the critical questions that Husserl encounters when exploring the question of time.

Let us begin by following what happens when Husserl applies his phenomenological method to the problematic concerning time-consciousness. When Husserl sets out to scrutinize how phenomena are given to consciousness, he discovers that temporality is characteristic of appearances in general. "On both sides—that is, both in the immanent and in the transcendent spheres of reality—*time* is *the irreducible form of individual realities* in their described modes" as Husserl emphasizes (*Hua* 10:274). Regardless of what is intended—external objects, other people, or internal phenomena—they can only appear as such in a temporal process. This condition not only applies to the intentional object but also to the act that intends this object. For example, if I listen to a melody, it is not only the notes but also my experience of the notes that passes away. As Husserl puts it, "the consciousness of a time itself [requires] time; the consciousness of a duration, duration; and the consciousness of a succession, succession."[4] This observation will prove to be deeply problematic for Husserl, since the intentional activity is supposed to ground the continuity of experience by identifying the phenomena as identical over time. The notes that run off and die away can appear as a melody only through an intentional act that apprehends them as an interconnected sequence. Furthermore, even each individual tone is temporally extended and can thus never be given as a simple unity but requires a minimal synthesis in order to be constituted as such.

Now, if the act of synthesis itself is temporal it cannot be given as an immediate unity. Rather, it must be synthesized by another act, which in turn must be synthesized by yet another act, and so on. In an appendix to his lectures on time from 1905, Husserl delineates the problem as follows:

> If I live in the appearing of the tone, the tone stands before me, and it has its duration or its alteration. If I focus my attention on the appearing of the tone, then this appearing stands before me and has its temporal extension, its duration or alteration. The appearing of the tone can therefore signify various things here. It can also signify the focusing of my attention on the continuity of adumbrations—now, just now, and so on. Now the stream . . . in its turn is supposed to be objective and to have its time. Here again a consciousness constituting this objectivity and a consciousness constituting this time would be necessary. On principle we could reflect again, and so *in infinitum*. Can the infinite regress here be shown to be innocuous?
>
> 1. The tone endures, becomes constituted in a continuity of phases.
>
> 2. While or as long as the tone endures, there belongs to each point of the duration a series of adumbrations running from the now in question on into the blurry past. We therefore have a continuous consciousness, each point of which is a steady continuum. But this continuum in its turn is a temporal series on which we can direct our attention. The drama therefore starts all over again. If we fix any point of this sequence, it seems that there must belong to it a consciousness of the past that refers to the series of past sequences, and so on.

> Now even if reflection is not pursued *in infinitum* and even if no reflection at all is necessary, that which makes possible this reflection—and, so it seems, makes it possible at least on principle *in infinitum*—must nevertheless be given. And there lies the problem. (*Hua* 10:114–15)

This problem will not cease to haunt Husserl's explorations into the temporality of consciousness. Husserl is always guided by the search for a fundamental, constituting level of consciousness, which will provide the ground for his phenomenology. But his search runs into the problem of an infinite regress when every instance, every moment, turns out to depend on other moments for its very constitution. As Husserl clearly realizes, the cause of the regress is the movement of temporalization, which divides every presence in its becoming and consequently prevents anything from ever being *in itself*. In phenomenological terms, this is why no intentional act can be "self-constituting." Precisely because it is temporal, the act cannot coincide with itself but requires another act to appear as such.[5]

To put an end to the regress, Husserl introduces a third level in the internal time-consciousness: what he calls "the absolute flow."[6] In contrast to the intentional acts and their objects, the flow is an "absolute subjectivity" that is not temporally constituted but immediately given to itself as a "living presence." In the following I will track how Husserl mobilizes a number of parallel strategies to safeguard originary presence. In spite of his ambition to provide a description of consciousness that is purged from metaphysical presuppositions, it remains axiomatic for Husserl that the subject must essentially be present to itself. This ideal is never abandoned on the programmatic level of his writings.

Thus, we can see why Derrida locates a modern form of the metaphysics of presence in Husserl's thinking. Phenomenology is not a traditional ontotheology or idealism, but Husserl nevertheless pledges to a version of the philosophical logic of identity. As previously mentioned, this logic prescribes that *what is* must be identical to itself. In Husserl such originary form is ascribed to the self-presence of the subject.

The self-presence of the subject, however, is called into question already by Husserl's most basic insight regarding intentionality. Husserl's insight concerns how the structure of any appearance is dyadic. Whatever is brought to appearance will appear *as* something for somebody and is thus said to be constituted by a transcendental subjectivity. In effect, the question arises as to how the constituting subjectivity appears to itself. If

the self-appearance of the transcendental subject also has a dyadic structure, then we are faced with an infinite regress, since the very condition of
appearance itself turns out to be conditioned. Husserl himself formulates
the problem as follows: "If one says that every content comes to consciousness only by means of an act of apprehension directed toward it,
then the question immediately arises about the consciousness in which
this act of apprehension, which is surely a content itself, becomes conscious, and an infinite regress is unavoidable."[7]

Structurally, this is the same problem that Kant discovered when inves-
tigating the relation between time and subjectivity in his *Critique of Pure
Reason*. As Kant noted, the unity of consciousness cannot itself be temporally constituted. If it were, the very ground for the synthesis of time
would itself be subjected to succession and thus in need of being synthesized by an instance other than itself, and so on. Husserl struggles with
the same regress, and his proposed solution is in certain respects similar
to Kant's. Where Kant contrasted the ever-changing empirical consciousness with a "pure, original, unchanging consciousness" (*Critique of Pure
Reason*, A 107), Husserl invokes an "absolute flow" that is exempt from
the condition of time. The crucial difference, however, is that Husserl is
forced to confront the question of how the transcendental subject appears
to itself. Kant elides the problem by appealing to a pure apperception,
which must be assumed as a condition for the unity of experience but
which itself cannot be intuited. Such a solution is not available for Husserl. The very possibility of a transcendental phenomenology hinges on
the possibility of undertaking a phenomenological analysis of transcendental subjectivity, which presupposes that this subjectivity can manifest
itself to itself.

Consequently, Husserl must account for how the absolute, time-
constituting flow can appear to itself. This self-appearance consists in
what Husserl calls a "longitudinal intentionality" (*Längsintentionalität*),
which does not exhibit the dyadic structure of objectifying consciousness.
Rather, the longitudinal intentionality is *pre*objective, *pre*reflexive, and
*pre*temporal. Husserl emphasizes the prefix in order to explain how the
absolute subjectivity of the flow can relate to itself without being divided
by the structure of reflexivity and without being intrinsically temporal.[8]
One should note, however, that Husserl's characterization of such a longitudinal intentionality must rely on negations. Husserl himself admits
that we can only speak of the flow in terms borrowed from the temporal,

objectifying, and reflexive consciousness. But with a classic gesture he attempts to explain away the problem by blaming it on the inadequate metaphors of language:

> We can say nothing other than the following: This flow is something we speak of *in accordance with that which is constituted,* but it is nevertheless not something that is temporally "objective." It is the *absolute subjectivity* and has the absolute properties of something to be designated *metaphorically* as a "flow"; the absolute properties of a point of actuality, a primordial source-point, "the now," etc. In the actuality-experience we have the primordial source-point and a continuity of moments of reverberation. For all of this, names are lacking. (*Hua* 10:75, trans. mod.)

Husserl's last sentence has come to fascinate a number of his commentators. In the declaration that "names are lacking" for describing the flow, they see a critique of the metaphysics inherent to reflexive phenomenology, in favor of a prereflexive intentionality that would be nonmetaphysical.[9] As is evident from Husserl's reasoning, however, it is rather the latter idea and its connection to an "absolute subjectivity" that answers to the phenomenological version of the metaphysics of presence. Husserl here claims that the flow of consciousness is an originary presence, a "primordial source-point" that constitutes time without itself being temporal. But whenever Husserl sets out to describe the pretemporal level, he will inevitably have recourse to a temporal vocabulary that questions the presupposed presence. This is not because the metaphors of language distort an instance that in itself is pretemporal but rather because the notion of an absolute subjectivity is a projection that cannot be sustained—a theoretical fiction.

To consolidate the above argument, we need to examine Husserl's various attempts to define the fundamental self-presence of consciousness. In several places, self-presence is explicitly identified with what Husserl calls the "primal impression" or "impressional consciousness." Like the absolute subjectivity of the flow, the primal impression is described as a source from which everything flows, a point of origin that depends on nothing but itself and is at the center of every experience:

> The primal impression is the absolute beginning . . . the primal source, that from which everything else is continuously produced. But in itself it is not produced; it does not arise as something produced but through *genesis sponta-*

nea; it is primal generation. It does not spring from anything (it has no seed); it is primal creation." (*Hua* 10:100)

At the same time, Husserl often admits that a pure Now is only an idealized abstraction, and he concedes that no phase of the flow can repose in itself. Whether on the side of intentional objects or intentional acts, even the most immediate experience has a certain temporal extension. It is thus dependent on what Husserl designates as three formal functions that are intrinsic to every experience: a "primary memory" (retention) that provides us with a consciousness of what has just passed, a "primal impression" that registers what happens, and a "primary anticipation" (protention) that marks the imminence of events to come. Moreover, Husserl maintains that perception itself is only possible through the retention and protention of impressions. Rather than being derived modifications of the primal impression, retention and protention are constitutive of presence as such.

Here we find the key to Derrida's deconstruction of Husserl. Following Husserl's admission that the now cannot be given as a punctual presence but must be retained and protended, Derrida argues that it is untenable to speak of a primordial self-presence.[10] The being of any moment is nothing but its own becoming past and becoming related to the future. On Derrida's account, then, the primacy of retention testifies to an intrinsic delay at the heart of subjectivity, just as the primacy of protention testifies to an intrinsic deferral.

I will seek to develop Derrida's argument, but one should note that it has met considerable resistance as an interpretation of Husserl. Among others, Zahavi has pointed out that Husserl guards himself against Derrida's interpretation by "extending" the concept of presence. According to the model of extended presence, the retention and protention are not past or future with respect to the now of the primal impression. Rather, these three functions (primal impression-retention-protention) constitute a "living presence" that is the fundamental *form* of all experience. According to this reading, Derrida is mistaken to interpret retention and protention as implying a "delay" or a "deferral" of presence. Although the *content* that is retained or protended cannot be present, the retention and protention are functions of the absolute flow, which grounds the continuity of experience in a presence that extends to include the recent past and imminent future.[11]

Husserl's analysis of an extended presence is one of his most celebrated, and it has strongly influenced philosophers such as Maurice Merleau-Ponty and Paul Ricoeur.[12] Ricoeur also mobilizes the "extended" concept of presence in an explicit polemic against Derrida, which anticipates the objections raised by Zahavi and others. The shared critique of Derrida is that his deconstruction only applies to the idea of a punctual Now, while Husserl offers us a model that overcomes this understanding of time by including retention and protention in an extended presence. Derrida does not accept the expansion of the field of self-presence but reads it as Husserl's attempt to evade the critical implications of retention and protention. Thereby, Derrida allegedly fails to assess the profound innovation in Husserl's phenomenology of time-consciousness.[13]

I will demonstrate, however, that the notion of an extended presence is based on the same metaphysical premise as the idea of a punctual Now, since both of these concepts presuppose that there is an instance that precedes temporality. The basic problem here is that self-presence and temporal extension are mutually exclusive attributes. Nothing that is temporally extended can ever be present in itself. Rather, it is necessarily divided between the past and the future. All philosophies of time are forced to confront this problem, which comes back to haunt Husserl on every level of constitution. The solution that Husserl proposes is based on a distinction between form and content. As we have seen, Husserl grants that the "content" of any experience is temporally extended. Accordingly, it is *no longer* or *not yet* present and must be retained or protended. Nonetheless, Husserl argues that the experience of the temporal content is given as an immediate presence, since the retention and protention function on the level of the absolute flow, which holds them together in an indivisible unity. Hence—if Husserl is right—the formal functioning of the flow (primal impression-retention-protention) *does not take any time*; it is given all at once as the "form" of an absolute subjectivity.[14]

Husserl's reference to a pretemporal subjectivity provides us with the most sophisticated version of a paradox that recurs in all theories that attempt to "extend" the notion of presence. It is here particularly instructive to compare Husserl's phenomenology of time with its Anglo-Saxon counterpart: William James's theory of "the specious present," which is often invoked as a precursor to Husserl's phenomenology of time. Like Husserl, James realizes that we can never experience a punctual Now. What we perceive is a "specious" presence, since it is divided between before and after, past and future. For James, however, the perception of this temporal succession is given immediately, since it is an indivisible act of consciousness. Only the *perceived* is temporally extended, while the act of *perceiving* is an immediate awareness that synthesizes successive moments without itself having to be synthesized.[15] The division of time is thus subordinated to an indivisible unity: a logic that Husserl also subscribes to when he appeals to a pretemporal subjectivity to found his theory of a "living presence."

Nevertheless, there is an important difference between Husserl's and James's respective theories, which makes Husserl's phenomenology potentially much more radical than James's empiricism. In contrast to James and his followers, Husserl realizes that both the object *and* the act of intentionality are temporal from the beginning. Not only the *perceived* present but also the *perceiving* presence is extended in time. And as Husserl himself observes, this entails that there will always be a delay—an ineradicable temporal difference—even in the sphere of immanent perception:

> Now let us exclude transcendent objects and ask how matters stand with respect to the simultaneity of perception and the perceived in the immanent sphere. If we take perception here as the act of reflection in which immanent unities come to be given, then this act presupposes that something is already constituted—and preserved in retention—on which it can look back: in this instance, therefore, the perception follows after what is perceived and is not simultaneous with it. (*Hua* 10:110)

Husserl's philosophical vigilance concerning the temporality of perception is exemplary, as is his attentiveness to the unsettling implications of such temporality. If the act of immanent perception also takes time, it cannot be given as an indivisible unity but exhibits a relentless displacement in the interior of the subject, where every phase of consciousness is intended by another phase of consciousness. Husserl, however, tries to evade the threat of an infinite regress by positing the foundational presence on a *third* level of consciousness, which he distinguishes from the temporality of *retention* as well as *reflection*:

> But—as we have seen—reflection and retention presuppose the impressional 'internal consciousness' of the immanent datum in question in its original constitution; and this consciousness is united concretely with the currently intended primal impressions and is inseparable from them: if we wish to designate 'internal consciousness' too as perception then here we truly have strict simultaneity of perception and what is perceived. (*Hua* 10:110–11)

Here, Husserl's description of "internal consciousness" answers to what he elsewhere calls the prereflective self-awareness of the absolute flow. The absolute flow is an unchanging dimension of consciousness and always coincides with itself: not because it is a mystical "beyond" but because it designates the immediate awareness of oneself, which remains even though the acts and the objects of intentionality pass away.

Thus, when Husserl locates the fundamental self-presence in the absolute flow rather than in the act of perception, he only provides us with a more profound version of James's theory. But it is also here that we can read Husserl's descriptions against his own conclusions. When closely scrutinized, his notion of the self-awareness of the flow operates according to two mutually exclusive models, which Husserl nonetheless tries to reconcile. As I have already emphasized, the flow must be immediately given to itself in order to escape the regressive movement of temporalization. Accordingly, Husserl often emphasizes that the flow is an *impressional* consciousness that appears to itself before any retentional modification. The description of the flow as impressional is consistent, since the self-presence of the flow would have to consist in *one* single moment in order to coincide with itself, as Husserl made clear in the passage quoted above. It is, however, precisely the notion of a single, self-identical now that Husserl himself undermines. At several crucial junctures he admits that even the flow itself can become constituted only through a retention that designates "the intentional relation . . . of phase of consciousness to phase of consciousness" (*Hua* 10:333). Contrary to Husserl's assertions, this retentional intentionality of the flow implies that it is always already temporal. If the flow were not temporal, its self-relation would not be disjoined into separate phases, and there would be no need for it to retain itself. Moreover, the irreducibility of time necessarily entails that nothing can ever be present in itself, that every moment is divided in its very event.

We can thus approach the crucial issue in Derrida's reading of Husserl, namely, the question of *autoaffection*. In phenomenology the question of autoaffection concerns how the subject is given to itself on the most fundamental level of consciousness. Nothing can appear without the subject being given to itself, so the conditions for autoaffection will also be decisive for determining the conditions for appearances in general.

To highlight the problem of autoaffection, Derrida dwells on Husserl's central distinction between two forms of intentional consciousness:

presentation (*Präsentation, Gegenwärtigung*) and re-presentation (*Verge-genwärtigung*). According to Husserl, the former is the primary dimension of experience: a "living presence" that constitutes time without itself being temporal. The living presence is the form of *presentation*, in which the subject is given to itself without mediation. Nonetheless, Husserl is well aware that there are many situations in which the subject must rely on mediation. As Derrida maintains, the necessity of mediation is especially clear in two of Husserl's most pervasive themes: the relation to the past and the relation to other subjects, which both presuppose the structure of *re-presentation*. When I recall a past event, the act of memory hinges on a structural division between two positions. A gap in time always separates me from my past, since the one who remembers cannot coincide with the one who is being remembered. In the same way, I cannot have a direct access to the consciousness of the other. His or her subjectivity has never been and will never be given to me in an immediate presentation; it can only be "appresented" (that is, intended *as* nonpresent and other) in my living presence. Because of this constitutive appresentation, our understanding of each other must rely on gestures, words, or other signs. These signs are necessarily mediated across a temporal distance and thus exhibit the same structure of re-presentation as the act of memory.

The comparison between the relation to the past and the relation to the other may seem fortuitous, but Derrida points out how Husserl keeps returning to the analogy between the movement of temporalization and the constitution of intersubjectivity.[16] To remember oneself is to be subjected to a temporal division, since the subject that intends is also the object that is being intended. By way of re-presentation I thus appear to myself *as an other*. In Husserl's analysis, the double perspective on oneself is the precondition for any intersubjective relation. Without the awareness that I am an other for the other, there would be no way of recognizing the other as an I for itself. Furthermore, Husserl makes it clear that the structure of re-presentation is necessary for the constitution of objectivity. Without memory one could not posit an identity over time, and without the relation to others there would be no sense of a shared, objective world.

That Husserl acknowledges the necessity of mediation does not mean, however, that he abandons his privileging of presence. On the contrary, Husserl understands both time and intersubjectivity as deriving from the form of the living present. What is past *has been* present, what is future *will be* present, and other subjects are in their turn given to themselves in an originary presentation, even though they can only be re-presented for me.

What Derrida wants to demonstrate is rather that the structure of re-presentation is the condition for the identity of the self from the first inception. The subject can never be given in an autonomous presentation but is constituted by relating to itself as an other. As I will attempt to demonstrate, this conclusion necessarily follows if one thinks time as irreducible on every level of constitution. The subject is always already divided by what Derrida calls "the movement of transcendental temporalization" (*SP*, 68/76), which does not allow anything to repose *in itself*.[17]

Husserl himself grants that the absolute flow must affect itself in order to be and maintains that autoaffection is retentional. For Husserl, however, the retentional autoaffection does not compromise the living presence of phenomenological subjectivity. Rather, the work of retention expands the sphere of immediate givenness without threatening its unity. It is important to dwell on this line of thought since several of Husserl's defenders have mobilized it against Derrida's deconstruction.[18] The polemical point is that Derrida does not pay proper respect to Husserl's distinction between retention and re-presentation. According to Husserl, the former is a "primary memory" that enables the *presentation* of presence as a continuous flow of impressions-retentions-protentions. In contrast, the latter is a discontinuous "secondary memory" that divides the self-awareness of the subject into two parallel "tracks" of consciousness. When something is presented for me, it is given as an unbroken flow in one track of consciousness (the present), whereas any re-presentation implies at least *two* tracks. The flowing presence of my consciousness *as* I remember is distinct from the past flow of presence *that* I remember.

Derrida does not deny that there are *descriptive* differences between these modes of consciousness. What he does deny is that there can be an *essential* difference between retention and representation such that the former type of consciousness would grant an immediate self-awareness, in contradistinction to the irreducible mediacy of the latter type of consciousness. Rather, both retention and representation testify to what Derrida designates as a general "representative structure" (*SP*, 50/56), since the distinction between them "only serves to separate two ways of relating to the irreducible nonpresence of another now" (65/73).

Let me try to clarify the argument in question. If I intend myself such as I was during a certain period last year, it is obvious that it is a matter of re-presenting myself to myself. My past existence is not immediately at hand, not accessible as a presence in itself, but must have been inscribed as a trace in order to be reactivated. Furthermore, the reactivation of the trace can never sublate the temporal difference that separates my past and present self. Husserl would not have contested this phenomenological fact. Derrida, however, ventures the much more radical claim that the inscription of memory—and the concomitant fracture in one's proper interiority—is the condition for any self-presence in the first place. Derrida thus insists on a "nonderived re-presentation" (*SP*, 84/94) whose division has not been preceded by any unity. Or as Derrida also puts it: "everything 'begins' by 're-presentation'" (45/50).

Many Husserl scholars have denounced Derrida's claim, but we can see how it follows from Husserl's own account of time-consciousness, insofar as his account admits that every now must be retained by another now in order to be constituted as such. In spite of Husserl's assertions, the structure of retentional consciousness cannot be essentially different from the structure of re-presentation. It would be impossible to perform the function of retention, to "hold on to" one now in another now, if this now had not been inscribed as a repeatable trace—that is, *re-presented as a memory for the future*—in its very event.

Proceeding from the general structure of re-presentation, Derrida reconfigures the notion of autoaffection that informs Husserl's phenomenology of time. Traditionally, autoaffection has been understood as a mode of interiority where there is no distance or difference between the one who affects and the one who is affected. In autoaffection, then, the subject would be so close to itself that any kind of mediation is excluded. The most prominent contemporary defenders of such a theory are the German philosopher Dieter Henrich (along with his followers in the so-called Heidelberg school) and the French phenomenologist Michel Henry. Both Henrich and Henry attack the idea of a *reflexive* self-presence as untenable, since the dyadic structure of reflexivity prevents the subject from ever coinciding with itself. Instead, they claim that the subject is given to itself on a prereflexive level, in the immediate unity of a pure immanence that precedes every form of objectification and temporalization. Given through an autoaffection without heteroaffection, the interiority of the subject is not dependent on anything exterior to itself.[19]

I call attention to Henrich's and Henry's idea of autoaffection because it is the clearest example of the notion of subjectivity with which Derrida takes issue.[20] Rather than trying to end the infinite regress of reflection—which stems from its incapacity to provide the ground of indivisible presence—Derrida accounts for it on the basis of what Rodolphe Gasché has called a "general theory of doubling."[21] As Gasché emphasizes, Derrida does not regard the constitutive difference of reflection as a problem to be solved; it is rather indicative of "a certain exteriority at the heart of all self-relation."[22] What precedes reflection is not a prereflexive unity or immediate sensation of self. On the contrary, it is the deferral and delay of *différance. Différance* makes reflection possible but at the same time makes it impossible for it to ever close upon itself. Consequently, heteroaffection inhabits even the most immediate autoaffection, since its very structure hinges on a difference between the affecting and the affected.

Nonetheless, Husserl attempts to save the level of absolute subjectivity from such heteroaffection. Although the autoaffection of absolute subjectivity is retentional, Husserl describes it as a "longitudinal intentionality" that is pretemporal, prereflexive, and preobjective. Rudolf Bernet has described longitudinal intentionality as an "intentionality without object," which he regards as a radical notion that contests Husserl's adherence to the metaphysics of presence.[23] But in fact, we can see how the theory of an intentionality without object is connected to one of Husserl's most traditional claims, namely, that "subjective time is constituted in the absolute timeless consciousness that is not an object" (*Hua* 10:112). Husserl's formulation is not incidental, since the purpose of the theory of prereflexive intentionality is to account for how the subject can be given to itself without mediation and consequently without the delay of temporal constitution.

Neither Husserl nor his followers can explain how such an intentionality could be possible at all. How can I appear to myself without being divided by the structure of reflexivity? And how can the retentional consciousness—which by definition involves a differential relation between phases of the flow—not be temporal? The only answer from Husserl and his followers is that there *must* be a more fundamental self-awareness than the reflexive one; otherwise, we are faced with an infinite regress where the intending subject in its turn must be intended and thus cannot be given to itself in an unmediated unity.[24]

The assumption that the regress is an unthinkable condition is a clear example of a modern version of the metaphysics of presence. Its underlying premise is that there must be an instance that is *in itself.* As long as this premise is operative, one cannot think the implications of time. What we call an infinite regress is nothing but the movement of temporalization, which undercuts the very idea of an origin or end, since every moment is divided in its becoming and refers to other moments that in turn are divided, and so on.

To consolidate Derrida's argument, then, one must demonstrate how the movement of temporalization is at work even on the deepest level in Husserl's account of time-consciousness. I propose to undertake such a demonstration here. My aim is to show that the necessary retention—far from being reconcilable with the unity of a living presence—is a re-presentation that divides the subject a priori.

In several places Husserl himself uses the terms "retention" and "representation" interchangeably, as though they answered to the same general structure. One should here consider a passage from the crucial § 39 in the lectures on internal time-consciousness. In Husserl's collected works it can be found in two almost identical versions. Husserl, however, describes the same phenomenon as "retention" in one version and as "reproduction" in the other—in spite of the fact that he usually relegates the latter term to the secondary memory of re-presentation. This seemingly marginal alteration is significant considering that Husserl is discussing the self-relation of the absolute flow. He writes:

> The flow of the consciousness that constitutes immanent time not only *exists* but is so remarkably and yet intelligibly fashioned that a self-appearance of the flow necessarily exists in it, and therefore the flow itself must necessarily be apprehensible in the flowing. The self-appearance of the flow does not require a second flow; on the contrary, it constitutes itself as a phenomenon in itself. The constituting and the constituted coincide, and yet naturally they cannot coincide in every respect. The phases of the flow of consciousness in which phases of the same flow of consciousness become constituted phenomenally cannot be identical with these constituted phases, and of course they are not. What is brought to appearance in the actual momentary phase of the flow of consciousness, in its series of retentional moments ["reproductive moments" in the other version], are the past phases of the flow of consciousness.[25]

A number of Husserl scholars have dwelt on this passage but without discussing the difference between the two manuscript versions and without properly assessing the critical implications. According to Zahavi, Husserl here provides us with an account of a prereflective self-manifestation that escapes the infinite regress of reflection. Symptomatically, Zahavi breaks off his quote after Husserl's claim that the flow "constitutes itself as a phenomenon in itself." Thus, he omits Husserl's subsequent admission that the phases of the flow do *not* coincide with themselves.[26] Bernet and Birnbaum do acknowledge the noncoincidence in the self-relation of the flow, but their conclusions remain different from mine. Bernet rightly observes that Husserl describes the flow as a process of alteration, where every phase appears as past due to a constitutive delay (*nachträglichkeit*). This observation, however, does not lead Bernet to question Husserl's central thesis that the flow is "non-temporal."[27] The inconsequential argumentation returns in Birnbaum, who follows Bernet's observation that the longitudinal intentionality of the flow is characterized by a delay. The flow intends itself, but it is not the same phase that intends and is being intended.[28] Nonetheless, Birnbaum maintains that the longitudinal intentionality is preobjective, prereflexive, and pretemporal. The delay that is irreducible on the deepest level of consciousness is, according to Birnbaum, a "pre-temporal delay" (152)—a notion that in my view is self-refuting. There can be no delay without temporalization, and one cannot formulate a "nonmetaphysical" theory of time as long as one posits a pretemporal level. Thus, Birnbaum's adherence to the idea of a pretemporal level dilutes his argument concerning a constitutive "delay." Birnbaum still adheres to Husserl's understanding of the primacy of the flow in relation to the temporal metaphors that he regards as secondary and misleading (133–34). To read Husserl against himself one must rather demonstrate how the becoming-space of time and becoming-time of space is irreducible on every level of constitution.

Hence, it is crucial that Husserl in the passage quoted above describes the absolute flow, which in his theory is the fundamental level of time-consciousness. The absolute flow is supposed to put an end to the threat of an infinite regress by being "self-constituting" and thereby safeguarding a primordial unity in the temporal flow. This solution requires that the subject appears to itself through a longitudinal intentionality that is not subjected to the constraints of a dyadic and temporal reflexivity. As we can see, however, Husserl's own text shows that the absolute flow cannot coincide with itself. Even on the deepest level it is relentlessly divided by temporal succession. No phase of consciousness can intend itself. It is always intended by another phase that in turn must be intended by another phase, in a chain of references that neither has an ulterior instance nor an absolute origin.

Once again, then, Husserl's search for a fundamental presence has led him to encounter an ineradicable temporal difference. Husserl repeatedly sets out to elucidate experience at its most immediate, only to discover that there can be no presence in itself.

Husserl's idea that the subject *constitutes* time is thus untenable. The subject does not constitute but is rather *constituted by* the movement of temporalization. The consequences of this inversion are considerable, since it is the supposed nontemporality of the absolute flow that allows Husserl to evade the most radical implications of retention and protention. If the reference to a nontemporal instance cannot be sustained, retention and protention cannot be posited as a unity in the "living presence" of subjectivity. Rather, these functions testify to the constitutive deferral and delay of *différance*. The delay is marked by the retentional awareness of being *too late* (in relation to what is no longer), while the deferral is marked by the protentional awareness of being *too early* (in relation to what is not yet). The deferral and delay not only applies to the content of experience but also to the autoaffection of the experiencing subject itself. I can appear to myself only by holding on to myself through retention and anticipating myself through protention. Accordingly, my self-relation is necessarily mediated across a temporal distance that prevents me from ever coinciding with myself.

Such a predicament remains unthinkable for Husserl and his defenders because it breaks with the logic of identity. If one follows the logic of identity, the paradoxes that Derrida mobilizes must be regarded as philosophically irresponsible or at least as seriously lacking explanatory force. This is, for example, the reason why Zahavi ultimately cannot accept Derrida's reading of Husserl, in spite of acknowledging some of its merits. Summarizing his critique of Derrida, Zahavi writes: "To claim that self-awareness is not a manifestation *sui generis*, but the result of a mediation, is basically to face all the problems of the reflection theory once again. To go further and claim that self-affection is always already a hetero-affection . . . is to advocate a position which, instead of contributing to a clarification of self-awareness, dissolves and eradicates the very phenomenon to be investigated."[29] Zahavi's argument is certainly correct if one assumes that *self-awareness as such is self-given*, which is axiomatic for Zahavi. But it is precisely this axiom that Derrida calls into question. The crucial problem, then, is how one can account for self-awareness without relying on the axiom that has been indispensable for all previous theories of self-awareness. Indeed, how can we speak of identity at all if there is no self-presence as such, but only incessant division between a past that never has been (present) and a future that never will be (present)?

It is precisely here that the necessity of arche-writing makes itself felt. Derrida's notion of arche-writing allows us to think the necessary synthesis of time without grounding it in a nontemporal unity. What is remarkable, then, is that the triadic structure Husserl describes as the minimal condition for the constitution of presence (primal impression-retention-protention) can be seen to exemplify arche-writing, insofar as we refuse to posit the triad as a unity in the absolute flow. The now of primal impression is then nothing but its own becoming past (through the intrinsic delay of retention), which at the same time is becoming projected toward the future (through the intrinsic deferral of protention). The primal impression is accordingly a *primal inscription* that enables repetition across the gap in time and exhibits the general structure of re-presentation. Without such inscription there would be nothing to retain or protend, no mediation between past and future, and consequently no perception or self-awareness at all.

Because of the necessity of inscription, autoaffection is always already heteroaffection. If the subject can constitute itself only through inscription, it is dependent on that which is exterior to itself. Accordingly, Derrida designates arche-writing as "the opening to exteriority in general" since it stems from the impossibility of anything ever being *in* itself. A dense and pivotal passage from *Speech and Phenomena* spells out the logic in question:

> The living present is always already a trace. This trace is unthinkable on the basis of a simple present whose life would be interior to itself. The self of the living present is originally a trace. The trace is not an attribute, and we cannot say that the self of the living present "originally is" a trace. One must think the being-originary on the basis of the trace and not the inverse. This arche-writing is at work at the origin of sense. Because sense, as Husserl recognized, by nature is temporal, it is never simply present; it is always already engaged in the "movement" of the trace, which is to say in the order of "signification." . . . Since the trace is the relation between the intimacy of the living present and its outside, the opening to exteriority in general, to the non-proper, etc., *the temporalization of sense is, from the very beginning, "spacing."*

As soon as we admit spacing at once as "interval" or difference and as opening to the outside, there is no longer any absolute interiority, the "outside" has insinuated itself in the movement by which the nonspatial inside, which is called "time," appears to itself, constitutes itself, "presents" itself. Space is "in" time, it is the pure going outside itself of time, it is the being outside itself of time as its self-relation. The exteriority of space, exteriority as space, is not something that supervenes upon time, it opens itself as pure "outside" "in" the movement of temporalization. . . . The theme of a pure interiority . . . is radically contradicted by "time" itself. . . . "Time" cannot be an "absolute subjectivity" precisely because one cannot think it on the basis of a present and the self-presence of a present being. The "world," like everything that is thought under this heading, and like everything that is excluded by the most rigorous transcendental reduction, is originally implicated in the movement of temporalization. (85–86/95–96; trans. mod.)

This passage consolidates my major claim in the present chapter: that the problem of time accounts for *why* writing in Derrida's sense is originary and for *how* this arche-writing should be understood. As I have argued, and as Derrida emphasizes here, the constitution of time is incompatible with the logic of identity because it cannot be thought on the basis of presence. Each now is succeeded by another now in its very event and thus requires the inscription of memory in order to be at all. Consequently, Derrida describes the movement of temporalization as the irreducible opening of one now to another now and specifies that the originary being outside itself of time is its *spacing*.[30] If there were one key word in Derrida's work, it would be *espacement*, which is shorthand for the coimplication of temporalization and spatialization. We must move slowly in this terrain, however, and clearly articulate not only *why* and *how* spacing should be understood as arche-writing, but also *what* this entails for our understanding of time and intersubjectivity.

The function of writing in general is to mediate between past and future through inscriptions that are characterized by the becoming-space of time as well as by the becoming-time of space. On the one hand, the written is always already an inscription of memory, a trace of the past that *spatializes time*. On the other hand, the written can only be read after its inscription and is thus marked by a relation to the future that *temporalizes space*. The reason for writing in the first place is to preserve what happens as a *memory for the future*, which constitutes both the possibility of repetition and its inevitable counterpart: the threat of extinction, of forgetting.

My reading of Husserl has sought to demonstrate the "transcendental" necessity of such spatiotemporal inscriptions even for the most minimal synthesis or most elementary self-awareness. Arche-writing, however, is not only a transcendental condition for the experience of a finite consciousness; it is an "ultratranscendental" condition for life in general.[31] As Derrida remarks in *Writing and Difference*, life as such is always already "threatened by the origin of the memory that constitutes it" (202/301). This is because the origin of memory—namely, the necessity of spatializing time, of inscribing traces of the past for the future—is an inherent temporal displacement that opens memory to forgetting from the first instance. The traces that retain the past for the future can only be inscribed by being exposed to erasure. Derrida describes the precarious time of arche-writing as follows:

> Traces thus produce the space of their inscription only by acceding to the period of their erasure. From the beginning, in the "present" of their first impression, they are constituted by the double force of repetition and erasure, legibility and illegibility. A two-handed machine, a multiplicity of agencies or origins—is this not the original relation to the other and the original temporality of writing, its "primary" complication: an originary spacing, deferring, and erasure of the simple origin, and polemics on the very threshold of what we persist in calling perception? . . . But this is because "perception," the first relation of life to its other, the origin of life, had always already prepared representation. (*WD*, 226/334)

Through our radicalization of Husserl we can see how such finitude is marked in autoaffection. Every retention is threatened from within by its complementary protention, which stems from the imminence of a future that can delete the inscription it is trying to maintain. Hence, temporal finitude is inscribed in autoaffection as such. Or as Derrida puts it: "The appearance of the *I* to itself in the *I am* is thus originally a relation to its own possible disappearance. Therefore, *I am* originally means *I am mortal*" (*SP*, 54/60–61).

Derrida's insistence on temporal finitude should help us to clarify what is at stake in his deconstruction of Husserl. Critics and followers of Derrida have often assumed that he takes Husserl to task for promoting an interiority that excludes the relation to the world and to the alterity of other human beings. Given this assumption, informed readers of Husserl have had little difficulty defending him from the alleged charges of deconstruction. Certainly, Husserl never wanted to exempt the subject from its relations to the world and to others; he only sought to analyze the conditions of possibility for this relationality on the basis of subjective intentionality. As we have seen, he thus discovered that the relation to alterity is opened by the structure of re-presentation, as exemplified by acts such as memory and empathy (*Einfühlung*). Through these acts the subject appears to itself as an other: either by remembering itself in the past or by imagining the perspective of an other and thus seeing itself as an other in relation to others. Derrida was in fact one of the first to emphasize the importance of these motifs in Husserl, and he has always maintained that Husserl is a sophisticated thinker of alterity, especially in an important polemic against Emmanuel Levinas.[32]

The decisive question for Derrida, however, is whether the structure of re-presentation is a condition for consciousness as such. Husserl denies this, in spite of recognizing the necessity of re-presentation for the constitution of time and intersubjectivity. As Husserl explains in the *Crisis*, the "self-temporalization" involved in remembering oneself and the "self-alienation" involved in relating to an alter ego must be regarded as derivative of an originary self-presentation, which he describes as "the immediate 'I,' flowingly-statically present" (185). The problem, then, is not that Husserl would exclude the relation to the world and to others, but that he grounds this relation in a living presence where we are given to ourselves without mediation. Husserl can thus write in the *Crisis*, among many other similar passages: "Each soul, reduced to its pure interiority, has its being-for-itself and its being-in-itself, has its life which is originally its own" (255). Again, Husserl does not exclude that the subject essentially is bound up with the world and with others. But he does think this essential bond on the basis of a fundamental integrity that belongs to everyone in his or her singularity. The form of such integrity would have to be pure autoaffection. Only pure autoaffection could secure a mode of self-relation where the subject is not dependent on anything that is exterior to itself. Thus, in pure autoaffection the subject would not have to "risk death in the body of a signifier that is given over to the world," as Derrida puts it with an apposite formulation (*SP*, 77/87).

In contrast, Derrida seeks to draw the rigorous consequences of the radical impossibility of such a fundamental integrity. Even the most elementary autoaffection of time presupposes the heteroaffection of space and the concomitant dependency on that which is exterior to oneself.

Such exterior support risks erasure in its very becoming and makes the subject essentially liable to betray itself as well as any other: to exclude, overlook, and forget. To think arche-writing is thus to think how death, discrimination, and obliteration are at work from the beginning and do not overtake an already constituted subject.

Consequently, the link between arche-writing and "arche-violence" is a key motif in Derrida. As he argues in *Of Grammatology*, metaphysics has always regarded violence as *derivative* of a primary peace or a fundamental integrity. The possibility of violence can thus only be accounted for in terms of a Fall, that is, in terms of a fatal corruption of a pure origin. By deconstructing this figure of thought, Derrida seeks to elucidate why violence is not merely an empirical accident that befalls something that precedes it. Rather, violence stems from an essential impropriety that does not allow anything to be sheltered from death and forgetting. "Anterior to the possibility of violence in the current and derivative sense . . . there is, as the space of its possibility, the violence of arche-writing."[33]

I have prepared the way for an account of arche-violence by analyzing the necessity of heteroaffection. To be dependent on that which is exterior to oneself is to be essentially compromised and threatened by "the other." In Derrida "the other" does not primarily designate another human being. On the contrary, alterity is indissociable from the spacing of time.[34] Such spacing is irreducibly violent because it breaches any interiority and exposes everyone—myself as well as any other—to the perils of finitude. Thus, when Derrida maintains the irreducibility of the other for the constitution of the self, he does not locate an *ethical* openness toward other human beings at the core of subjectivity. Rather, what is at stake is the primordial opening to corruption and dissimulation, which opens the possibility of every relation, including the relation to oneself. In his reading of Husserl, Derrida refutes the possibility of an unmediated presentation and insists on a primordial re-presentation in order to think the violent opening that threatens consciousness from within. In a certain way, then, my endeavors in the present chapter can be seen as the preparation for a reading of the following proposition from *Of Grammatology*: "Arche-writing is the origin of morality as of immorality. The nonethical opening of ethics. A violent opening" (140/202).

§ 3 Arche-Violence:
Derrida and Levinas

> There is a transcendental and preethical violence. . . . This transcendental violence, which does not spring from an ethical resolution or freedom, or from a *certain way* of encountering or exceeding the other, originally institutes the relationship . . .
>
> —Derrida, *Writing and Difference* (128/188)

During the last fifteen years, a standard way of defending deconstruction has been to endow it with an "ethical motivation." According to this line of argument, Derrida's undermining of metaphysical presuppositions and totalizing systems emanates from an ethical concern to respect "the Other." The most prominent advocates for such a perspective are Robert Bernasconi, Drucilla Cornell, and Simon Critchley, to whom I will return further on, since their readings exemplify the account of deconstruction with which I take issue in this chapter. What these readings have in common is the attempt to assimilate Derrida's thinking of alterity to Emmanuel Levinas's ethical metaphysics. Consequently, they understand deconstruction in terms of an "aspiration to a nonviolent relationship to the Other," as Cornell puts it in her book *The Philosophy of the Limit* (62). Such an approach certainly makes sense from within a Levinasian framework, where the Other answers to the Good and recalls us to an originary ethics. "War presupposes peace, the antecedent and non-allergic presence of the Other," Levinas asserts in his central work *Totality and Infinity* (199/173–74). As I will argue, however, the idea of a primary peace is incompatible with deconstructive thinking. In Derrida's work there is no support for positing the other as primordially Good or for prescribing a nonviolent relationship to him or her or it. On the contrary, Derrida's notion of alterity is inextricable from a notion of constitutive violence. Violence does not supervene on a peaceful Other but marks the possibility of every relation, as my epigraph makes clear. The epigraph is from Derrida's early essay "Violence and Metaphysics," but we will see how Derrida's thinking continued to be informed by the notion of a constitutive violence, all the way up to his late work on responsibility, justice, and hospitality.

A recurrent topos in contemporary discourse is to locate a "turn" toward the ethical in Derrida's later texts. Such a narrative is misleading not only because it fails to consider that ethical questions have been a major concern for Derrida ever since his first books, but also because it disregards how the logic of deconstruction transforms the fundamental axioms that inform the discussion of ethics. The appropriation of Derrida as an "ethical" philosopher rests on the inability to understand his complex logic of violence and the concomitant failure to assess the critical implications of central deconstructive terms such as "alterity" and "undecidability."

Specters of Marx is a good place to start, since it is often regarded as the book that initiates the "turn" in Derrida's thinking, where he explicitly begins to address questions of justice. The supposed turn has either been welcomed as the confirmation of an ethical injunction in deconstruction or dismissed as a complacent utopianism, with Derrida piously invoking a "justice" that has no bearing on the real political challenges of the contemporary world. There are good reasons, however, not to accept these readings, since they misconstrue the way in which Derrida works with ethicopolitical concepts. It is true that *Specters of Marx* is to a large extent a book on justice. But what Derrida calls justice is not an ethical ideal. On the contrary, Derrida questions the very idea of an ideal state of being, which entails a profound reconfiguration of our inherited assumptions about the goals of ethics and politics.

An important clue is the phrase that reverberates throughout the book: "The time is out of joint." This line from Shakespeare's *Hamlet* is the leitmotif in *Specters of Marx*. By exploring its resonance we can begin to assess what is at stake in the book. As Derrida points out, Hamlet's line has often been quoted and translated as a critique of the prevalent state of society. The disjointure of time is then understood in terms of a moral or social decay, in which the founding principles of community have been perverted or gone astray. Such a critique opposes the disjointed time— which keeps losing its course and does not hold together—to a society that is harmoniously synchronized with itself, regardless of whether the synchrony is posited as a lost origin or as a consummated future. The same opposition characterizes the traditional critique of ideology: in contrast to how things are, in contrast to the prevailing injustice and oppression, the demand for justice is raised as a demand concerning how things *ought* to be.

In *Specters of Marx*, Derrida reconfigures the understanding of what it means that "the time is out of joint." As many readers have noted, Derrida is firm in his contention that we cannot do away with a notion of emancipation and progress. He repeatedly emphasizes the importance of pursuing political critique, of not closing one's eyes before the innumerable victims of global capitalism, and of reaffirming a certain "Marxist" spirit. These points are reinforced through a critique of the neoliberal rhetoric that proclaims the death of Marx and Marxism, represented in *Specters of Marx* by Francis Fukuyama's book *The End of History and the Last Man*. Protesting against Fukuyama's neoevangelism, which celebrates the end of ideologies and emancipatory narratives in the capitalist paradise, Derrida paints a "blackboard picture" of the contemporary world, recalling that "never have violence, inequality, famine and thus economic oppression affected as many human beings in the history of the earth and of humanity" (85/141). This remark may seem to be nothing but a version of the traditional critique of ideology. Apparently, Derrida maintains that our time is "out of joint" and that we have to combat the disjointure in the name of a better, a more just society. The pivotal difference, however, is that the classical concept of emancipation—like the Marxist form of political critique—is tied to the notion that the ideal condition would be an absolute peace. While the world is de facto marked by violence, exclusion, and discrimination, one thus postulates that justice in principle (de jure) should put an end to violence.

The challenge of Derrida's thinking is that he undermines the notion of an ideal justice, without renouncing the struggle for justice. For Derrida, the disjointure of time is neither something that supervenes on a state of being that precedes it nor something that one can or should finally overcome. Hence, the provocative thesis in *Specters of Marx* is that violence and discrimination are not opposed to justice; they are inextricable from its very possibility. Of course, Derrida does not regard violence or discrimination as positive in themselves. Rather, he argues that the machinery of exclusion is at work in the formation of every identity and cannot finally be eliminated. The disjointure of time is the condition for there to be any ethics and politics, as well as any society and life to begin with.

By tracking the notion of a necessary disjointure, we can discern the continuity of Derrida's thinking. Derrida's deconstructive logic is always concerned with the impossibility of being *in itself.* In previous chapters I demonstrated how Derrida's logic follows from the implications of temporality. The temporal can never be in itself but is always disjoined between being no longer and being not yet. Thus, time itself is constitutively out of joint. Or more exactly: time itself is the impossibility of any "itself." This is not a paradox but follows from analyzing the minimal definition of time. Even the slightest temporal moment must be divided in its becoming: separating before from after, past from future. Without such division there would be no time, only a presence forever remaining the same.

Consequently, time is unthinkable without the synthesis of the trace (arche-writing). To think the tracing of time as the condition for life in general is to think a constitutive finitude, which from the very beginning exposes life to death, memory to forgetting, identity to alterity, and so on. Derrida always proceeds from the logic of such a double bind. What I want to emphasize here is that the understanding of the trace that informs deconstructive logic is radically different from Levinas's understanding of the trace. Indeed, both Derrida and Levinas appeal to "the trace of the other" as the trace of a past that has never been present. The shared vocabulary has often been adduced as evidence of their proximity, but a closer study of the terms in question reveals that the analogy is misleading.[1]

The most instructive reading is Levinas's essay "The Trace of the Other," where he elucidates the notion of the trace that is operative in his writings. Levinas's main concern is to establish that "a trace does not effect a relationship with what would be less than being, but obliges with regard to the infinite, the absolutely other" (357). The absolutely other is here the positive infinity of God, which Levinas describes as analogous to the Good beyond being in Plato and the One in Plotinus. The One is an absolute past because it "has already withdrawn from every relation and every dissimulation" (356). While absent in the world, the One is nevertheless present as a trace in the ethical encounter with a human face: "it is in the trace of the other that a face shines; what is presented there is absolving itself from my life and visits me as already ab-solute" (359). Levinas even goes so far as to venture the following claim: "Only a being that transcends the world can leave a trace" (358).

That the other appears as a trace does not mean, then, that it is dependent on mediation or subjected to the movement of signification. On the contrary, Levinas insists that the other "comes without mediation; he signifies by himself" (351). The immediacy of the face is not an incidental feature of Levinas's argument; it is crucial for his notion of an original "uprightness" in the ethical encounter. As Levinas explains, it is the "absoluteness of the presence of the other, which has justified our interpreting the exceptional uprightness of thou-saying as an epiphany of this absoluteness" (358). Thus, we should not be surprised when Levinas's description of the absolute presence of the other turns out to be interchangeable with his notion of the absolute past.[2] Levinas himself accounts for the equivalence between the absolute presence of the face and the absolute past of the Absent One: "the supreme presence of a face is inseparable from this supreme and irreversible absence" (356).

Derrida's notion of the trace can be seen to systematically undermine these Levinasian premises. First, in Derrida the trace of a past that has never been present does not refer to an Absent One. On the contrary, it designates a constitutive spacing that undermines the very idea of the One. Second, spacing explains why there can be no instance (such as the absolute Other in Levinas's account) that precedes its own "dissimulation." As Derrida puts it in *Of Grammatology*, the "presentation of the other as such, that is to say the dissimulation of its 'as such,' has always already begun" (47/69). Third, the spacing of the trace undermines the possibility of anything being *in itself* and accounts for erasure as a necessary risk. Thus, it undercuts Levinas's theological appropriation of the trace. As Derrida formulates it in *Writing and Difference*: "An unerasable trace is not a trace, it is a full presence, an immobile and uncorruptible substance, a son of God, a sign of parousia and not a seed, that is, a mortal germ" (230/339).

Last but not least, for Derrida the trace is concomitant with the necessity of mediation. This precludes the "immediacy" that grounds Levinas's notion of "uprightness." Levinas repeatedly refers to uprightness when he sets out to promote the primacy of ethics. In *Totality and Infinity* the face-to-face relation figures as the guarantee for a supposedly "straightforward" and "immediate" encounter that is "foreign to all compromise and all contamination," relying on "the absolute authenticity of the face" and a "primordial word of honour" in relation to which the deceitful powers of rhetoric are denounced as "corrupting."[3] Levinas's other major philosophical work, *Otherwise Than Being*, follows the same logic in maintaining an opposition between the "sincerity" of the primordial Saying and its "alienation" in the Said.[4] To sustain the distinction between the Saying and the Said, Levinas explicitly relies on the opposition between speech and writing. As Levinas explains, sincerity can only emanate from a *spoken* language, in the proximity of one-for-the-other, since there is nothing in a piece of writing (or more generally: in language as a system of signs) that can guarantee its sincerity. Thus, Levinas emphasizes that "saying could not be interpreted as a sincerity, when one takes a language as a system of signs. One enters into language as a system of signs only out of an already spoken language, which in turn cannot consist in a system of signs" (*Otherwise Than Being or Beyond Essence*, 199n9/183n1). This is an excellent example of the phonocentrism that Derrida has analyzed as one of the most pervasive versions of the metaphysics of presence. As Derrida demonstrates in *Of Grammatology*, the privileging of (idealized) speech over writing derives from the premise that there was good before evil, peace before violence, and so on.

Levinas's adherence to the opposition between speech and writing is symptomatic. The primacy of ethics requires that there *first* was sincerity and peaceful hospitality, *before* these values were compromised by insincerity and violent hostility. Derrida targets precisely this logic of opposition. It proceeds from what he calls the "ethico-theoretical decision" of metaphysics, which postulates the simple to be before the complex, the pure before the impure, the sincere before the deceitful, and so on.[5] Accordingly, all divergences from the positively valued term are explained away as symptoms of "alienation," and the desirable is conceived as the return to what supposedly has been lost or corrupted. In contrast, Derrida argues that what makes it *possible* for anything to be at the same time makes it *impossible* for anything to be in itself. The integrity of any "positive" term is necessarily compromised and threatened by its "other." Such constitutive alterity answers to an *essential corruptibility*, which undercuts all ethico-theoretical decisions concerning how things *ought* to be in an ideal world.[6]

A key term here is what Derrida calls "undecidability," which opens everything to the coming of time that cannot be predicted. As I argued in Chapter 1, there is no opposition between undecidability and the making of decisions. On the contrary, one has to make decisions *because* it is impossible to calculate what will happen. Thus, Derrida emphasizes that one always acts in relation to what cannot be predicted, that one always is forced to make decisions even though the consequences of these decisions cannot finally be established. Any kind of decision (ethical, political, juridical, etc.) is more or less violent, but it is nevertheless necessary to make decisions. Once again, I want to stress that violent differentiation by no means should be understood as a Fall, where violence supervenes on a harmony that precedes it. On the contrary, discrimination has to be regarded as a constitutive condition. Without divisional marks—which is to say, without segregating borders—there would be nothing at all.

In effect, every attempt to organize life in accordance with ethical or political prescriptions will have been marked by a fundamental duplicity. On the one hand, it is necessary to draw boundaries, to demarcate, in order to form any community whatsoever. On the other hand, it is precisely because of these excluding borders that every kind of community is characterized by a more or less palpable instability. What cannot be included opens the risk as well as the chance that the prevalent order may be transformed or subverted.

In *Specters of Marx*, Derrida pursues this argument in terms of an originary "spectrality." A salient connotation concerns phantoms and specters as haunting reminders of the victims of historical violence, of those who have been excluded or extinguished from the formation of a society. The notion of spectrality is not, however, exhausted by these ghosts that question the good conscience of a state, a nation, or an ideology. Rather, Derrida's aim is to formulate a general "hauntology" (*hantologie*), in contrast to the traditional "ontology" that thinks being in terms of self-identical presence. What is important about the figure of the specter, then, is that it cannot be fully present: it has no being in itself but marks a relation to what is *no longer* or *not yet*. And since time—the disjointure between past and future—is a condition even for the slightest moment, spectrality is at work in everything that happens. An identity or community can never escape the machinery of exclusion, can never fail to engender ghosts, since it must demarcate itself against a past that cannot be encompassed and a future that cannot be anticipated. Inversely, it will always be threatened by what it cannot integrate in itself—haunted by the negated, the neglected, and the unforeseeable.

Thus, a rigorous deconstructive thinking maintains that we are always already inscribed in an "economy of violence," where we are both excluding and being excluded. No position can be autonomous or absolute; it is necessarily bound to other positions that it violates and by which it is violated. The struggle for justice can therefore not be a struggle for peace, but only for "lesser violence." Derrida himself only uses this term briefly in his essay "Violence and Metaphysics," but I will develop it in a direction that I argue is crucial for Derrida's rethinking of the political.[7] The starting point for my argument is that all decisions made in the name of justice are made in view of what is judged to be the lesser violence. If there is always an economy of violence, decisions of justice cannot be a matter of choosing what is nonviolent. To justify something is rather to contend that it is less violent than something else. This does not mean that decisions made in view of lesser violence are actually less violent than the violence they oppose. On the contrary, even the most horrendous acts are justified in view of what is judged to be the lesser violence. For example, justifications of genocide clearly appeal to an argument for lesser violence, since the extinction of the group in question is claimed to be less violent than the dangers it poses to another group. The disquieting point, however, is that all decisions of justice are implicated in the logic of violence. The desire for lesser violence is never innocent, since it is a desire for violence in one form or another, and there can be no guarantee that it is in the service of perpetrating the better.

Consequently, my argument is not that the desire for lesser violence answers to a normative ideal or that it is inherently good. Such an argument presupposes that there is a way to objectively define and measure violence, which is an untenable presupposition. Every definition and every measure of violence is itself violent, since it is based on decisions that are haunted by what they exclude. The criteria for what counts as violence are therefore always open to challenge. Indeed, there would be no chance to pursue political critique and to transform the law if the definitions of violence were not subject to possible alteration. A contemporary example is the extension of animal rights. What formerly went unrecognized as violence in the juridical sense—the abuse and killing of animals—has begun to be recognized as an illegal violence. A similar transformation of the criteria for what counts as violence is still under way with regard to subordinated classes, races, and genders. If there were an objective norm for what is less violent, the range of such political critique would be limited in advance, and there would be an end to politics. In contrast, Derrida argues that politics is endless since any definition of violence is itself violent and given over to possible contestation.

Deconstruction cannot teach us what the "lesser violence" is in any given case. On the contrary, deconstruction spells out why the question of violence remains forever undecidable. The supposed lesser violence may always be more violent than the violence it opposes, and there can be no end to the challenges that stem from the impossibility of calculation. Derrida's argument here is neither negative nor positive; it neither deplores nor celebrates the constitutive violence. Rather, it accounts for violence as the condition for both the desirable *and* the undesirable. Because of the economy of violence, there is always the possibility of less violence (and the risk of more violence). Otherwise there would be no politics in the first place. If there were not the chance of less violence (and the threat of more violence), there would be no political struggle, since nothing could ever be changed.

A possible objection here is that we must strive toward an ideal origin or end, an *arkhe* or *telos* that would prevail beyond the possibility of violence. Even if every community is haunted by victims of discrimination and forgetting, we must try to reach a state of being that does not exclude anyone, namely, a consummated presence that includes everyone. However, it is with precisely such an "ontological" thesis that Derrida's hauntological thinking takes issue. At several places in *Specters of Marx* he maintains that a completely present life—which would not be "out of joint," not haunted by any ghosts—would be nothing but a complete death. Derrida's point is not simply that a peaceful state of existence is impossible to realize, as if it were a desirable, albeit unattainable end. Rather, he challenges the very idea that absolute peace is desirable. In a state of being where all violent change is precluded, nothing can ever happen. Absolute peace is thus inseparable from absolute violence, as Derrida argued already in "Violence and Metaphysics." Anything that would finally put an end to violence (whether the end is a religious salvation, a universal justice, a harmonious intersubjectivity, or some other ideal) would end the possibility of life in general. The idea of absolute peace is the idea of eliminating the undecidable future that is the condition for anything to happen. Thus, the idea of absolute peace is the idea of absolute violence.

The aim of the present chapter is to elucidate how Derrida pursues his thinking of violence via a reading of Levinas. I will thus seek to clarify why Derrida has devoted so much attention to Levinas's work. What interests Derrida is Levinas's insistence that the ethical must be thought on the basis of an alterity that cannot be appropriated. But alterity has a radically different sense in Derrida's work. It does not testify to a Good beyond being, and "the other" does not primarily designate another human being. On the contrary, alterity is indissociable from the spacing of time. Spacing is "arche-violent" because it breaches any interiority and exposes everyone—myself as well as every other—to the essential corruptibility of finitude.

Hence, when Derrida reads Levinas he seeks to demonstrate that the relation to the other cannot be ethical as such, but is a nonethical opening that cannot be appropriated by any ethics. For the same reason, the metaphysical and religious qualities that Levinas ascribes to the other are for Derrida incompatible with a rigorous thinking of alterity. As Derrida underscores in "Faith and Knowledge," the alterity of spacing "will never have entered religion and will never permit itself to be sacralized, sanctified, humanized, theologized. . . . Radically heterogeneous to the safe and sound, to the holy and the sacred, it never admits of any *indemnification*" (58/34) and is neither "the Good, nor God, nor Man" (59/35). The implicit dissociation from Levinas is further reinforced when Derrida concludes the same paragraph by designating his conception of spacing as "an utterly *faceless* other" (my emphasis).

Derrida first developed his strategy of reading Levinas against himself in "Violence and Metaphysics." The point of departure is Levinas's designation of ethics as "first philosophy." Levinas's claim is based on his now famous notion of a face-to-face encounter with the other human being. According to Levinas, the distinctive trait of the encounter is a fundamental asymmetry. The subject is subordinated to the other through an ethical injunction to respect him as an absolute Other. Despite the clear resonances of power and dominance in his description (where the other appears as the Master, the High, the Transcendent, and so on), Levinas holds that the subjection to the other answers to the ethical Good. "To be for the Other is to be good," he asserts in *Totality and Infinity* (261/239).

Levinas's thinking describes a metaphysical opposition between a positive principle—which *ought* to reign supreme—and a negative principle that unfortunately has taken hold of our existence. The primary imperative is said to be "thou shalt not kill," an injunction that according to Levinas emanates from the immediate revelation of the face and confronts the subject with an unconditional moral responsibility. To be sure, Levinas recognizes that such a prohibition cannot prevent transgressions. But following his infinitist metaphysics, Levinas seeks to *derive* these violations from what he calls the Same, which compromises the positive infinity of the absolutely Other.

The dichotomy between the Same and the Other is the guiding principle for Levinas's critique of the philosophical tradition. The problem with traditional metaphysical concepts of unity and identity is not, for Levinas, that they rely on an idea of originary peace. Rather, these concepts ultimately exercise violence by erecting a *finite totality* (the Same) that excludes the transcendence of *infinite alterity* (the Other). Thus, Levinas employs the concepts of alterity and totality in a very idiosyncratic manner. Derrida devotes large parts of "Violence and Metaphysics" to demonstrating how the above outlined conceptual schema is untenable, in order to read Levinas against himself.

Derrida's principal argument is that the finite cannot be a totality. On the contrary, alterity is irreducible because of temporal finitude. That every slightest moment is disjoined by time entails that neither I nor anyone else can ever be protected *in ourselves*. Hence, alterity cannot be understood in terms of goodness and nonviolence. If alterity is irreducible, then violence is a necessary risk since, far from being "absolute," one is always dependent on others that may violate, negate, or exploit.

Accordingly, the idea of absolute peace has traditionally been linked to the idea of a closed totality that is liberated from any form of negativity or difference. Only such a unity could guarantee serenity by not allowing any disintegrating forces or polemical antagonisms—which is to say, no alterity whatsoever—to enter. The idea of such absolute unity is the idea of the absolutely Same, and we can see how it concurs with Levinas's idea of the absolutely Other. Contrary to what Levinas avows, the unity of totality has never been identified with the finite but is projected as a positive infinity beyond the violent conditions of history. It is to this line of thought that Levinas himself adheres.

Levinas's favorite examples from the history of philosophy are Descartes' idea of the Infinite and Plato's Good beyond being. These concepts—which for Levinas testify to the absolutely Other—are cardinal examples of the idea of the absolutely Same. They define a state of perfect unity, liberated from any restraining relation and thereby from all forms of alterity. Or as Levinas himself puts it:

> The One of which Plato speaks . . . is *other* absolutely and not with respect to some relative term. It is the Unrevealed, but not unrevealed because all knowledge would be too limited or too narrow to receive its light. It is unrevealed because it is *One*, and because making oneself known implies a duality

which already clashes with the unity of the One. The One is not beyond being because it is buried and hidden; it is buried because it is beyond being, wholly other than being. ("The Trace of the Other," 347)

Apparently unaware of the inconsistency, Levinas thus criticizes the philosophy of identity, totality, and monadic being by invoking an absolute that reinstates these ideals. Indeed, Levinas speaks of the wholly Other instead of the wholly Same. But the shift in terminology makes no essential difference since the two extremes—as Derrida maintains in "Violence and Metaphysics"—invert into each other and at bottom are founded on the same ideal.

The convergence between the wholly Other and the wholly Same is even more apparent if we examine Levinas's fascination with the idea of the Infinite that Descartes puts forward in the third of his *Meditations*, in a classic attempt to prove the existence of God. What interests Levinas here is the sharp opposition between the finite and the infinite that Descartes establishes. When Descartes attempts to think the positive infinity of God, he discovers that such an idea of the Perfect is beyond his power of imagination. This leads Descartes to the conclusion that such an idea of the Infinite cannot have originated in his own finite consciousness, but testifies to an absolute transcendence (i.e., God). According to Levinas, such absolute transcendence is revealed in the face of the other, which thus bears a "resemblance" to the divine. In *Totality and Infinity* Levinas even claims that Descartes' opposition between the *primary* (the perfection of the infinite) and the *secondary* (the imperfection of the finite) "remains entirely valid" (41/12). The perfection of the infinite answers to Levinas's understanding of the absolutely Other as something "beyond history," which is "absolved" from a limiting play of relations.

The treatment of Descartes is an instructive example of how Levinas misconstrues what is at stake in traditional philosophical notions of identity and alterity. Indeed, one can say that Descartes' idea of the Infinite is absolutely Other in relation to the finite subject. But the idea of the Infinite is absolutely Other because it transcends the condition of alterity. Descartes cannot imagine the Perfect because it would be a state of pure autonomy, uncontaminated by anything other than itself. If the other were such a positive infinity, it would be absolutely identical to itself and not allow for any alterity at all. Alterity requires a play of relations, where any given term is *other than* something else and cannot be "absolved" from limitation.

For the same reason, the other cannot be respected *as such*—as given in itself—but only by being related to the perspective of another. The "violence" of not being respected as such is not something that supervenes on an instance that precedes it but is the trait of constitutive alterity. If the other could appear for me as him- or herself, from his or her own perspective, he or she would not be an other. Hence, we may always misunderstand or disregard one another, since none of us can have direct access to the other's experience. The face-to-face encounter cannot be characterized by the "immediacy" to which Levinas appeals. Rather, the encounter is always mediated across a temporal distance. Temporal distance opens the space for all kinds of discords, but it is nevertheless the prerequisite for there to be relations at all.

Moreover, the same temporality constitutes the self-relation of the subject, as we saw in the previous chapter on Husserl. Even the most intimate autoaffection can only take place through the violent passage of time, which requires the spatialization of traces in order to be marked as such but also risks deleting these traces in the concomitant movement of temporalization. To think the spacing of time is thus to think how death, discrimination, and obliteration are at work from the beginning and do not overtake an already constituted subject. Every experience is threatened by erasure in its very becoming and makes the subject essentially liable to violate itself as well as any other: to exclude, overlook, and forget.[8]

Thus, Derrida articulates a double argument concerning the relation between self and other. On the one hand, he emphasizes that the subject cannot go outside of itself. The openness to the other is mediated through one's own experience and thus necessarily limited. On the other hand, the subject can never be in itself but is always exposed to an alterity that exceeds it.[9] Alterity does not stem from the Good beyond being but from the spacing of time that breaches the integrity of self and other from their first inception.

The spacing of time entails that alterity is undecidable. The other can be anything whatsoever or anyone whosoever. The relation to the other is thus the nonethical opening of ethics. This opening is violent because it entails that everything is exposed to what may corrupt and extinguish it.

Hence, Derrida emphasizes that the other *as other* is the other *as mortal*.[10] It is this originary finitude that raises the demand of responsibility in the first place. If the other could not be violated or annihilated (and inversely, if the other could not violate or annihilate me), there would be no reason to take responsibility or pursue reflections on ethical problems. As Derrida writes in *Politics of Friendship*, the violent opening of ethics is already revealed in the decree "thou shalt not kill." For Derrida, this injunction does not testify to a primary peace but indicates that violence is an imminent threat (otherwise there would be no need for a prohibition). Assaults and violations are always possible since relations can be forged only between finite beings, where the one is exposed to being murdered by the other and vice versa. Even the most affectionate love or intimate friendship is therefore haunted by the sentence "I can kill you, you can kill me," as Derrida puts it in *Politics of Friendship* (122/143).

As a result, Levinas's injunction of unconditional submission before the other cannot be sustained. Although Levinas claims to proceed from the face-to-face relation, he evidently postulates that the subject in the ethical encounter either gazes upward (toward the Other as the High) or downward (toward the Other as someone who is helplessly in need, bearing "the face of the poor, the stranger, the widow and the orphan" as a refrain declares in *Totality and Infinity*). But regarding all the situations where you are confronted with an other who assaults you, turns down the offered hospitality, and in turn denies you help when you need it, Levinas has nothing to say. If the other whom I encounter wants to kill me, should I then submit myself to his or her command? And if someone disagrees with me, should I then automatically accept this criticism as a law that is not to be questioned or counterattacked?

Questions like these make it clear that Levinas does not at all found his ethics on an intersubjective encounter. Rather, he presupposes that the ethical encounter exhibits a fundamental asymmetry, where the other is an absolute Other who reveals the transcendence of the Good. Accordingly, Levinas condemns every form of self-love as a corruption of the ethical relation, and prescribes that the subject should devote itself entirely to the other. To be ethical is for Levinas to be purely disinterested, to take responsibility for the other without seeking any recognition on one's own behalf.[11]

It suffices, however, to place yourself face-to-face with someone else to realize that the asymmetry assumed by Levinas is self-refuting. If you and I are standing in front of each other, who is the other? The answer can only be doubly affirmative since "the other" is an interchangeable term that shifts referent depending on who pronounces the words. I am an other for the other and vice versa, as Derrida reinforces in "Violence and Metaphysics."

Derrida's argument not only contradicts Levinas's idea of the absolutely Other but also undercuts his rhetoric. That "the other" is a reversible term means that all of Levinas's ethical declarations can be read against themselves. To say that the I should subject itself to the other is at the same time to say that the other should subject itself to the I, since I am a you and you are an I when we are others for each other. To condemn the self-love of the I is by the same token to condemn the self-love of the other. Indeed, whoever advocates a Levinasian ethics will be confronted with a merciless irony as soon as he or she comes up to someone else and face-to-face declares, "You should subject yourself to the Other," which then literally means, "You should subject yourself to *Me*, you should obey *My* law."

Levinas cannot think these inversions of his own prescriptions since he refuses to realize that alterity cannot be ethical as such. Rather, alterity marks that nothing can be *in itself*. Levinas cannot assimilate this insight because his philosophy requires that alterity ultimately answers to the Good. Even when Levinas describes the ethical in apparently violent terms—as in *Otherwise Than Being*, where the other "accuses," "persecutes," and "traumatizes" the subject—he understands violence as an instance of the Good, which disrupts the evil egoism of the subject by subordinating it to the demands of the other. It is thus quite crucial for Levinas that the subordination to a tyrant—who also accuses one of self-love and demands that one follow his command—can be rigorously distinguished from the subordination to an ethical other.[12] But it is precisely the possibility of such a distinction between the "good" other and the "bad" other that the deconstructive analysis calls into question. To posit the other as primordially Good is to deny the constitutive undecidability of alterity. The other cannot be predicted, and one cannot know in advance how one should act in relation to him, her, or it. Consequently, there is nothing intrinsically ethical about subjecting oneself to the other, who may always be a brutal tyrant. There can be no encounter that *precedes* such risks, which are implicated in every relation from the beginning.

The relation to a finite other is, accordingly, what makes ethics *possible* but at the same time what makes it *impossible* for any of its principles to have a guaranteed legitimacy, since one may always confront situations where they turn out to be inadequate. When one speaks of "the other," one can never know in advance what or whom one invokes. It is thus impossible to decide whether the encounter with the other will bring about a chance or a threat, recognition or rejection, continued life or violent death.

Remarkably, we can articulate the link between alterity and violence by following passages in Levinas's own texts. For example, some of the most fascinating pages in *Totality and Infinity* demonstrate that it is *mortality* that exposes being to a constitutive alterity. To be mortal is to be susceptible to forces that one's own will cannot finally master. In this context Levinas admits that violence must be regarded as an essential risk, since the inevitable death to come figures as a relentless threat. Regardless of how tranquil death may appear, it is always a "murder" that one neither can guard against nor prepare for. One can only try to delay death for as long as possible, haunted by an irreducible insecurity as regards one's own future. Interestingly enough, Levinas connects this fundamental vulnerability with the relation to the other. Precisely because of my disquietude before what will happen, I become aware of my limitation and my dependence on others, which cannot be pacified by any transcendent Good. Levinas himself writes that "the fear of violence" is extended into "fear of the Other, of the absolutely unforeseeable" (235/212), which ought to mean that alterity does not point toward a positive infinity but toward an unpredictable and violent future.

The same line of thought can be read in *Otherwise Than Being*. Here, alterity is linked to the diachrony of time and an originary exposure of the subject, described by Levinas in terms of a temporality where it is always already "out of phase with itself." The subject comes into being through a relation to the past and the future that exceeds its control. Therefore, it can never be a closed entity. The subject is rather conditioned by an inherent alterity, which stems from the diachrony of time and is accentuated by the risk of being violated in the interaction with others.

If Levinas followed this argument consistently (adding that the diachronic temporality not only is the condition for the subject but for every other as well), then alterity could never be compatible with a metaphysical idea of Goodness. However, Levinas disarms the critical implications of diachrony by understanding alterity as a trace of the divine. As he explains in "The Trace of the Other," such a trace testifies to the absolute transcendence of God, which he also describes as "an absolute past which unites all times" (358). Thus, Levinas's religious understanding of the other reintroduces the idea of an instance beyond diachronic temporality despite the fact that Levinas himself describes diachrony as the condition of alterity.

The appeal to an instance beyond temporality is salient in both *Totality and Infinity* and *Otherwise Than Being*. In *Totality and Infinity* Levinas holds out the promise of a "messianic peace," which is to abolish "the ontology of war." This eschatological vision quite literally projects an overcoming of time, to which I will return in the next chapter. Here I need only to point out that the messianic "triumph," according to Levinas, will put an end to the destructive forces of time by "converting" the temporal into the eternal (285/261). In fact, such a closure is necessary for his doctrine of the Good beyond being. As Levinas asserts in *Otherwise Than Being*, "the Good as the infinite has no other" since "nothing escapes its goodness" (187n8/13).

Hence, to read Levinas against himself one must be vigilant regarding how two radically different notions of "alterity," "transcendence," and "infinity" are at work in his text. The infinite alterity of diachronic temporality is incompatible with the infinite alterity of the Good beyond being. In "Violence and Metaphysics" Derrida pursues this argument by drawing on Hegel's distinction between negative and positive infinity. The concept of *negative infinity* names a process of displacement without end. The classical example comes from mathematics, where no number can be the greatest but is always superseded by another number, which in turn is superseded by yet another number, and so on. In *Science of Logic* Hegel provides a general definition of such negative infinity by analyzing it as intrinsic to temporal finitude. As Hegel demonstrates, the finite is an incessant "ceasing-to-be" that prevents it from ever being in itself and thus opens the "*relation* to an *other*" (250). Finite relationality necessarily entails a negative infinity since none of the terms can be absolute; each is always transcended by another finitude, which in turn is transcended by another finitude, and so on. For Hegel such negative infinity is a "spurious infinity" (*schlechte Unendliche*). The movement that is driven by the negativity of time is rather a process of self-actualization, which is governed by the true infinity of the Notion. The Notion is *positive infinity*, which is completely in itself and thereby sublates spatial limitation and temporal alteration. By negating the negation of time, "the image of the true infinity, bent back upon itself, becomes the *circle*, the line which has reached itself, which is closed and wholly present, without *beginning* and *end*" (149).

Consequently, if one wants to take issue with Hegel's totalization, one must undermine the idea of positive infinity. Derrida claims that "the only effective position to take in order not to be enveloped by Hegel" is "to consider the spurious infinity (that is, in a profound way, original finitude) irreducible" (*WD*, 119/176). In a parenthesis a few lines further on, he points out that the spurious infinity as such is "time."[13] This is the key to Derrida's argument. The relentless displacement of negative infinity answers to the movement of temporalization, which is the spacing of *différance*. Accordingly, *différance* can be described as an *infinite finitude*.[14] As I demonstrated in Chapter 1, this conception of finitude does not entail a return to the Idea of infinity that Hegel criticizes in Kant. The infinite finitude of time is not oriented toward a positive infinity that remains forever out of reach. On the contrary, the thinking of infinite finitude refutes the very Idea of positive infinity by accounting for finitude *not* as a negative limitation but as constitutive of being in general.[15] Positive infinity is neither an immanent actuality (Hegel) nor a transcendent Idea (Kant); it is *self-refuting as such* since everything is subjected to a temporal alteration that prevents it from ever being in itself. Alterity is thus irreducible because of the negative infinity of finitude, which undermines any possible totality from the outset.

In contrast to Derrida's deconstructive logic, Levinas attempts to criticize philosophies of totality by referring to the other as a positive infinity. Levinas's argument is untenable, since such an absolute Other would be an absolute Same. The idea of a positive infinity is precisely the idea of a totality that is not limited by a relation to something other than itself and thus abolishes alterity. Derrida writes in "Violence and Metaphysics":

> The infinitely other, the infinity of the other, is not the other *as* a positive infinity, as God, or as resemblance with God. The infinitely Other would not be what it is, other, if it was a positive infinity, and if it did not maintain within itself the negativity of the indefinite. . . . The other cannot be what it is, infinitely other, except in finitude and mortality (mine *and* its). (*WD*, 114–15/168–69)

Derrida's argument here is pivotal for understanding the notion of the "infinitely other" that is operative in his writings. Derrida's employment of the term infinitely other does *not* signal an adherence to Levinas's conception of the Other as a positive infinity. Rather, it designates the negative infinity of finitude. Finitude entails that the other is infinitely other, not because the other is absolved from relations and reposes in itself but because finitude entails that alterity cannot ever be eliminated or overcome.

The same logic informs Derrida's use of terms like "absolutely other" or "wholly other" (*tout autre*), which must be rigorously distinguished from Levinas's use of these terms. For Derrida, the "absolutely" or "wholly" does not refer to a positive infinity or to any other form of divinity but to the radical finitude of every other. Every finite other is absolutely other, not because it is absolutely in itself but on the contrary because it can never be in itself. Thus, it is always becoming other than itself and cannot have any integrity as such (for example, as "ethical").

For the same reason, Derrida's notion of "infinite responsibility" should not be conflated with Levinas's. For Derrida, the infinitude of responsibility answers to the fact that responsibility always takes place in relation to a *negative infinity* of others. The negative infinity of responsibility is both spatial (innumerable finite others that exceed my horizon) and temporal (innumerable times past and to come that exceed my horizon). Far from confirming Levinas's sense of responsibility, the negative infinity of others is fatal for his notion of an originary encounter that would give ethics the status of "first philosophy" and be the guiding principle for a metaphysical "goodness." Even if it were possible to sacrifice yourself completely to another, to devote all your forces to the one who is encountered face-to-face, it would mean that you had disregarded or denied all the others who demanded your attention or needed your help. For there are always *more than two*, as Richard Beardsworth has aptly put it.[16] Whenever I turn toward another, I turn away from yet another and thus exercise discrimination. As Derrida points out in *The Gift of Death*, "I cannot respond to the call, the demand, the obligation, or even the love of another without sacrificing the other other, the other others" (68/68). Consequently, Derrida emphasizes that the concept of responsibility lends itself a priori to "scandal and aporia" (68/68). There are potentially an endless number of others to consider, and one cannot take any responsibility without excluding some others in favor of certain others. What makes it *possible* to be responsible is thus at the same time what makes it *impossible* for any responsibility to be fully responsible. Responsibility, then, is always more or less discriminating, and infinite responsibility is but another name for the necessity of discrimination.

The necessity of discrimination is at the core of Derrida's thinking, and anyone who wishes to articulate a deconstructive understanding of ethicopolitical problems needs to elaborate it. I insist on this point since it calls for an approach that is opposed to the numerous attempts to forge an alliance between Derrida and Levinas. One of the first to argue for such an alliance was Robert Bernasconi, who paved the way for later Levinasian readings of Derrida.[17] In his essay "The Trace of Levinas in Derrida," Bernasconi claims that "Violence and Metaphysics" should not be understood as taking issue with Levinas's philosophy, but only as pointing out certain necessities that impose themselves on philosophical discourse. Derrida's critique of Levinas would then be limited to the way Levinas uses metaphysical language, and Bernasconi insists that "this should not be confused with passing judgment on what Levinas says" (26). Thus, Bernasconi disregards the central arguments in Derrida's essay and does not even address the notion of violence that is elaborated there. Bernasconi asserts that "we let the finite stand for the totalizing thought of the tradition of Western ontology, as the infinite stands for the attempt to surpass it" (15). This is a misleading matrix for discussing Derrida's essay, since Derrida demonstrates the incoherence of such a setup. Derrida argues that the finite cannot be a totality and that the idea of totality is the idea of the (positive) infinity that Levinas posits as a challenge to the idea of totality. Hence Derrida's insistence on taking "history, that is, finitude, seriously . . . in a sense which tolerates *neither finite totality, nor positive infinity*" (*WD*, 117/172; my emphasis). Because Bernasconi disregards the logic of this argument—which pervades Derrida's entire essay—he misconstrues the difference between Derrida and Levinas. In his later essay "Deconstruction and the Possibility of Ethics" (128), Bernasconi claims that Derrida's argument concerning how alterity already is *in* the Same has been adequately responded to by Levinas, through the latter's recognition that the idea of the Other is reflected within history and within Western ontology, in Plato's Good beyond being and Descartes' idea of the Infinite. But in fact, none of Derrida's criticisms are answered by this move. Derrida's argument is, on the contrary, that alterity cannot be thought in terms of the positive infinity that Levinas subscribes to in Plato and Descartes. Rather, alterity is indissociable from the violence of spacing, which is always already at work in the infinite finitude of *différance*. Instead of recognizing this argument, Bernasconi reiterates his claim that Derrida is not really at odds with Levinas. According to Bernasconi, Derrida never intended to show that "certain of Levinas's central terms were incoherent" (129). Rather, Bernasconi formulates the ethics of deconstruction in Levinasian terms, as originating in a face-to-face relation.

Bernasconi's thesis is further developed by Simon Critchley in his widely influential *The Ethics of Deconstruction.* Critchley asserts that ethics in Levinas's sense is "the goal, or horizon, toward which Derrida's work tends" (2). The motivation of deconstruction would thus be an "unconditional ethical imperative" (31) that Critchley links to Derrida's notion of an originary "yes." For Critchley, the originary "yes" is the "ethical moment" in deconstruction, which commits it to an "affirmation of alterity, of the otherness of the Other" (189). This assertion is repeated passim, without Critchley considering Derrida's analysis of the intrinsic link between alterity, violence, and temporality. Rather, Critchley argues that the "undecidability" of deconstructive reading has an ethical underpinning, since it supposedly hesitates and suspends judgments in order to respect the alterity of the other. Critchley thinks this is a compelling ethics, but he worries about how it can be transposed to the domain of politics, which always involves decisions, discords, and conflicts. According to Critchley, Derrida avoids these phenomena for the benefit of an "undecidable" approach, so deconstruction does not provide an adequate account of the necessary "passage" from the ethical to the political. As Critchley puts it:

> Deconstruction fails to thematize the question of politics *as* a question—that is, as a place of contestation, antagonism, struggle, conflict, and dissension on a factical or empirical terrain. The rigorous undecidability of deconstructive reading fails to account for the activity of political judgment, political critique, and the political decision. (189–90)

Thus, Critchley believes he has discovered an "impasse" in Derrida's thinking and attempts to show us a "way out" of it through Levinas's philosophy.

Critchley's account is fallacious for several reasons. First, what Derrida calls the originary "yes" does not designate an ethical affirmation of the other, but answers to the trace structure of time that is the condition for life in general. Whatever we do, we have always already said "yes" to the coming of the future, since without it nothing could happen. But for the same reason, every affirmation is essentially compromised and haunted by negation, since the coming of the future also entails all the threats to which one may want to say "no." The unconditional "yes" is nothing in itself; it only marks the opening of an unpredictable future that one will have to negotiate, without any affirmative or negative response being given in advance.

Second, Derrida's notion of "undecidability" has nothing to do with a pious respect for the Other. As I have argued, undecidability elucidates what it means to think temporality as an irreducible condition. Accordingly, everything must be understood on the basis of a constitutive duplicity, which at the same time makes possible both promises and threats, life and death, fidelity and betrayal, and so on. What is at stake is to think temporal alterity as the nonethical opening of ethics. Temporal alterity gives rise to both the desirable *and* the undesirable, to every chance *and* every menace. Hence, alterity cannot answer to someone or something that one ought to "respect" unconditionally. Rather, it precipitates affirmations *and* negations, confirmations *and* resistances, in relation to undecidable events that stem from the "same" infinite finitude. There is thus no opposition between undecidability and decisions in Derrida's thinking. On the contrary, it is the undecidable future that necessitates decisions. One is always forced to confront temporal alterity and engage in decisions that only can be made from time to time, in accordance with essentially corruptible calculations.

Third, there is no support in Derrida's thinking for the Levinasian distinction between ethics and politics. Critchley's claim that Derrida fails to account for the political as "conflict, and dissension on a factical or empirical terrain" is simply false, since Derrida maintains that violence is irreducible—that we are always already involved in the process of making decisions that are more or less violent. Critchley's critique is all the more misleading since it is actually he and Levinas who defend the thought of a primary "ethical experience," which would precede the conflicts they ascribe to the political. They are thus confronted with the question of how to find a "passage" from a supposedly primary "ethics" to a supposedly secondary "politics." It is in Levinas's answer to this question that Critchley thinks he has found a "way out" of what he perceives as the Derridean impasse. But, in fact, one can track how the Levinasian argument that Critchley adopts is a clear example of the metaphysical logic Derrida deconstructs. As we have seen, Levinas wants to promote ethics as "first philosophy" with reference to an "immediate" encounter, in which the subject is submitted to the Other as the incomparably High. This would be the de jure of ethics: its categorical imperative. However, on Levinas's own account it turns out that such an approach is de facto untenable, since the encounter between two is called into question by "the third" (*le tiers*), who interrupts the ethical relation and demands that we consider others than the Other. We are thus caught up in what Levinas designates as the domain of the political, where it is necessary to interrogate and calculate intersubjective relations in order to achieve social justice. Levinas's observation does not, however, entail that he renounces his notion of a singular, ethical encounter with the Other, which would precede the political. Instead, he holds that the political community should be guided by the respect for the Other, who here turns out to be no one less than God the Father, recalling us to "the human fraternity."

Even if one disregards the theologicopatriarchal humanism in Levinas's line of reasoning, one should note how he attempts to explain away the incoherence of his conceptual schema. Both Levinas and Critchley admit that "the third" haunts the face-to-face encounter, at the same time as they describe the arrival of the third as a passage from one order to another, from the immediate to the mediate, the originary to the derivative, the ethical to the political. The same argumentative structure recurs in Bernasconi's essay "Justice Without Ethics?" Bernasconi points out that there are always already others, which contradict the ethics of submission before an absolutely singular Other, but he does not draw the deconstructive consequences of this contradiction. That the third party is de facto there from the beginning does not, for Bernasconi, call into question the de jure definition of ethics as "a face to face relation with the Other without the third party" (65). Indeed, Bernasconi categorically excludes that Levinas's ethical ideal can be contested by the problem of the third: "one cannot argue that, because there can never be a face to face with the Other without the others, the notion of ethics makes no sense" (ibid.). Thus, Bernasconi precludes the deconstructive thinking of originary discrimination and retains the Levinasian distinctions between the Other and the others, the ethical and the political. But if there are always already more than two, then there is no justification whatsoever for the Levinasian demarcation of ethics from politics. The very idea of a primary "ethical experience" in the face-to-face encounter is untenable, since any encounter always excludes others and thus exercises discrimination.

Derrida makes precisely this point in *Adieu to Emmanuel Levinas*. Here, Derrida insists that "the third does not wait" and undermines the primacy of ethics.[18] Where Levinas holds that there is a "primordial word of honor" in the "uprightness" of the ethical encounter, Derrida argues that such a pledge of unconditional fidelity necessarily commits perjury, either by betraying its relation to other others in favor of a certain other or inversely. In *Adieu* the nonethical opening of ethics is described as an arche-perjury or arche-betrayal that makes us doubly exposed to violence: "exposed to undergo it but also to exercise it" (33/66). Moreover, there have always been innumerable others, whom one cannot sort into categories such as "the other" and "the third." Consequently, Derrida maintains that one can only choose "between betrayal and betrayal, always more than one betrayal" (34/68).

Levinas draws a quite different conclusion from his thinking of the third. Instead of regarding the ineluctable relation to the third as refuting the idea of an originary ethical encounter, Levinas claims that it paves the way for a universal justice under the heading of God.[19] Levinas's reference to God is not fortuitous; it is necessary to consolidate his vision of "a society where there is no distinction between those close and those far off, but in which there also remains the impossibility of passing by the closest," as he puts it in *Otherwise Than Being* (159/203). The only way to achieve such an ideal society would be through a totalizing instance, which would have the ability to survey every aspect of every relation and thereby be absolutely assured against the risk of committing mistakes or exercising discrimination. Of course, Levinas claims to be refuting philosophies of totality. But he does not assess the consequences of such a refutation. If not everything and everyone can be included—which is to say, if totalization is impossible—it will always be necessary to exclude. This is what Derrida's deconstructive logic underscores. Moreover, deconstructive logic undermines the notion that it would be desirable to attain an absolute peace (an ideal that guides Levinas's "ethical" vision of unconditional submission before the Other, as well as his "political" vision of a society that would respect alterity without exclusion). Such a peace would in fact abolish the very possibility of relations and thus be the equivalent of an absolute violence. For Derrida, then, Levinas's ideal ethical relation between two is not only untenable but undesirable; it would be "the worst violence," Derrida writes in "Faith and Knowledge" (100/99). In contrast to Levinas, Derrida argues that "more than One is at once more than two" (ibid.). This originary dissemination of others can never be mastered by any ethics or politics. Rather, it opens the space and time for all kinds of violence, dramatically abbreviated by Derrida as "perjury, lies, remote-control murder, ordered at a distance even when it rapes and kills with bare hands" (ibid.). Such threats of violence cannot be eliminated—since they are concomitant with the very possibility of relations—but can only be mitigated in essentially precarious processes of negotiation.

We can specify the deconstructive logic of violence by considering Drucilla Cornell's book *The Philosophy of the Limit*.[20] Like Bernasconi and Critchley, Cornell wants to endow deconstruction with an ethical motivation, reading it as "driven by an ethical desire to enact the ethical relation" (62). Although Cornell is critical of certain aspects of Levinas's philosophy, her understanding of the ethical relation is strongly informed by his notion of the Other as the Good. According to Cornell, to be ethical would be to "respect" alterity and "enact a nonviolent relation to otherness" (64). Cornell repeatedly speaks of such an "enactment" of the ethical, but for the most part she limits herself to positing it as an ideal, as something toward which we can "aspire" but never quite reach. Hence, while Cornell recognizes that "we can never fully meet the promise of fidelity to otherness" (90), she does not question the desirability and ethical status of such fidelity. On the contrary, Cornell explicitly adheres to a notion of how things *ought* to be by subscribing to "the *ideal* of community as the hope for a nonviolent ethical relationship to the other" (56), a hope she also rehabilitates in terms of the utopian "dream" of a "communalism understood as belonging together without violence" (60).

The utopian dream of peace pervades Cornell's book and is symptomatic of her misconception of the deconstructive thinking of alterity. As I have argued, the notion of a nonviolent relation to the other is based on a suppression of alterity, since it must presuppose that the other is not violent in its turn and consequently denies the radical unpredictability of the other. Only if one assumes that the other is primarily peaceful does it make sense to prescribe a nonviolent relation, since the command to "respect" the alterity of the other does not make any sense if the other wants to destroy me. Moreover, the dream of a community without violence is the dream of a community in which there would be *nothing other* than peace, excluding anyone or anything that does not want to engage in the "ethical" relation. Hence, the supposedly ethical dream is unethical on its own terms, since it dreams of eliminating the susceptibility to radical alterity, which cannot be dissociated from the susceptibility to violence and the concomitant attempts to combat it.

It is only by coming to terms with the deconstructive "logic" of violence that one can assess the ethicopolitical significance of deconstruction. The deconstructive logic of violence does not prevent one from criticizing social injustices or any other forms of violence, but it exposes the internal contradictions of the doctrines that hold it to be desirable to eliminate exclusion once and for all. Discrimination is a constitutive condition. The negotiation of it cannot be governed by a regulative idea or harbor any assurance of its own legitimacy. For precisely this reason it will always be urgent to reflect on ethicopolitical questions, to work out strategies for a "lesser violence" that is essentially precarious. Those who, like Levinas, proceed from metaphysical premises of how things *ought* to be will in one way or another attempt to deny this predicament for the benefit of one ideal or another. But the argument here is that one thereby blinds oneself to the condition that makes responsibility *possible*, while at the same time making it *impossible* to sustain the metaphysical values by which Levinas lets himself be guided.

Nevertheless, there is a widespread assumption that Derrida has come to adopt these values, especially with regard to the themes of justice and hospitality that have been salient in his work ever since *Specters of Marx*.[21] The source of misreading is that Derrida seems to operate with an opposition between two principles, as in the distinction between law and justice that I elaborated in Chapter 1, or in the similar distinction between conditional and unconditional hospitality. In his sequel to *The Ethics of Deconstruction*, entitled *Ethics-Politics-Subjectivity*, Critchley takes advantage of these supposed oppositions in order to consolidate his proposed liaison between Derrida and Levinas in terms of a shared demarcation of ethics from politics.[22] According to Critchley's schema, the political sphere does not leave room for the proper ethical relation, since it requires consideration of innumerable others, without any given criteria as to who or which one should prioritize. As Critchley puts it, *politics* is therefore a matter of making more or less ungrounded, unjust decisions. "Each choice I might make in favour of *x* might work against *y* and *z*, not to mention *a*, *b* and *c*" (108). But Critchley's observation does not prevent him from advocating an *ethics* that precedes the condition of politics. Thus, Critchley claims that Derrida's notions of law (*droit*) and conditional hospitality belong to the political, while justice and unconditional hospitality answer to the ethical.

On closer inspection, however, it turns out that Derrida undermines the basic premise of Critchley's reasoning. Derrida argues that injustice is inscribed in the very possibility of justice and thus not something that comes about secondarily, through an alleged passage from ethics to politics. It is indeed true that, like Levinas, Derrida repeatedly speaks of justice in terms of a relation to "the other." But this does not mean, as Critchley believes, that Derrida adheres to the Levinasian notion of an originary ethical experience in the face-to-face encounter.[23] On the contrary, the disjointure that opens the relation to the other is inseparable from the nonethical opening of an undecidable future. Derrida writes in *Specters of Marx*, concerning what it means that time is, and must be, *out of joint*:

> . . . if adjoining in general, if the joining of the "joint" supposes first of all the adjoining, the correctness (*justesse*), or the justice of time, the being-with-itself or the concord of time, what happens when *time itself* gets "out of joint," dis-jointed, disadjusted, disharmonic, discorded or unjust? . . . But with the other, is not this disjuncture, this dis-adjustment of the "it's going badly" necessary for the good, or at least the just, to be announced? Is not disjuncture the very possibility of the other? How to distinguish between two disadjustments, between the disjuncture of the unjust and the one that opens up the infinite asymmetry of the relation to the other, that is to say, the place of justice? (22/48)

And he continues a few pages further on:

> Beyond right, and still more beyond juridicism, beyond morality, and still more beyond moralism, does not justice as relation to the other suppose on the contrary the irreducible excess of a disjointure or an anachrony, some *Un-Fug*, some "out of joint" dislocation in Being and in time itself, a disjointure that, in always risking the evil, expropriation, and injustice (*adikia*) against which there is no calculable insurance, would alone be able to *do justice* or to *render justice* to the other as other? (27/55)

That Derrida's answer to this question is yes, that he is thinking the undecidable relation between justice and injustice as a constitutive condition, should be clear. On the following page Derrida speaks of the "unpredictable singularity of the *arrivant as justice*" (28/56). But one should then keep in mind that the coming (*l'arrivant*) is made possible by the disjointure, the being *out of joint*, which is also what "can do harm and do evil, [and] it is no doubt the very possibility of evil," as Derrida emphasizes (29/57).

It is here important that *l'autre* and *l'arrivant* can be understood in two ways: as the one *who* is other and coming, as well as *what* is other and coming. The oscillation between the who and the what is always undecidably at play in Derrida's work, since he reinforces that *l'autre* and *l'arrivant* can be anything whatsoever or anyone whosoever. Accordingly, deconstruction does not allow for a primary ethical relation that would be characterized by "goodness," but elucidates the fundamental exposure to the undecidable coming of the other. Or as Derrida puts it with a seemingly enigmatic phrase that he often repeats: deconstruction is what happens. The French phrase here is *ce qui arrive*: whatever or whoever that comes, happens, arrives and that one is forced to negotiate, in the more or less imminent danger that even the very situation of negotiation will be shattered by the force of what happens.

For the same reason, what Derrida calls unconditional hospitality is not an ethical ideal that we unfortunately have to compromise due to political realities. Rather, Derrida demonstrates that "hospitality and exclusion go together," as he writes in *Specters of Marx* (141/223). If I did not discriminate between what I welcome and do not welcome, what I find acceptable and unacceptable, it would mean that I had renounced all claims to be responsible, make judgments, or pursue any critical reflections at all. Moreover, it would mean that I had opened myself without reservations to whatever is violently opposed to me and can extinguish everything that is mine, including my principles of hospitality.

Hence, it is *not* the case that an ethics of unconditional hospitality is what we *ought* to strive for, while we regrettably have to make hospitality conditional. On the contrary, an ethics of unconditional hospitality is impossible for *essential* reasons, since it would require that I could not react in a negative or protective manner but automatically must welcome everything. An ethics of unconditional hospitality would short-circuit all forms of decisions and be the same as a complete indifference before what happens.[24]

Now, this does not prevent Derrida from saying that conditional hospitality is bound to an "unconditional hospitality." But what he then invokes is not an ethical ideal. As distinct from the ethics of unconditional hospitality he deconstructs, Derrida's notion of unconditional hospitality designates the exposure to the unpredictable, which can always be violent and to which one cannot know in advance how one should relate. The "hospitality" to otherness is unconditional *not* because it is ideal or ethical as such, but because one is necessarily susceptible to violent visitations. Even the most conditional hospitality is unconditionally hospitable to that which may ruin it. When I open my door for someone else, I open myself to someone who can destroy my home or my life, regardless of what rules I try to enforce on him or her or it.[25]

Accordingly, Derrida distinguishes between the conditional hospitality of *invitation* and the unconditional hospitality of *visitation*.[26] No matter how many or how few I invite into my life, I cannot be immune from the visitation of others whom I have not invited and who exceed my control. Indeed, Derrida underscores that *nothing happens* without the unconditional hospitality of visitation (*Rogues*, 149/205). Unconditional hospitality is thus another name for the violent alteration of time, which opens me both to what I desire and what I fear. The exposure to visitation is intrinsic to the hospitality I desire, since no one can arrive and nothing can happen without the unpredictable coming of time. But by the same token, the hospitality I desire also opens the door to what I fear. Hospitality can never be reduced to the invitation of an other who is good; it must be open to the risk of an evil visitation. Even the other who is welcomed as peaceful may turn out to be an instigator of war, since the other may always change.

We can thus understand why Derrida says that unconditional hospitality is at once indissociable from *and* heterogeneous to conditional hospitality. On the one hand, unconditional hospitality is *indissociable* from conditional hospitality, since it is the exposure to the visitation of others that makes it necessary to establish conditions of hospitality, to regulate who is allowed to enter. On the other hand, unconditional hospitality is *heterogeneous* to conditional hospitality, since no regulation finally can master the exposure to the visitation of others. Even the most securely guarded borders may be transgressed or compromised from within. Otherwise there would be no need for protection in the first place. In effect, all limitations of hospitality are at the same time exposed to what they seek to exclude, haunted by those who—rightly or not—question the legitimacy of the determined restrictions.

In *Rogues*, Derrida explicitly recalls that his notion of unconditional hospitality cannot be aligned with "the ethical" or with any form of normative prescription (172–73n12/204n1). Nothing can establish a priori that it is better to be more hospitable than to be less hospitable (or vice versa). More openness to the other may entail more openness to "bad" events, and less openness to the other may entail less openness to "good" events. Consequently, the law of unconditional hospitality does not provide a rule or a norm for how one should act in relation to the other, but requires one to make precarious decisions from time to time. The only unconditional law of hospitality is that one will have been forced to deal with unforeseeable events.

Derrida's thinking of hospitality thus articulates yet another version of the nonethical opening of ethics. To think the nonethical opening is to think why there will always be problems and why the process of dealing with them has no end. The ethics and politics of hospitality (here understood in the widest possible sense: as all kinds of demarcations and decisions) take place in an "economical" negotiation, where no position can be autonomous or absolute but is necessarily bound to other positions. Since the play of relations cannot ultimately be controlled, one is always exposed to the threat (and the chance) of interactions that will challenge or overturn the premises of the negotiation.

Neither justice nor hospitality can therefore be understood as an ethical ideal. If Derrida is easily misunderstood on this point, it is because he uses a "positively" valorized term ("hospitality," "justice") to analyze a condition that just as well can be described with a "negatively" valorized term ("violent exposition," "irreducible discrimination"). This is not a valid excuse for those who want to turn Derrida into an ethical philosopher. But it reminds us that we have to be vigilant concerning the strategies Derrida applies in his deconstruction of traditional concepts. When Derrida invokes an "unconditional" hospitality or an "undeconstructible" justice, it may indeed seem as if he invokes the ideal of something that would be good in itself. I have argued, however, that the unconditional and the undeconstructible are the disjointure of time and make it impossible for anything to be good in itself. Even the most ideal hospitality or justice must be open to the corruption of evil, since the undecidable coming of time is inscribed in the very idea of hospitality or justice.

To be sure, the essential corruptibility of hospitality and justice can have the most devastating effects. But for Derrida corruptibility is also the possibility for anything to happen. A hospitality or justice that would be immune from the violent coming of the other would cancel out the possibility of hospitality and justice. The only way to secure an absolute peace would be to extinguish everything that could possibly break the peace and thereby extinguish the undecidable time to come that is the condition for anything to happen.

Hence, deconstructive thinking exercises a critical vigilance against all ideals of an absolute peace: as we have seen, absolute peace would be absolute violence. This vigilance, however, does *not* entail that the deconstructive thinker automatically can be ascribed any ethicopolitical insights; he or she is as liable as anyone else to make mistakes or erroneous judgments in a given situation. But to deny this inevitable risk, to deny the essential corruptibility of responsibility or to project its consummation in an ideal future, is to deny the condition that makes responsibility possible in the first place.

§ 4 Autoimmunity of Life: Derrida's Radical Atheism

> One cannot want God for a friend.
> —Derrida, *Politics of Friendship* (223/251)

In book 4 of his *Confessions*, Augustine recounts a fatal episode from his time as a teacher of rhetoric in Tagaste. The young Augustine has found a friend to whom he is deeply attached, but after less than a year his friend dies. Augustine is overcome with grief. In loving his friend, he has bound his desire to a mortal being. Consequently, Augustine is shattered by the loss of his mortal friend and cannot find any remedy for his mourning. Rather, the work of mourning reveals a double bind at the heart of his desire. The source of what Augustine desires—the mortal life he wants to guard and keep—is also the source of what he fears. In loving the mortal, Augustine wants to protect it from death and prolong its life as much as possible. But his desire to keep the mortal intensifies the fear of losing it. As Augustine explains: "the more I loved my friend, the more I hated and feared death which, like a cruel enemy, had taken him away from me."[1] The crucial problem here is that the enemy, the threat of death, does not come from the outside as an evil accident but is interior to life. As Augustine realizes, it was *always possible* that his friend could die. Every mortal bond is bound to be broken, so one friend was fated to mourn the other. Augustine writes: "I was unhappy and so is every soul unhappy which is tied to its love for mortal things; when it loses them, it is torn in pieces, and it is then that it comes to realize the unhappiness which was there even before it lost them" (4.6).

More than fifteen hundred years after Augustine, Derrida finds himself in a similar situation of mourning. In response to the death of his friend Paul de Man, Derrida writes a series of lectures under the heading of *Mémoires*. Like Augustine, Derrida makes clear that the friendship always

was haunted by the knowledge that both would die and one of them before the other. Indeed, he emphasizes that "there is no friendship without
this knowledge of finitude."[2] The friend can only be given "as a mortal,
to us mortals," and it is the mortal friend "whom we love as such" (32/52).
That the beloved friend is mortal does not mean, however, that his death
is acceptable. On the contrary, Derrida cannot accept the death of his
friend and is "inconsolable before the finitude of memory" (34/53). This
is not a paradox but follows from the double bind that is inherent in the
desire for mortal life. It is because Derrida wants to hold on to a mortal
life that he is devastated by the extinction of this mortal life and cannot
come to terms with death. The double bind is irresolvable, since the death
that he defends against is internal to the life that is defended.

The same double bind is operative if I limit myself to being my own
friend. As I have argued in the previous chapters, even the most immediate autoaffection is only given through the coming of time. Hence, I am
necessarily divided into being a mortal other for myself. At every moment
I have to hold on to myself as a memory for the future, which may be lost
and lead to mourning. Consequently, Derrida maintains that "mourning
in the sense of a general possibility" regulates "all our relations with the
other *as other*, that is, as mortal for a mortal, with the one always capable
of dying before the other" (39/57). The mortal other can here designate
both my relation to myself as an other—as I experience my survival at the
expense of a past self—and my relation to another other who can die. In
either case the self and the other can be given to themselves only through
the structural possibility of mourning. The *actual* experience of mourning
is preceded by the *possible* mourning that is at work from the first moment of experience, since every experience is temporal and will be lost.

The same link between the problem of mourning and the problem of
time occupies Augustine throughout his *Confessions*. Augustine forcefully
demonstrates that the temporal never can repose *in itself* but is marked
by the movement of disappearance from the beginning. The past is no
longer, the future is not yet, and the present itself can come into being
only by becoming past. As Augustine observes in book 11, "if the present were always present and did not go by into the past, it would not be
time at all, but eternity" (11.14). Every presence is thus divided in its very
event; it "flies suddenly out of the future into the past" (11.15). Whether
we examine an hour, a minute, or a second, we discover this flight of time

that makes it impossible for anything to be present as such. Even the most immediate presence is divided from within and passes away as soon as it comes to be. Nothing can prevent this loss of time that is inherent to life, since "the cause of its being is that it shall cease to be" (11.14).[3]

The actual mourning that befalls Augustine on the death of his friend is an intensification of the possible mourning that is at work from the first inception of desire. Because the temporal can never be in itself, every slightest movement of desire is shadowed by the risk of loss. In Augustine's words: "wherever man's soul turns . . . it is fixed to sorrows" because all things "hurry toward ceasing to be" and offer "no place to rest, since they do not stay. They pass away and no one can follow them with his bodily senses. Nor can anyone grasp them tight even while they are present" (4.10).

Hence, both Augustine and Derrida demonstrate that it is essentially perilous to desire the mortal, since it makes one dependent on what will disappear. But their responses to the same predicament are radically different. Augustine's conversion to Christianity is explicitly a turn away from the attachment to mortal life. In opposition to the treacherous time of finite relations, Augustine posits the eternal presence of God. In God nothing can ever pass away, since everything is given in *one* absolute presence that is unrivaled by succession, *one* absolute unity that reposes in itself. Thus, Augustine argues that man should love his friends and fellow men only insofar as he loves God through them and does not become attached to their mortal singularity. "If souls please you, love them in God, because by themselves they are subject to change" (4.12). The aim of Augustine's strategy is quite explicitly to preclude mourning. The man who loves God in his friends "loses no one dear to him, for they are all dear to him in one who is not lost" (4.9). Following the same logic, Augustine condemns the mourning of his friend as a "madness" (4.7) that stemmed from his mortal love. The reason he became susceptible to mourning was that he poured out his soul "like water onto sand by loving a man who was bound to die" (4.8). What the Christian Augustine must learn is rather to detach himself from the mortal and turn his desire toward the immortal.

In contrast, Derrida maintains that we love the mortal *as mortal* and that there can be nothing beyond mortality. For Augustine, to love the mortal as mortal is deplorable and misguided. If one is bound to the mortal, the positive can never be released from the negative. Any mortal bond is a double bind, since whatever is *desirable* cannot be dissociated from the *undesirable* fact that it will be lost.

It is precisely on such a double bind that Derrida insists. In addition to *Mémoires*, it is here instructive to consider the collection of texts that Derrida wrote in response to the death of personal friends: *Chaque fois unique, la fin du monde.*[4] Across a great number of singular occasions, these texts persistently return to mourning as a force that cannot be overcome and that emanates from the love of what is mortal. For example, in the text dedicated to the memory of Jean-Marie Benoist, Derrida writes:

> To have a friend, to look at him, to follow him with your eyes, to admire him in friendship, is to know in a more intense way, already injured, always insistent, and more and more unforgettable, that one of the two of you will inevitably see the other die. One of us, each says to himself, the day will come when one of the two of us will see himself no longer seeing the other and so will carry the other within him a while longer, his eyes following without seeing, the world suspended by some unique tear, each time unique, through which everything from then on, through which the world itself—and this day will come—will come to be reflected quivering, reflecting disappearance itself: the world, the whole world, the world itself, for death takes from us not only some particular life within the world, some moment that belongs to us, but, each time, without limit, someone through whom the world, and first of all our own world, will have opened up in a both finite and infinite—mortally infinite—way. (107/137–38)

This passage delineates the double bind of mortal being that is accentuated in the experience of mourning. On the one hand, mortality makes every other a unique living being. If the other were not mortal, there would be nothing to distinguish the other from anything else, since the other would not be irreplaceable. On the other hand, the mortality that constitutes the essence of the other also makes the other altogether destructible. The world that opens through the other is thus "mortally infinite." No one can replace the other; no one can experience what he experienced, see what she saw, feel what it felt. The extinction of this unique origin of the world is a poignant reminder of what I have analyzed as the infinite finitude of life. The other is infinitely other—its alterity cannot be overcome or recuperated by anyone else—because the other is finite.

Derrida captures the absolute mortality of life in his notion of death as the end of the world. The guiding thread in his reflections on mourning is that each death is the end of the world. When someone dies it is not simply the end of someone who lives in the world; it is rather *the end of the world as such*, since each one is a singular and irretrievable origin of the world. As Derrida emphasizes in the preface to *Chaque fois*, such an end of the world "does not leave any place, not the slightest chance, neither for the replacement nor for the survival of the sole and unique world, of the 'sole and unique' that makes every living being . . . a sole and unique living being" (11; my translation). Derrida explicitly maintains his argument against the idea of God. He glosses "God" as the idea that death cannot put an end to *the* world—to the true and ultimate world—even if it puts an end to the mortal world of a singular living being. The idea of God is thus the idea that there can be something that is immune from destructibility. For Derrida, on the contrary, it is a matter of thinking that every possible world is absolutely destructible.

The atheism that Derrida expresses does not only deny the existence of God and immortality; it also answers to what I call radical atheism. Radical atheism proceeds from the argument that everything that can be desired is mortal in its essence. A version of this argument is presented in Derrida's essay "Force of Law," following his claim that love is always a love of ruins. The point is not that one loves ruins per se, but that whatever one loves bears its own ruin within itself:

> One cannot love a monument, a work of architecture, an institution as such except in an experience itself precarious in its fragility: it has not always been there, it will not always be there, it is finite. And for this very reason one loves it as mortal, through its birth and its death, through one's birth and death, through the ghost or the silhouette of its ruin, one's own ruin—which it already is, therefore, or already prefigures. (278/105)

Both the experience of love *and* the beloved are necessarily finite. Such finitude is not something that comes to inhibit desire but precipitates desire in the first place. It is *because* the beloved can be lost that one seeks to keep it, and it is *because* the experience can be forgotten that one seeks to remember it. As Derrida strikingly puts it, *one cannot love* without the experience of finitude. This is the premise from which radical atheism necessarily follows. If one cannot love anything except the mortal, it follows that one cannot love God, since God does not exhibit the mortality that makes something desirable. The absolute being of God is not only unattainable but *undesirable*, since it would annul the mortality that is integral to whatever one desires.

A remarkable example of radical atheism can be found in Derrida's book *Politics of Friendship*. At the end of chapter 8 Derrida discusses Aristotle's account of perfect friendship. The basic problem here is the one we have traced in Augustine's and Derrida's reflections on mourning, namely, that all friends are mortal. The mortality in question does not only entail that friends can die but also that they can deceive, betray, and violate the intimate relation. The decisive question, then, is why there cannot be a perfect friend that is exempt from mortal corruptibility. God is the model of such a perfect friend, since only an absolutely self-sufficient being can be immune from betraying either itself or the other. But as Derrida stresses in his reading of Aristotle, *one cannot want* such a perfect friend. A self-sufficient being cannot think about anything other than itself and is consequently incapable of entertaining any relation whatsoever. As Derrida puts it, the absolute being of God "could not care less about friendship because it could not care less about the other" (223/251). Derrida's argument opens the possibility of a radically atheist answer to the question why there cannot be a perfect friendship. The classic answer is to posit perfection as the *telos* of friendship, as the ideal that drives the desire for friendship even though it remains inaccessible for mortal beings. Traditional atheism remains within this model for desire. While it denies the existence of God, it does not dispute that we desire such an absolute being. Aristotle's account of perfect friendship, however, makes it possible to read this teleological conception of desire against itself. As Derrida emphasizes, the inaccessibility of perfect friendship can be interpreted "*otherwise*—that is to say, in terms of a thought of alterity which makes true or perfect friendship not only inaccessible as a conceivable *telos*, but inaccessible *because it is inconceivable* in its very essence, and hence in its *telos*" (221–22/249–50). What Derrida here calls the thought of alterity answers to what I call radical atheism. According to the logic of radical atheism, perfect friendship is not an inaccessible ideal but inconceivable as such. A perfect friendship would destroy the possibility of friendship, since there can be no friendship without mortality.

We can further develop the notion of radical atheism via Derrida's notion of "radical evil." The term comes from Kant's treatise *Religion Within the Limits of Reason Alone*, but it receives a quite different meaning in Derrida's work. The notion of radical evil can be seen as an intervention in one of the most fundamental theological debates, which concerns the origin of evil. The classic theological problem is how the omnipotence of God can be compatible with the existence of evil. If God created evil he is not absolutely good, but if he did not create evil he is not almighty. Augustine formulated the most influential solution to the problem by arguing that evil does not belong to being as such. Only the good has being, and evil is nothing but the privation of goodness, a corruption that supervenes from without and does not affect the supreme good of being in itself. As Augustine writes in *The City of God*: "Evil has no positive nature; but the loss of good has received the name 'evil'" (11.9). Thus, God can be the creator of everything that is (since all that has being is good) without being responsible for evil. The source of evil rather resides in the free will of human beings, which makes them liable to prefer mortal matters instead of turning toward God.

Kant pursues a similar argument by reducing evil to an effect of the free will, which may lead one to follow the incentives of one's sensuous nature rather than the moral law. For Kant, radical evil designates that the propensity to evil cannot finally be extirpated by human powers.[5] But Kant does not call into question the Idea of a good that is exempt from evil. In contrast, Derrida's notion of radical evil undercuts the very Idea of something that would be good in itself:

> The thought of "radical evil" here is not concerned with it as an eventuality. It is simply that the *possibility* of something evil, or of some corruption, the *possibility* of the non-accomplishment, or of some failure, is *ineradicable*. And it is so because it is the condition for every felicity, every positive value—the condition for ethics for instance. So if you want to eradicate the *possibility* of this negative then you destroy what you want to save. Thus ethics could not be ethical without the ineradicable *possibility* of evil. . . . The *possibility* of infelicity, non-fulfillment, is part of what it is that we want to save under the name of ethics, politics, felicity, fulfillment, and so on.[6]

The possibility of evil is not a deplorable fact of our human constitution, which prevents us from achieving an ideal Good. Rather, the possibility of evil is intrinsic to the good that we desire, since even the most ideal fulfillment must remain open to the possibility of nonfulfillment. This argument presupposes a rethinking of fulfillment as essentially temporal. Derrida himself does not explicitly undertake such a rethinking, but it is indispensable for developing the logic of his argument. If fulfillment is essentially temporal, it follows that it must remain open to the possibility of nonfulfillment, since it can never repose in itself and is altered by the coming of the future. For the same reason, everything that is good must be open to becoming evil. This threat of evil does not supervene on the good; it is part of the good that we desire.

Hence, Derrida can be seen to affirm the desire that Augustine stigmatizes as the source of evil. In his treatise *On Free Choice of the Will*, Augustine derives evil from the desire for "things that cannot be possessed without the fear of losing them" (1.4). If one did not fear to lose what one desires, one would never feel hatred or resentment, and one would never have recourse to violence, since one would never feel threatened. Consequently, Augustine argues that the impetus for doing evil is the desire for mortal life. All evil and all sin stem from "the love of those things which a man can lose against his will" (1.4). The most fundamental example of such love is of course one's attachment to the mortal life that one may lose against one's will. The path to overcoming evil is thus to convert one's desire for mortal life into a desire for the immortal life of God.[7]

In contrast, Derrida articulates the desire for mortal life as a constitutive force. His notion of radical evil designates that the possibility of evil is intrinsic to the beloved itself, since the beloved is mortal. The mortality of the beloved precipitates both the desire for proximity and the fear of loss. As Derrida writes in *Politics of Friendship*, "love is the evil, love can be evil's vehicle and evil can always come out of love, the radical evil of the greatest love" (257/287–88). Derrida does not elaborate this claim, but we can trace the argument in his analysis of the phrase "I love you," which occurs earlier in the book. Derrida's analysis proceeds from what he describes as "the desire for a unique friendship, an indivisible bond, an 'I love you' one single time, one single time forever, one single time for all time(s)" (215/243). There is an internal contradiction in this desire for an indivisible bond, since it is a desire to keep the temporal forever. As Derrida points out, "indivisibility is immediately infinite in its finiteness. It appears as such only in the desire for repetition and multiplication, in the promise and the memory that divide the indivisible in order to maintain it" (216/244). Even the most indivisible bond is thus divided from within, since it must be kept as a memory for the future. The exposition to the future is both what gives the chance of keeping the bond and the threat of breaking the bond. The binding declaration "I love you" can only be delivered before an undecidable future, which opens the possibility of good and evil at the same time:

"I love you" cannot and must not hope to prove anything at all. Testimony or act of faith, such a declaration can decide only providing it wants to remain theoretically undecidable, improbable, given over in darkness to the exception of a singularity without rule and without concept. Theoretically, it can always flip into its opposite. Without the possibility of radical evil, of perjury, and of absolute crime, there is no responsibility, no freedom, no decision. . . . Furthermore—another side of the same law—the request or offer, the promise or the prayer of an "I love you," must remain unilateral and dissymmetrical. Whether or not the other answers, in one way or another, no mutuality, no harmony, no agreement can or must reduce the infinite disproportion. This disproportion is indeed the condition of sharing, in love as well as in friendship. In hatred as well as in detestation. Consequently, the desire of this disproportion which *gives* without return and without recognition must be able not to count on "proper agreement," not to calculate assured, immediate or full comprehension. It must indeed desire that which goes to make the essence of desire: this non-assurance and this risk of misunderstanding. (219–20/247–48)

The declaration "I love you" cannot be assured of its destiny, since the feeling is mutable and the other may not reciprocate. The claim here is that such nonassurance belongs to the *essence* of desire. According to Derrida, a declaration of love *could not* ever have counted on an assurance that would make it immune from mutability "but above all *it had to* and *desired not to want* to count on such an assurance, which would destroy in advance the possibility of addressing the other as such" (219/247). My argument is that this logic of desire follows from thinking the spacing of time as a constitutive condition. The spacing of time opens the possibility of alteration at every juncture and makes nonassurance intrinsic to every relation. If I were certain what the beloved would do to me, I would not desire him or her or it, since there would be no time or space to relate to the other. The desire for the other can never be a desire for the immutable, since the other is inherently mutable.

The possibility of being together is thus inseparable from the peril of being deserted. This double bind cannot even hypothetically be resolved, since mortality is the condition for both everything one desires *and* everything one does not desire. In accordance with the notion of radical evil, it gives rise to friendship and love, as well as to hatred and detestation. As Derrida writes elsewhere in *Politics of Friendship*: "Not only could I enter into a relationship of friendship only with a *mortal*, but I could love in friendship only a mortal at least exposed to so-called violent death—that is, exposed to being killed, *possibly by myself.* . . . To love in love or friendship would always mean: I can kill you, you can kill me, we can kill ourselves" (122/143). Hence, the desired good and the feared evil have the same source, since whatever good one desires is mortal.

Following the logic of radical atheism, I will demonstrate how all attempts to assimilate Derrida's thinking to a religious framework are wrongheaded. During the last two decades there has been an upsurge of studies that give a theological account of deconstruction. These readings have sought an alibi in the proliferation of apparently religious terms in Derrida's later works, which engage with notions such as faith, messianicity, and God. I will argue, however, that Derrida reads these notions against themselves in accordance with a radically atheist conception of desire.

The question of desire is at the heart of John D. Caputo's widely influential book *The Prayers and Tears of Jacques Derrida: Religion Without Religion*. Along with Caputo's numerous other texts on the subject, and with no less than two collections of essays devoted to Caputo's work, *The Prayers and Tears* has established Caputo as the most powerful proponent for the religious turn in Derrida scholarship.[8] My refutation of religious readings of Derrida will focus mainly on Caputo, not only because of his influence but also because he goes as far as possible in attempting to make deconstruction compatible with religion. That Caputo systematically misreads Derrida testifies to the radical atheism of deconstruction. Indeed, I will demonstrate that Derrida's work undermines Caputo's basic presuppositions.

The central claim in Caputo's work is that deconstruction and religion share the same conception of desire or "passion." Thus, when Caputo discusses the relation between deconstruction and negative theology, he notes Derrida's recurrent objections to negative theology, but for Caputo these objections are only the beginning and not the end of the story. According to Caputo, Derrida's critique of negative theology is a "first, preparatory and merely negative point," which is superseded by an affirmation of the desire that drives negative theology: "deconstruction says yes, affirming what negative theology affirms whenever it says no. Deconstruction desires what negative theology desires and it shares the passion of negative theology."[9] Caputo's assertion is a good place to start, since a comparison between the conception of desire in negative theology and deconstruction brings out the radical atheism of the latter.

Contrary to Caputo's assertion, negative theology says no to what deconstruction affirms. The desire for mortal life that is affirmed in deconstruction is precisely the desire that is denigrated in negative theology. A rigorous example is offered by the work of Meister Eckhart, one of the most influential negative theologians of all time and Caputo's main reference. The highest virtue for Eckhart is "absolute detachment from all creatures," since the desire for mortal creatures is incompatible with reposing in the absolute fullness of God.[10] God is given in himself, in absolute presence, so that for God "nothing is past and nothing is future" (93).[11] To desire a mortal creature is, on the contrary, to desire something that can never be *in itself* but is constituted by its relation to an irretrievable past and an unpredictable future. Eckhart's famous concept of *Gelâzenheit* is precisely about detaching oneself from such bonds to the finite; a detachment that is supposed to release one from concern with what has been and what will come, in order to let things be in themselves and approach the timeless presence of God. The crucial move is to direct one's desire away from the temporal and become indifferent to the fate of mutable beings:

> The man who is in absolute detachment is carried away into eternity where nothing temporal affects him nor is he in the least aware of any mortal thing. The world is well and truly dead to him, for he has no taste for any earthly thing. . . . True detachment means a mind as little moved by what happens, by joy and sorrow, honor and disgrace, as a broad mountain by a gentle breeze. Such motionless detachment makes a man superlatively godlike. For God is God because of his motionless detachment; he gets his purity and his simplicity and his unchangeableness from his detachment. If, then, a man is going to be like God, so far as any creature can resemble God, it will be by detachment. This leads to purity, and from purity to simplicity, and from simplicity to immovability. (91)

For Eckhart, then, the best would be a state of repose in which *nothing can happen*. If something can happen, there is exposure to the passage of time, which prevents everything from coming to rest. "Any event, however insignificant, will always cause some troubling of detachment" (90). Absolute detachment is rather a stillness that "stays in itself," and Eckhart emphasizes that "no going outside of oneself, however excellent, is better than staying still" (89). Hence, human beings should aim at becoming absolutely still to become like God, to whom nothing can happen since God is exempt from time.

Eckhart's ideal is epitomized in his definition of God as the negation of negation.[12] Finite being is necessarily inhabited by negation, since its being entails that it may *not* be. God is the negation of negation, since finite being is negated in the absolute fullness of God. The same logic applies to the question of desire. Man must negate the desire for finite beings in order to become one with God.

Hence, Eckhart formulates a clear version of the religious ideal of absolute immunity. He refuses to predicate God insofar as the predicate of being entails temporal finitude. Every being is bound to disappear and carries its own death within itself as an autoimmune threat. To say that God is not a being is thus a way of making him immune from finitude.

However, if we approach Eckhart's texts with the deconstructive logic of autoimmunity we can read the ideal immunity of God against itself. Eckhart subscribes to the notion of God as absolute presence and absolute fullness, but he also shows that it is inseparable from absolute absence and absolute emptiness. God is Nothing, since everything that is finite (which is to say everything) must be eliminated in God. While Eckhart affirms the paradox in the name of God's ineffable perfection, the logic of deconstruction enables us to read the paradox in the opposite direction. If God only can be conceived as Nothing, it is not because He is ineffable but because the pure life of God would be nothing but pure death. Eckhart himself is quite clear that the way to unity with God (the *via negativa*) is achieved through an inner "destruction" of all bonds to created beings for the benefit of the uncreated God. The object of detachment must be "absolutely nothing" (95), since everything that is something is created and mortal:

> Perfect detachment pays no attention to creatures. It is without lowliness and loftiness. It has no interest in being below or above. It is intent on being master of itself, loving no one and hating no one, having neither this nor that, being neither like nor unlike any creature. The only thing it would like to be is the same. But it has no desire at all to be either this or that. He who is this or that is something; but detachment is absolutely nothing. (90)

Eckhart here describes the absolute immunity that according to his conception of desire is "the best." But if we follow the logic of autoimmunity, we can see that it is "the worst." As I have argued, there can be no cure for the autoimmunity of finitude, since the threat of death is located *within* whatever is desired. This autoimmunity of finitude answers to what Derrida calls radical evil. It precipitates both love and hate, attraction and fear. For Derrida, such radical evil is not a negative predicament that it is desirable to overcome. Rather, the absolute good that would be the antidote to radical evil is the same as absolute evil, since it would destroy the possibility for anything to be. The same logic is evident in Eckhart's reasoning, but he draws the opposite conclusion. Given that hate is intrinsic to love, Eckhart negates both love and hate; and given that the desire for either this or that is a desire for the finite, Eckhart negates both the desire for this and that. Eckhart's stance is certainly consistent since, if there is an autoimmune threat intrinsic to everything, the only way to have absolute immunity is to negate everything. But the radically atheist argument is that *one cannot want* absolute immunity and that it has never been the aim of desire.

The problem for Eckhart is indeed that desire is *not* directed toward the absolute nothingness of God; it is rather a desire for mortal life. There would be no reason to preach *detachment* from mortal beings if people were not *attached* to mortal beings. Eckhart is very attentive to how the lure of mortal desire is at work even in the purest concept of God. Not only human beings as created beings but also God as an object of thought must be eliminated in the *via negativa*. One should not settle for a God that can be *thought* because when the thought perishes the God perishes as well.[13] Instead, Eckhart prays God to rid him of God, since all the concepts he can form of "God" are subject to the constraints of mortality.[14]

The same argument can be traced in Pseudo-Dionysius, who warns against beautiful descriptions of God or the angels. If one dwells on beautiful imagery, one remains on the level of the mortal senses and runs the risk of becoming attached to images that will perish rather than to God himself. It can thus be better to represent God as a worm or some other repulsive thing to remind oneself that all images are inadequate to God and that one must go beyond everything that appeals to the senses to approach the "immaterial reality" of the divine.[15] What must be overcome is the desire for the material, which Pseudo-Dionysius describes as "that chronic urge to dwell with the ephemeral, that living, mastering longing to remain with whatever is applauded by the senses" (151).

For Derrida, on the contrary, it is a matter of thinking a constitutive desire for mortal life that undercuts the religious ideal of immunity from within. If one can only desire the mortal, one cannot desire immortality, since it would eliminate the mortal *as mortal.* Hence, I will demonstrate that Derrida relies on the desire for mortal life to read even the most religious ideas against themselves. Messianic hope is for Derrida a hope for temporal survival, faith is always faith in the finite, and the desire for God is a desire for the mortal, like every other desire.

The common denominator is Derrida's claim that desire is a desire for *the impossible.* The desire for the impossible is quite central for Caputo, who argues that it testifies to "the religious aspiration of deconstruction" (xxi). According to Caputo, "the impossible, being impassioned by the impossible, is the religious, is religious passion" (xx). This argument, however, is based on a fundamental misunderstanding of what Derrida means by the impossible. Caputo quotes and often alludes to a statement by Jesus in the New Testament: "For mortals it is impossible, but not for God; for God all things are possible" (Mark 10:27).[16] This statement is the matrix for Caputo's systematic misreading of Derrida. When Derrida writes that something is impossible, Caputo takes it to mean that it is impossible for us mortals but not for God. Caputo asserts that "with God all things are possible, above all *the* impossible" (114); and again, "with God everything is possible, even *the* impossible" (133). Derrida's passion for the impossible would thus answer to religious passion and especially to the passion of prophetic eschatology that Caputo detects in Derrida's writings on justice and the gift. For Caputo, absolute justice is impossible within our present legal orders but not in "the kingdom of God, where God rules" (224). *Our* juridical systems are always more or less unjust, but in his kingdom God "will count our every tear" (113), letting "justice flow like water over the land" and "letting justice come 'for all of God's children'" (114). Similarly, Caputo holds that it is impossible for us to give a pure gift, but for God it is possible. "God is love and what God gives is best, because God's will, God's heart, is good through and through" (225), and "every good gift is from God" (229).

The impossible is thus figured as an ideal possibility that we desire, even though it is inaccessible for us. What we desire is impossible given our mortality, but we dream of it becoming possible in the kingdom of God. The dream of such an impossible kingdom is the dream of an absolute immunity, where the good would be immune to evil, justice immune to injustice, and the gift immune from being a poison.

Caputo's notion of the impossible is instructive, since it is the opposite of Derrida's. What Derrida calls the impossible does not refer to something that is unattainable because of our human limitations, such as the kingdom of God. Derrida explicitly emphasizes that the impossible is *not* an inaccessible ideal; it is rather "what is most undeniably *real.*"[17] The impossible is not an inaccessible ideal but what is most undeniably real, since it answers to the spacing of time that divides everything within itself. The spacing of time makes X *possible* while making it *impossible* for X to be in itself. Such spacing is quite incompatible with the religious ideal of absolute immunity. As Derrida writes in "Faith and Knowledge," the spacing of time "will never have entered religion and will never permit itself to be sacralized, sanctified, humanized, theologized. . . . Radically heterogeneous to the safe and sound, to the holy and the sacred, it never admits of any *indemnification*" (58/34).

The spacing of time makes it impossible for anything to be good in itself, since it opens the possibility of alteration and corruption from the first inception. This impossibility of being in itself has traditionally been understood as a negative predicament that we desire to overcome. Derrida's radically atheist argument, however, is that the impossibility of being in itself is *not* a negative predicament. As he puts it in a compact formula: "what makes possible makes impossible the very thing that it makes possible and introduces—as its chance—a non-negative chance, a principle of ruin into the very thing it promises or promotes."[18] Hence, there is no opposition between the possible and the impossible. That we desire the impossible does not mean that we desire something above or beyond the possible. On the contrary, it means that whatever we desire is constituted by temporal finitude, which makes it impossible for it to be in itself:

> Possibilization allows itself to be haunted by the specter of its impossibility, by its mourning for itself: a self-mourning carried within itself that also gives it its life or its survival, its very possibility. This *im*possibility opens its possibility, it leaves a trace—chance and threat—*within* that which it makes possible. (359/305)

The chance of what we desire is inseparable from the threat of losing it. Derrida locates this double bind on the most elementary level by tying it to life as a matter of *survival.* The movement of survival is necessarily haunted by mourning, both in relation to what has been lost in the past and what will be lost in the future. As Derrida writes in *Politics of Friendship*, survival is "the other name of a mourning whose possibility is never to be awaited. For one does not survive without mourning" (13/31). Derrida goes on to specify that this "tautology of survival" is an "invincible tautology for every living being" and that "even God would be helpless" (14/31). There is thus *no exception* to the law of survival, which is inscribed in the movement of life as such. To live is necessarily to affirm the time of survival, since it gives the possibility to live on in the first place. But to live is also to fear the time of survival, since it entails that one may always become dead or be left to mourn the death of the beloved.

Derrida's logic of the impossible spells out that the double bind of temporal survival cannot even ideally be resolved. The impossibility of being in itself is necessary because it answers to the "exposure to what comes or happens. It is the exposure (the desire, the openness, but also the fear) that opens, that opens itself, that opens us to time, to what comes upon us, to what arrives or happens, to the event."[19] The impossible is thus what happens all the time; it designates the impossibility of being in itself that is the condition of temporality. This impossibility of being in itself is not a privation, since *nothing could happen* if being were given in itself. Rather, the impossibility of being in itself opens the possibility of everything we desire and the peril of everything we fear.

Hence, we can see how Caputo reads the paradox of impossibility in the wrong direction. For Derrida, the impossibility of being in itself opens the possibility for everything. The impossible must remain impossible, since only the impossibility of being in itself allows anything to happen. Inversely, if the impossible were to become possible (as in Caputo's kingdom of God) everything would become impossible, since nothing could happen.

In previous chapters I have demonstrated how the logic of impossibility informs Derrida's analyses of justice and the gift. The gift is impossible because it is a gift of time. Time makes the gift possible, since nothing can be given without being temporal. But time also makes it impossible for the gift to be given in itself, since the temporal can never be in itself. Hence, even the most desirable gift must run the risk of becoming a poison, since it cannot be immune from its own alteration. If this impossibility of a good gift were to be overcome—for example, in the kingdom of God—there would be no gift since there would be no time. When Caputo describes how the impossible gift becomes possible in the kingdom of God, he thus describes how the condition of the gift is canceled out. If the gift is altogether good (which is how Caputo envisages God's gift) it cannot be given, since nothing can be given without a temporal interval that opens the possibility of violent loss and corruption.

Analogously, Derrida maintains that there can be no justice without the coming of time. The coming of time makes justice possible, since there would be no question of justice without unpredictable events that challenge the generality of the law. But by the same token, the coming of time makes absolute justice impossible, since it opens the risk that one has made or will have made unjust decisions. When Derrida argues that the coming of time is the undeconstructible condition of justice, he thus emphasizes that it is a "de-totalizing condition," which inscribes the possibility of corruption, evil, and mischief at the heart of justice itself.[20] If this impossibility of absolute justice were to be overcome, all justice would be eliminated. Accordingly, Caputo's account of how the impossible justice becomes possible in the kingdom of God cancels out the very condition of justice. For God to count our every tear and do justice to all, he would have to be a totalizing instance that can encompass everyone and everything. If he were not a totalizing instance, he would have to pay attention to some at the expense of others and commit the injustice of discrimination. Absolute justice is thus incompatible with the coming of time, since the coming of time exceeds any totalization. But by the same token absolute justice entails that nothing can happen to cause the concern for justice in the first place. As Caputo points out, there is no reason to worry about tomorrow in the kingdom of God, since God will provide everything we need.[21]

Derrida's argument is, on the contrary, that it is quite impossible for there to be an absolute justice that is immune to injustice or a gift that is immune from being a poison. This impossibility is not negative, but the possibility of any justice or gift. Justice must be open to injustice and the gift must be open to being a poison, since neither justice nor the gift can be given in itself.

The absolute immunity that Caputo holds out as desirable is thus not simply unattainable; it is *undesirable* because it would close the autoimmune opening of life itself. Religious readers of Derrida necessarily fail to assess this logic of desire, since it reveals that their ideal of the most desirable (the best) is the most undesirable (the worst). A prominent example is Richard Kearney, who along with Caputo has been a major force in the attempt to accommodate deconstruction to religion. Kearney largely endorses (Caputo's version of) deconstruction, but he raises a critical question that takes us to the heart of the issue.[22]

Kearney proceeds from Derrida's argument that there is an unconditional openness to the coming of "the other." As we have seen, Derrida emphasizes that the other who comes can be anyone whosoever or anything whatsoever. This is the claim that troubles Kearney. Following Caputo, Kearney assumes that deconstruction "awaits the coming of the just one."[23] Kearney links the coming of the just one to the notion of "a transcendent God who will come to save and liberate" ("Desire of God," 127), but he is worried about how the coming of such a Good God can be compatible with the exposure to a radically unpredictable future. Caputo ignores the problem by launching two mutually exclusive arguments. On the one hand, he reiterates Derrida's claim that justice concerns the relation to an other who cannot be predicted. On the other hand, he asserts that the other is always "the victim, not the producer of the victim. It would never be the case that the 'other' to come would be Charles Manson, or some plunderer or rapist."[24] Caputo's assertion is quite contrary to Derrida's logic of alterity. The other to come can always be a plunderer or rapist, since the other who comes cannot be anticipated and can change its character at any juncture.

Unlike Caputo, Kearney recognizes that there is a serious problem here. Given that the other who comes is always "able to change in order to become no matter what other" (as Derrida writes in *Sauf le nom*), Kearney asks how we can discriminate "between true and false prophets, between bringers of good and bringers of evil, between holy spirits and unholy ones" (127). The point for Kearney is that there ought to be criteria that enable us to "substantively distinguish" (143) between whether the other is good or evil and thus to separate "those thieves that come in the night to rob and violate" from "those who come to heal and redeem" (126). By not providing such criteria, Derrida supposedly underestimates "the need for some kind of critical discernment—based on informed judgment, hermeneutic memory, narrative imagination, and rational discrimination" (139). For the same reason, Kearney is concerned that Derrida does not illuminate how we can make decisions "if we can never *know* (for certain), or *see* (for sure) or *have* (a definite set of criteria)" (127).

It is true that Derrida does not provide substantive criteria for how to distinguish between whether the other who comes is good or evil. But this does not mean that he underestimates the need for identification, recognition, and discriminatory decisions. On the contrary, Derrida argues that such acts are necessary *because* of the undecidable future that exceeds them. We seek to identify, recognize, and make decisions because we cannot know in advance what the other will bring about. If we knew (for certain) or saw (for sure) or had (a definite set of criteria), we would know in advance what the other would do and thus be able to predict the future. But by the same token there would be no need for any decisions. If the future could be predicted, there would be nothing to decide on and no reason to act in the first place.

Every recognition is thus haunted by a possible misrecognition, every identification by a misidentification, and every decision by an undecidable future that may call it into question. When Kearney asks for criteria that would relieve this problem, he asks for criteria that would allow us to decide *once and for all* whether the other is good or evil. But such a final identification is incompatible with the relation to the other, since the other may always change. The structural uncertainty in the relation to the other has nothing to do with a cognitive limitation that would prevent us from having access to the true nature of the other. There is no true nature of the other, since the other is temporal and cannot know what it will become. The reason why the other cannot finally be identified or recognized is not because it is an ineffable Other that belongs to another realm, but because it is inherently mutable and may come to contradict any given identification or recognition.

Hence, Derrida maintains that even the other who is identified as good may always *become* evil and that "this is true even in the most peaceful experiences of joy and happiness."[25] Even when I invite a good friend and we have a great time, it is an irreducible condition that "the experience might have been terrible. Not only that it *might* have been terrible, but the threat remains. That this good friend may become the devil, may be perverse. The perversity is not an accident which could be once and for all excluded, the perversity is part of the experience" (9).

We return here to the thought of radical evil, which reinforces that the chance of the good is inseparable from the threat of evil. As Derrida puts it: "for an event, even a good event to happen the possibility of radical evil must remain inscribed as a possibility," since "if we exclude the mere possibility of such a radical evil, then there will be no event at all. When we are exposed to what is coming, even in the most generous intention of hospitality, we must not exclude the possibility that the one who is coming is coming to kill us, is a figure of evil" (9). The *must* in Derrida's reasoning does not refer to an ethical obligation to be open to the other, since it is not a matter of choice. The exposure to the coming of the other—which is inseparable from the coming of time—precedes every decision and exceeds all mastery. The reason why we must not exclude the possibility of evil is because nothing could happen without it. Indeed, Derrida's argument does not only entail that nothing could happen but also that *nothing would be desirable* without the possibility of evil, since it is intrinsic to the experience of the good itself. Following his example of the friend, Derrida writes: "when I experience something good, the coming of a friend for example, if I am happy with a good surprise, then in this experience of happiness, within it, the memory of or the lateral reference to the possible perversion of it must remain present, in the wings let's say, otherwise I could not enjoy it" (9). Hence, Derrida reconfigures the most fundamental assumption about the good that we desire. The threat of evil does not testify to a lack of the good; it is internal to whatever good that we desire.

The same logic of radical evil informs Derrida's analysis of *faith*. Derrida argues that faith is constitutive of every relation to the other, since one cannot *know* what the other will do or *see* what the other has in mind. "I do not *see* the other, I do not *see* what he or she has in mind, or whether he or she wants to deceive me. So I have to trust the other—that is faith. Faith is blind."[26] Consequently, faith must be open to being deceived, trust must be open to being violated, and the credit granted to the other must be open to being ruinous. As Derrida remarks in *Politics of Friendship*, "this break with calculable reliability and with the assurance of certainty—in truth, with knowledge—is ordained by the very structure of confidence or of credence as faith" (16/34). Faith is unreliable not only because I can never have direct access to the other's intentions, but also because the other is mutable in itself and can change its mind at any juncture.

There can be no relation to the other and no experience in general without such faith in the mutable. We can never know for sure what will happen because experience is predicated on the unpredictable coming of time. Whatever we do, we place our faith in a future that may shatter our hopes and lay to waste what we desire. In *Rogues*, Derrida underscores that "this ex-position to the incalculable event" is "the irreducible spacing of the very faith, credit, or belief without which there would be no social bond, no address to the other, no uprightness or honesty, no promise to be honored, and so no honor, no faith to be sworn or pledge to be given" (153/210–11). It follows that one cannot maintain a strict opposition between good and evil or between sworn faith and perjury. Rather, Derrida argues that "as soon as reason does not close itself off to the event that comes, the event of what or who comes," it must take into account that "only the infinite possibility of the worst and of perjury can grant the possibility of the Good, of veracity and sworn faith. This possibility remains infinite but as the very possibility of an autoimmune finitude" (153/211).

The autoimmunity of faith is central to Derrida's main essay on religion: "Faith and Knowledge." Derrida here distinguishes between faith and the religious ideal of absolute immunity (the unscathed). The two are usually conflated in the notion of religious faith, which is understood as the faith in an absolute Good that is safe from the corruption of evil. The logic of radical evil, however, allows us to read the religious ideal of absolute immunity against itself. To have faith in the good is not to have faith in something that can be trusted once and for all. On the contrary, the good is autoimmune because the possibility of evil is inherent in its own constitution:

> Nothing immune, safe and sound, *heilig* and holy, nothing unscathed in the most autonomous living present without a risk of autoimmunity. As always, the risk charges itself twice, the same finite risk. Two times rather than one: with a menace and with a chance. In two words, it must take charge of—one could also say: take in trust—the *possibility* of that radical evil without which good would be for nothing. (82/71)

The division of time (that there is always "two times rather than one") accounts for the condition of radical evil. Whatever one has faith in is itself subjected to the undecidable future, which requires one to "take in trust" what may be a menace. This condition of radical evil cannot be removed, since it is the condition of life itself. If it were removed, it would amount to the "annulment of the future" (83/72) and hence the annulment of life itself.

We can thus specify how Derrida undermines the religious ideal of absolute immunity, which informs both Caputo's and Kearney's reasoning. They lay claim to thinking beyond the metaphysics of presence, but in fact their arguments rely on an absolute presence. Without the presupposition that the other is absolutely present in itself, nothing could safeguard Caputo's assertion that the other *is* a victim who cannot turn out to have been or to have become a producer of victims. Moreover, the other could never be "the Other whose good is absolute," as Caputo has it.[27] The ideal of such an absolutely good Other is also the ideal that informs Kearney's reasoning. His model for who should come is explicitly a transcendent God who will bring salvation and redemption. For Kearney the best would be if the other who comes were good once and for all so that we could safely distinguish between what comes to heal and what comes to violate.

For Derrida, on the contrary, the coming of such a Good God would be the worst, since it would have to eliminate the coming of time that compromises any final salvation and makes every good other susceptible to becoming evil. By excluding the possibility of evil, the supposedly ideal relation to the other would eliminate every relation to the other. The other who comes can be anyone whosoever or anything whatsoever *except* the wholly Good other that Caputo and Kearney think that we hope for, since such an other would cancel itself out along with everything else.

Hence, we can trace how Derrida's thinking of the other deconstructs the religious idea of salvation. In *Rogues* he proposes "to separate as irreconcilable the notion of *salut* as greeting or salutation to the other from every *salut* as salvation (in the sense of the safe, the immune, health, and security)" (114/160). Moreover, he proposes to question the very desire for salvation: "to consider the greeting or salutation of the other, of what comes, as irreducible and heterogeneous to any seeking of *salut* as salvation" (114/160). These propositions resonate with a number of texts from the last ten years of Derrida's life, where he employs the resources of the French word *salut* in order to emphasize that the religious notion of salvation is incompatible with the opening to the other.[28] *Salut* can signify both the salvation of (*salut de*) someone or something and the greeting to (*salut à*) someone or something. Derrida links the former meaning to the religious ideal of the unscathed. To be granted *salut* as salvation would be to become wholly immune to evil, safe from any possible harm. To address the greeting *salut* is, on the contrary, to open oneself to an other who can always cause harm or do evil and in any case opens the possibility of loss that compromises any salvation. As Derrida explains, the greeting *salut* is pronounced "at a moment of encounter or separation, at the moment of parting or meeting again, and each time it is both the moving away and the moving toward but each time, even at the instant of departure or of death, it is a 'salut' at the coming of what comes."[29] Thus, the greeting *salut* signifies an experience of temporal survival; it is addressed to a mortal other that is coming or going. Such a greeting of the other characterizes *experience in general*, since the coming and going of the other answers to the coming and going of time. Even in my most immediate self-relation I am always greeting myself on the verge of leaving and arriving, since I can only exist by becoming past and becoming future.

Derrida's strong claim is that the greeting of the other is incompatible with the very hope for salvation: "the *salut à* presupposes a renunciation of the *salut de*. To address a greeting *to* the other, a greeting from one's own self to the other as other, for this greeting to be what it must be it must break off all hope of salvation or redemption, all return and restitution of the 'safe'" (269–70/184). The radicality of Derrida's argument emerges if one bears in mind that greeting the other is not a matter of choice. Whatever one does, one is greeting the other, since nothing can happen without the coming of the other. Thus, in spite of Derrida's recourse to voluntary metaphors, the "renunciation" of the hope for salvation is concomitant with the advent of life as such. Whatever one desires, one cannot desire the absolute immunity of salvation, since it would close the opening to the other that is the condition for whatever one desires.

Hence, Derrida writes that "the desire for immunological salvation always tragically contradicts itself according to an autoimmunological necessity that loses its own protection and goes so far as to ruin its own most elementary defenses" (395n9/183n1). Derrida does not develop this claim, but my argument is that it follows from thinking the unconditional affirmation of survival. As I demonstrated in Chapter 1, the affirmation of survival is unconditional because every moment of life depends on the trace structure of time. The trace that makes life possible is always living on from the past by being left for a future that may erase it. The unconditional affirmation of such mortality does not entail an acceptance of death. On the contrary, to affirm mortal life is to oppose death, to resist and defer it for as long as possible. But since mortal life is essentially linked to death, it is internally bound to what it opposes.

There is thus an "autoimmunological necessity" that contradicts the desire for salvation from within. If one did not affirm mortal life, there would be no desire to save anything from death, since only mortal life can be threatened by death. Without the affirmation of mortal life, then, there would be no desire for salvation. But for the same reason, the desire for salvation cannot be a desire for the absolute immunity of immortality. The state of immortality cannot answer to the desire to save the mortal, since it would put an end to the time of mortal life. The desire for salvation is rather a desire for survival that is essentially autoimmune, since the death that it defends against is internal to what is defended.

We must therefore distinguish between salvation as immortality and salvation as survival. The religious idea of salvation as absolute immunity is necessarily an idea of immortality, since every mortal being is autoimmune. Traditional atheism denounces the religious hope for salvation as an illusion, without questioning that we desire the absolute immunity of salvation that religion promises. In contrast, radical atheism locates an internal contradiction in the desire for salvation and enables us to read the religious idea of salvation against itself. We can trace such a radically atheist move in Derrida's writing on *salut*. The *salut* as a greeting or salutation to the other answers to the movement of survival, which allows us to reconceptualize the desire for salvation:

> To salute is to name the other precisely where the other is called, that is, called from another place which will have had to be her end—and I shall add, *that* is mourning and the cureless obsession, precisely where the other can no longer call herself, save herself and salute, only be saluted, where the two meanings of *salut* part and say goodbye to one another. . . . *Le salut* as health or salvation, redemption or resurrection, must never be like *le salut* as a call or as "calling out to one another." Absolute heterogeneity, irreconcilable difference between the two *saluts*. Whether one delights in it or deplores it, this dissociation is Necessity. . . . To be able to call, oneself as well as another, to call oneself or call out to one another, in order to be able to call, where saluting is more than naming, it is necessary that *le salut* of salvation or health, *le salut* of redemption or resurrection never be assured. Not that it is out of the question, but it is necessary that it always *could* be refused, threatened, forbidden, lost, gone: the *no-way-out* or the endlessness of the aporia, the endlessness of the end that is never-ending. The possibility of the *non-salut* of salvation or health must haunt *le salut* as calling. . . . One can only call out to the other, and salute, while living, as one of the living, that is, while dying, as one of the dying, in the other's passing-on [*sa mourance*] and in one's own, in a survival that is neither life nor death.[30]

Derrida here launches two apparently contradictory claims. On the one hand, there is an "absolute heterogeneity, irreconcilable difference" between *le salut* as salvation and *le salut* as a greeting that calls out to the other. Given that there cannot be anything without the greeting of the other (who may be "oneself as well as another" in accordance with the division of time that informs every self-relation), it follows that the absolute immunity of salvation is excluded from the start. As Derrida writes earlier in the same text, whatever one does "in order to save oneself, get through it safe and sound, immune, unharmed, intact, there is no salvation. No *salut*, no *run for your life* or merely a *run for your life* without hope of salvation" (216/202). The religious notion of salvation is thus emphatically negated. On the other hand, Derrida writes in the passage above that salvation is not "out of the question" but should rather be understood as something that is never assured.

These apparently contradictory claims become consistent if we apply my distinction between immortality and survival. Insofar as salvation is understood as the absolute immunity of immortality, it is out of the question. There can be no such salvation, since nothing can happen without the greeting of an other that can come to compromise any immunity. However, insofar as salvation is understood as a survival that saves one from death by giving one more time to live, it is not out of the question. It is rather a precarious possibility that always can "be refused, threatened, forbidden, lost, gone" because of the infinite finitude of time ("the endlessness of the end that is never-ending"). The reason why salvation is never assured is not because there is an immortal salvation that one may be refused by God, but because the salvation in question is a matter of temporal survival. Such survival can never be assured because it is always—as long as it lives on—threatened from within.

We can thus understand why Derrida writes that the two meanings of *salut* part at the moment of death, when "the other can no longer call herself, save herself and salute, only be saluted." The *salut* as health or salvation cannot outlive death, since it is a matter of a mortal health or mortal salvation. In contrast, the *salut* as a salute to the other can outlive death but only by itself being subjected to the temporal finitude that marks any call to the other. As Derrida points out, one can only call out to the other "while living," which is to say "while dying," in the movement of survival that gives and takes the time for every *salut*.

Hence, when Derrida speaks of the *salut* without salvation, he is not only rejecting the religious idea of salvation. Such a rejection would remain within the bounds of traditional atheism. Derrida's notion of the *salut* without salvation is radically atheist because it does not designate a lack of salvation, but enables us to reconceptualize the very desire for salvation. It is not a matter of renouncing struggles for health or of denouncing hopes for salvation. Rather, it is a matter of demonstrating that these struggles and hopes were never concerned with the absolute immunity that is promoted as the religious ideal. The struggle for health and the hope for salvation have never been driven by a desire to be immortal but by a desire to live on as mortal.

The same radical atheism can be traced in Derrida's notion of the messianic without messianism. More than any other term in Derrida's vocabulary, the messianic has invited the misconception that Derrida harbors a religious hope for salvation. Such readings are due to misunderstanding Derrida's distinction between the messianic and every form of "messianism." In Derrida's vocabulary the messianic is another name for the relation to the undecidable future, which opens the chance for what is desired but at the same time threatens it from within, since it is constituted by temporal finitude. In contrast, messianism is the religious or political faith in a future that will come and put an end to time, replacing it with a perpetual peace that nothing can come to disrupt. Consequently, Derrida emphasizes that what he calls the messianic is without messianism and without religion. The only common trait concerns the formal structure of a *promise of the coming*, which is what Derrida takes advantage of in order to read messianism against itself.

Derrida's reading is easily misunderstood since the respective meanings of the promise of the coming are quite incompatible. What Derrida designates as the to-come (drawing on the French word for future, *avenir*, which literally means to-come, *à-venir*) can never come to repose in a presence but always opens itself to yet another future. The promise of the coming is thus intrinsic to experience in general, which always has to commit itself to a future that in turn is threatened by the coming of another future. Far from supporting the promise of messianism, the promise of deconstruction undercuts it a priori. There can never be a peaceful resolution, since the opening toward the undecidable future is the condition for anything to happen. Messianism, on the contrary, promises a Messiah that will come and *close* the opening toward the undecidable future.

A clear example of messianism is the "messianic triumph" Levinas invokes toward the end of *Totality and Infinity*. Levinas notes that the metaphysical "truth" of ethics is incompatible with a temporality that does not admit of any definitive judgments but is always related to yet another future, where the criteria of judgment can be revised. Given this temporal predicament, no ethical principles can be protected against critical interrogation or violent deformation and no God can ever come to impose a verdict on the injustices of history. For Levinas, then, the *negative* infinity of time—time as infinitely finite displacement—must be overcome by the *positive* infinity of the Good beyond being. Or as Levinas literally puts it: there must be a transcendent truth that in the last instance will "seal" the opening toward the contingent future by "converting" the temporal into the eternal. Levinas hails this conversion as the "pure" messianic triumph, which is "secured" against the "evil" that an endless temporality cannot prohibit (285/261).

What Derrida calls the messianic is thus the opposite of what Levinas calls the messianic.[31] Indeed, Derrida's notion of the messianic runs counter to the entire religious tradition. The common denominator for religious notions of the messianic is that they posit the messianic as a promise of timeless peace. In contrast, Derrida links the messianic to the coming of a future that undercuts the very idea of timelessness. Derrida's key formula for describing the messianic is *il faut l'avenir*, which can either be translated as "it is necessary [that there be] the future" or as "there must be the future." Derrida glosses the phrase as follows:

> There is an "it is necessary" for the future. Whatever may be its indetermination, be it that of "it is necessary [that there be] the future" ["*il faut l'avenir*"], there is some future and some history. . . . We must insist on this specific point precisely because it points to an essential lack of specificity, an indetermination that remains the ultimate mark of the future: *whatever may be the case concerning the modality or the content* of this duty, this necessity, this prescription or this injunction, this pledge, this task, also therefore this promise, this necessary promise, *this "it is necessary" is necessary, and that is the law.* This indifference to the content here is not an indifference, it is not an *attitude* of indifference, on the contrary. Marking any opening to the event and to the future as such, it therefore conditions the interest in and not the indifference to anything whatsoever, to all content in general. Without it, there would be neither intention, nor need, nor desire, and so on. . . . Apparently "formalist," this indifference to the content has perhaps the value of giving

one to think the necessarily pure and purely necessary form of the future as such, in its being-necessarily-promised, prescribed, assigned, enjoined, in the necessarily formal necessity of its possibility—in short, in its law. It is this law that dislodges any present out of its contemporaneity with itself. Whether the promise promises this or that, whether it be fulfilled or not, or whether it be unfulfillable, there is necessarily some promise and therefore some historicity as future-to-come. It is what we are nicknaming the messianic without messianism. (*Specters of Marx*, 73/123–24)

Here as elsewhere Derrida defines the messianic promise as the formal condition for all experience and all hope, since it marks the opening to an undecidable future. The "content" of the messianic promise can be anything whatsoever or anyone whosoever, but whatever it is, it cannot be exempt from time. Rather, it is necessarily subject to the law of time that "dislodges any present out of its contemporaneity with itself." As Derrida points out, even if the messianic promise were fulfilled there would still be time in the form of "historicity as future-to-come." It follows that the messianic promise cannot be a promise of timeless peace, since the fulfillment of such a promise would put an end to time.

Derrida can thus be seen to invert the logic of religious eschatology. Instead of promoting the end of time, Derrida emphasizes that the coming of time exceeds any given end. As he explains, there is "an extremity that is beyond any determinable end of being or of history, and this eschatology—as extreme beyond the extreme, as last beyond the last—has necessarily to be only the absolute opening toward the non-determinability of the future. . . . What I call the eschatological or the messianic is nothing other than a relation to the future so despoiled and indeterminate that it leaves being 'to come.'"[32] The promise of the messianic is inseparable from a threat, since it is the promise of an unpredictable future that may negate what one hopes for. Accordingly, Derrida points out that "the eschatological or the messianic, even if they have the form of expectation, hope, promise—motifs that are apparently so striking—is also the experience of death. . . . Only a mortal can speak of the future in this sense, a god could never do so. So I know very well that this is a discourse—an experience, rather—that is made possible as a future by a certain imminence of death" (23).

Nevertheless, it is above all the messianic that has served as an alibi for the religious reading of Derrida. For Caputo the messianic is "the point at which the path of deconstruction swings off in an unmistakably prophetico-messianic direction" and "where we touch upon the heart of Derrida's religion, of the call for a justice, a democracy, a just one to come, a call for peace among the concrete messianisms."[33] Proceeding from this premise, Caputo undertakes an elaborate misreading of Derrida's distinction between the messianic and messianism. According to Caputo, Derrida's distinction "spells the difference between war and peace. . . . The concrete messianisms have always meant war, while the meaning of the messianic is, or should be, *shalom, pax*" (190). The messianic is thus aligned with the promise of a divine peace, which Caputo regards as perverted by the concrete messianisms insofar as they posit themselves as specially chosen by God and thereby exclude others. In Caputo's schema "religion is most dangerous when it conceives itself as a higher *knowledge* granted a chosen *few*, a chosen people of God: that is a formula for war. . . . As if God took the side of one people against another, or granted special privileges to one people that are denied to others."[34] In contrast to such messianism, Caputo promotes "the God who said that He does not delight in ritual sacrifice but in justice, religion as a powerful prophetic force which has a dream of justice for *all* of God's children—that is the religion that emerges from an hour on the couch with deconstruction. That religion is good news, for the oppressed and everybody else" (160). Accordingly, deconstruction is figured as "a blessing for religion, its positive salvation" since "deconstruction discourages religion from its own worst instincts" and "helps religion examine its conscience, counseling and chastening religion about its tendency to confuse its faith with knowledge, which results in the dangerous and absolutizing triumphalism of religion, which is what spills blood" (159). All of Caputo's works on a supposedly deconstructive religion are structured around this opposition between a "good" religion that welcomes others and a "bad" religion that excludes others. For Caputo, Derrida's work helps us to move away from "the bloody messianisms" in favor of "the messianic" promise of a divine kingdom that is open to everyone.[35]

Such a reading of the messianic is quite untenable. It is true that Derrida describes the messianic as a "universal" structure of experience, but this universality does not promise a divine kingdom of peace. On the contrary, the universal structure of the messianic designates the "irreducible movement of the historical opening to the future," which is the common denominator for all experience.[36] As such, it gives rise to all kinds of violence. Derrida explicitly defines the messianic as the exposure to a radically unpredictable future, which entails that "the other and death—and radical evil—can come as a surprise at any moment."[37] For the same reason, "the messianic is threatening" and "frightening."[38] As Derrida points out in *Politics of Friendship*, the messianic "carries within it an irresistible disavowal," since it is haunted by a "structural contradiction" that "converts *a priori* the called into the repressed, the desired into the undesired, the friend into the enemy" (174/198). The structural contradiction is due to the messianic opening to an undecidable future. One cannot desire the coming of the future "without simultaneously fearing it" since it can "bring nothing but threat and chance at the same time" (174/198). Moreover, what is engaged in such a "*double bind* is not only myself, nor my own desire, but the other, the Messiah, or the god himself" (174/198). It follows that the Messiah or the god is as mortal as every other who may come. Derrida glosses the other to come as "the Messiah, the thinker of the dangerous 'perhaps,' the god, *who*ever would come in the form of the event—that is, in the form of the exception and the unique" (174/198). The common denominator is that whoever comes must be subject to the double bind of temporal finitude, which makes every chance liable to become a threat. Whatever is desired must "be capable of not answering—my call, my invitation, my expectation, my desire" (174/198). Accordingly, Derrida maintains that "the expectation of the Messiah" may be "a fear, an unbearable terror—hence the hatred of what is thus awaited" (173/198). Far from promising a final peace, the messianic precipitates war. It is the opening of a mortal future that is the source of all hope but also of all paranoia, fear, and hatred, since it entails that the desired other can always be or become a menace.

The crucial question, then, is why Derrida chooses to retain the term *messianic* to designate the opening to the undecidable future. Derrida's use of the term may seem counterintuitive and easily invites religious appropriations. My argument, however, is that Derrida's notion of the messianic without messianism follows the radically atheist logic that we traced in his notion of the *salut* without salvation. A radical atheism cannot simply denounce messianic hope as an illusion. Rather, it must show that messianic hope does not stem from a hope for immortality (the positive infinity of eternity) but from a hope for survival (the negative infinity of time).[39]

It is here instructive to look closer at Derrida's account of the promise, which is explicitly parallel to his account of the messianic. Derrida defines "the structure of the promise" as "*the memory of that which carries the future here and now.*"[40] This definition of the promise highlights the division between past and future that is the condition of temporal survival. On the one hand, to promise is to commit oneself to the future, since one can only promise something that is to come. On the other hand, to promise is to commit oneself to the past, since it entails a promise to remember the promise. Whatever I promise, I necessarily promise to keep the memory of the promise. There is thus an interval of time that divides the promise within itself, which answers to the interval that divides every now from its inception.

Because of the necessary interval in the experience of the promise, there is always time for the promise to be broken. The moment I make a promise is immediately succeeded by another moment that may alter or revoke the promise. That the promise may be broken is not something that is extrinsic to the act of promising; it is intrinsic to its being as such. A promise *must* be breakable in order to be a promise. If it were certain that the promise would be kept, there would be no promise, since the promise is made in relation to an unpredictable future. As Derrida puts it: "a promise must *be able not to* be kept, it must threaten not to be kept or to become a threat in order to be a promise."[41] The possibility of failure is thus "not only inscribed as a preliminary risk" (362/308) in the promise. Rather, "the possibility of failure must continue to mark the event, even when it succeeds, as the trace of an impossibility, at times its memory and always its haunting" (362/309).

Derrida's argument follows from thinking the promise as a *promise of time.* If the promise (whatever its content) is a promise of time, it follows that even the most ideal fulfillment of the promise must be haunted by the possibility of nonfulfillment, since the temporal must remain open to its own alteration. It is thus misleading to say that the promise cannot be fulfilled. Rather, the promise *does not promise fulfillment* insofar as fulfillment is understood as the consummation of time. The promise does not promise a future that will be present in itself, which would put an end to time. Whatever it promises, it promises the coming of a future that in its turn will have the structure of a promise. Indeed, the structure of experience will always be the structure of the promise. Even the most immediate experience must be inscribed as a memory for the future and thus promise to remember itself.

If the promise is inherent in every experience, we must further complicate the relation between promise and threat. As Derrida points out, "a healthy, classical theory of the promise cannot take into account an ill-intentioned, harmful or maleficent promise. A promise belongs to the order of benediction. I can only promise 'good.' I cannot promise the other that I will kill him, rob him, lie to him or curse him. That would be a threat and not a promise."[42] It is precisely the axiomatic distinction between promise and threat, however, that Derrida calls into question by aligning every act with the structure of the promise. It follows that even when I threaten to rob or kill, I am making a promise. The threat that is intrinsic to the structure of the promise does not only consist in that the promise may be broken; it can also consist in that the promise may be kept. Derrida epitomizes the interdependence of promise and threat in his claim that "the threat is not something that comes from the outside to place itself next to the promise." Rather, "the threat is the promise itself, or better, threat and promise always come together *as* the promise. This does not mean just that the promise is always already threatened; it also means that the promise is *threatening*."[43]

We can thus understand why Derrida maintains that "a promise pledges only to what is mortal. A promise has meaning and gravity only on the condition of death."[44] Although Derrida does not elaborate this claim, I argue that it is presupposed by all his accounts of the promise. According to Derrida's criteria, a promise must be able to be broken and to break other promises; it must be susceptible to being threatened and to become a threat. Only a promise of mortality can meet these criteria. A promise of immortality can never be broken, since it can never be contradicted by anything that happens to the mortal. When someone dies, it is not a promise of immortality that is broken, since the death of mortal life cannot have any bearing on the status of immortality. When someone dies, it is rather a promise of mortal survival that is broken. What follows from Derrida's criteria, then, is that every promise is a promise of mortal survival. A promise of mortal survival is both threatened (since even when it is fulfilled it may be negated by death) and threatening (since it can be fulfilled only at the expense of what does not survive).

In *Specters of Marx*, Derrida employs the structure of the promise to pursue what he calls "an atheological heritage of the messianic" (168/266). The messianic is here linked to the promise of justice, which is directed both toward the past (as a promise to remember victims of injustice) and toward the future (as a promise to bring about justice). The messianic promise of justice is radically atheist because it proceeds from the unconditional affirmation of survival. Without the affirmation of survival, there would be no struggle for justice in the first place. If I did not desire the survival of someone or something, there would be nothing that compelled me to fight for the memory of the past or for a better future.

The affirmation of survival is never innocent, however, since the movement of survival always entails the obliteration or eradication of what does *not* survive. As Derrida writes in *Specters of Marx*, any watch over the dead that seeks to remember what has been excluded "will fatally exclude in its turn":

> It will even annihilate, by watching (over) its ancestors rather than (over) certain others. At this moment rather than at some other moment. By forgetfulness (guilty or not, it matters little here), by foreclosure or murder, this watch itself will engender new ghosts. It will do so by choosing already among the ghosts, its own from among its own, thus by killing the dead: law of finitude, law of decision and responsibility for finite existences, the only living-mortals for whom a decision, a choice, a responsibility has meaning and a meaning that will have to pass through the ordeal of the undecidable. (87/144)

Every promise of justice will thus have to reckon with the dead; it will have to "bury" them, either in the sense of commemorating or repressing them. In Derrida's words: "it will always be necessary that still living mortals bury the already dead living. The dead have never buried anyone, but neither have the living, the living who would be only living, the immortal living. The gods never bury anyone" (114/187). The figure of burying the dead is thus a figure of mortal survival. The same figure of burying the dead runs throughout *Specters of Marx* and reaches a crucial formulation toward the very end of the book:

> Only mortals, only the living who are not living gods can bury the dead. Only mortals can watch over them, and can watch, period. Ghosts can do so as well, they are everywhere where there is watching: the dead *cannot do so*—it is impossible and they must not do so.
>
> That the without-ground of this impossible can nevertheless *take place* is on the contrary the ruin or the absolute ashes, the threat that must be *thought*, and, why not, exorcised yet again. To exorcise not in order to chase away the ghosts, but this time to grant them the right, if it means making them come back alive, as *revenants* who would no longer be *revenants*, but as other

arrivants to whom a hospitable memory or promise must offer welcome—without certainty, ever, that they present themselves as such. Not in order to grant them right in this sense but out of a concern for *justice*. Present existence or essence has never been the condition, object, or the *thing* [chose] of justice. One must constantly remember that the impossible ("to let the dead bury their dead") is, alas, always possible. One must constantly remember that this absolute evil (which is, is it not, absolute life, fully present life, the one that does not know death and does not want to hear about it) can take place. One must constantly remember that it is even on the basis of the terrible possibility of this impossible that justice is desirable: *through* but also *beyond* right and law. (175/277–78)

The experience of survival—as the burial of the dead—is here presented as what raises the concern for justice. If life were fully present to itself, if it were not haunted by what has been lost in the past and what may be lost in the future, there would be nothing that could cause the concern for justice. Consequently, "present existence or essence has never been the condition, object, or the *thing* of justice." The struggle for justice is rather a struggle for survival that commits the struggle for justice to the spectral experience of time. There can be no justice without a memory of what is *no longer* that is kept for a future that is *not yet*. Justice can only be brought about by "living-mortals" who will exclude and annihilate by maintaining the memory and life of certain others at the expense of other others. The discrimination between others is not the privation of an ideal justice; it is the "law of finitude, law of decision and responsibility" that gives both the chance of justice and the threat of injustice.

Hence, the commitment to survival that makes justice *possible* is also what makes absolute justice *impossible*. It is this impossibility of absolute justice that Caputo thinks is desirable to overcome. According to Caputo, we "dream" of the impossible becoming possible in the kingdom of God. In Caputo's conception of desire such a kingdom is "the best," whereas in Derrida's conception of desire it is "the worst." In the passage quoted above, Derrida makes the argument with reference to Jesus's imperative "to let the dead bury their dead." In response to a man who wants to bury his father, Jesus says, "Let the dead bury their dead, but you go and proclaim the kingdom of God" (Luke 9:60). Jesus's demand is certainly consistent, since as long as one is concerned with burying the dead—and hence with mortal survival—one is blocking the kingdom of God. The absolute peace of the kingdom of God is incompatible with survival, since the violence of loss is inscribed in the movement of survival as such. If one survived wholly intact, one would not be surviving; one would be reposing in absolute presence. The only way to have absolute peace is to have "absolute life, fully present life, the one that does not know death." But as Derrida points out, such an absolute life would be the "absolute evil" of "absolute ashes" that eliminates every trace of time. That the impossible ("to let the dead bury their dead") is impossible is thus not a negative predicament. On the contrary, if the impossible became possible everything would be extinguished.

Ironically, when Caputo encounters the passage quoted above, he claims that it is about "another Derridean *impossible*, not one of which we dream but an impossible of which we live in dread."[45] In fact, Derrida here pursues the same logic of impossibility that pervades his entire work and that Caputo systematically misreads. Caputo thinks we desire that the impossible will become possible, while Derrida argues that we dread that the impossible will become possible. If the impossible were to become possible, everything would be erased. The dead would have buried their dead, and the violent traces of survival would be eliminated. Such an end of finitude is "alas, always possible"—since everything is absolutely destructible—but it is resisted in the movement of survival, which keeps traces of the past for the future.[46] Such tracing of time is the minimal protection of life but it also attacks life from the first inception, since it breaches the integrity of any moment and makes everything susceptible to annihilation.

It is the autoimmunity of life that in turn causes the autoimmunity of justice. In *Archive Fever* Derrida recalls that he thinks "justice, the justice which exceeds but also requires the law, in the direction of the act of memory, of resistance to forgetting, whether this be of the injunction in general or of its place of assignation: other people, living or dead" (76n14/122n1). However, the resistance to forgetting that is the exercise of justice is also "the place of all violences. Because if it is just to remember the future and the injunction to remember, namely the archontic injunction to guard and to gather the archive, it is no less just to remember the others, the other others and the others in oneself" (77/123). Thus, "I shall no doubt be unjust out of a concern for justice" (63/101–2), since the memory of some entails the forgetting of others. Moreover, "the injustice of this justice can concentrate its violence in the very constitution of the *One* and the *Unique*" (77/123). Even the most elevated One is differing and deferring from itself because of its temporal constitution, which makes it liable to forget what it has been and indeed compromises its own defense of the past in opening itself to the future. As Derrida puts it: "at once, at the same time, but in a same time that is out of joint, the One forgets to remember itself to itself, it keeps and erases the archive of this injustice that it is" (78/125). The One is thus not only violent to others but also to itself: "The One makes itself violence. It violates and does violence to itself but it also institutes itself as violence" (78/125). Neither the most minimal life nor the most ideal justice can be exempt from such violence, since they depend on the movement of survival that always involves loss and erasure.

As we recall from *Politics of Friendship*, there is no exception to the law of survival and "even God would be helpless" (14/31). Derrida's argument is radically atheist because it entails that nothing—including whatever is posited as "God"—can be exempt from temporal finitude. As Derrida points out in *Rogues*, "the story of a god who deconstructs himself in his ipseity" is the story of a god who is "a vulnerable nonsovereignty, one that suffers and is divisible, one that is mortal" (157/215–16). Genesis is an example of such a story. In his reading of Genesis, Derrida focuses on the scene where God gives Adam the task of naming the animals. What interests Derrida is that God delegates the task to Adam *in order to see* what he will do (Gen. 2:19). God himself is thus subjected to the undecidable future, since otherwise he would not have to wait and see:

> This "in order to see" marks at the same time the infinite right of inspection of an all powerful God *and* the finitude of a God who does not know what is going to happen to him with language. And with names. In short, God does not yet know what he really wants; this is the finitude of a God who does not know what he wants with respect to the animal, that is to say with respect to the life of the living as such, a God who sees something coming without seeing it coming, a God who will say "*I am that I am*" without knowing what he is going to see when a poet enters the scene to give his name to living things. This powerful yet deprived "in order to see" that is God's, the first stroke of time, before time, God's exposure to surprise, to the event of what is going to occur between man and animal, this time before time has always made me dizzy. As if someone said, in the form of a promise or a threat, "you will see what you will see" without knowing what was going to end up happening.[47]

When Derrida reads the story of God, he does not treat the temporal terms as inadequate for describing God. On the contrary, he argues that finitude is inscribed in the genesis itself and exposes God to the unpredictable coming of time from the first instance.

Hence, Derrida's treatment of God is the inverse of the treatment of God in negative theology. Negative theology proceeds from the premise that whatever story we tell about God, whatever image or predicate we employ to describe God, cannot be adequate to the positive infinity of God. To describe God is to make him dependent on conditions that apply to temporal finitude. It is in order to save God from such mortal contamination that negative theology refuses to predicate God. Derrida's argument is exactly the opposite, since he holds that God is as dependent on temporal finitude as everyone else. When Derrida employs the name of God, or reads a story that involves God, it is to show that even the supposedly indivisible is divisible and that whoever says *I am* confesses that he is mortal.

Such radical atheism follows from the thinking of the trace that informs Derrida's writing from beginning to end. The structure of the trace entails that everything is subjected to the infinite finitude of time and consequently that God himself is "an *effect of the trace*."[48] It follows that any notion of God as a positive infinity is contradicted from within by the spacing of time, which cannot be appropriated by religion. As Derrida writes in "Faith and Knowledge," the spacing of time "will never have entered religion and will never permit itself to be sacralized, sanctified, humanized, theologized" (58/34).

I recall these premises because they are at odds with another major attempt to accommodate Derrida's thinking to religion: Hent de Vries's *Philosophy and the Turn to Religion*. According to de Vries, there is a shift in Derrida's work from the notion of a generalized writing that he developed in the 1960s to what de Vries calls "a *generalized religion*" (434). Derrida never speaks of a generalized religion, yet de Vries claims that it is the most important term for understanding what is at stake in Derrida's work: "the shift from generalized writing to generalized religion is by no means trivial or the mere transposition of an old discussion and a fixed 'conceptual matrix.' . . . The turn to religion studied here constitutes, in my opinion, also the most significant."[49] As I have argued throughout this book, there is no such "turn" in Derrida's thinking. The early work on arche-writing articulates the spacing of time that informs all of Derrida's subsequent work. In *Sauf le nom* Derrida recalls that spacing is "undeconstructible, not as a construction whose foundations would be sure, sheltered from every internal or external deconstruction," but as the very movement of deconstruction that is at work in everything that happens (80/104). De Vries never addresses the spacing of time and he never tries to elucidate what Derrida means by arche-writing, while relegating it to secondary importance. De Vries does quote the passage where Derrida states that spacing "will never have entered religion," but he takes no note of it.[50] Rather, de Vries maintains that the aim of his book is to demonstrate that Derrida's work is on the way "not to writing, let alone to a science of writing, but, rather, to 'God' (*à dieu*) or to what comes to substitute for the totally other. . . . Substituting for the 'infinite' and ultimately the Infinite, nothing less is at issue in the formula of the *à dieu*" (26).

De Vries takes issue with Rodolphe Gasché, who has underscored that Derrida "is certainly closer to philosophy than to theology."[51] Gasché argues that the trace is more originary than God, since God is an effect of the trace. De Vries, however, objects that God is "the most exemplary name" for the trace, so "the latter is no more originary than the former. Rather, the trace and God—or whatever absolute comes to substitute in His place—could be said to be co-originary" (357).[52] De Vries does not provide an account of what he thinks Derrida means by the trace, but it is clear from his argument that he has not understood what is at stake. The trace is not an absolute that can be substituted for God. It is rather what marks the infinite finitude of life. As Derrida emphasizes, "the trace is always the finite trace of a finite being. So it can itself disappear. An ineradicable trace is not a trace. The trace inscribes in itself its own precariousness, its vulnerability of ashes, its mortality."[53] Derrida's thinking of finitude is persistently avoided by de Vries.[54] The one time he does quote Derrida's definition of *différance* as an infinite finitude, it is to dismiss its importance. According to de Vries, "for all the insistence on finitude—'la différance infinie est finie'—and for all the emphasis on ends of man far more radical than, say, Kant and Heidegger, Kojève and Sartre, would have dreamed, we are nonetheless dealing here, in Derrida's texts, with a certain quasi-mystic *deification*" (129). The reason de Vries offers for his assertion is that in Derrida "the self becomes as other as the totally other for which 'God' is still the most exemplary—in a sense, the most substitutable—name" (129). De Vries here draws an analogy between Derrida's notion of the wholly other and Pseudo-Dionysius's notion of an ecstasy where "we should be taken wholly out of ourselves and become wholly of God, since it is better to belong to God rather than to ourselves" (quoted in de Vries, 129). In fact, the two notions could not be more different. For Pseudo-Dionysius, to become wholly of God is to transcend temporal finitude and be united with the positive infinity of the divine. For Derrida, on the contrary, every one is wholly other because the alterity of time cannot be overcome. Every one is wholly other because every one is a temporal singularity that always can be lost and never be reappropriated by anyone else.

The proximity between negative theology and deconstruction suggested by de Vries is thus misleading. At one point de Vries lists Derrida's numerous objections to negative theology, but he nevertheless holds that deconstruction is analogous to "the most heterodox or to the most orthodox—in any case the most rigorous—apophatic theologies" (100).[55] De Vries does not explain what such theologies would be or how they would answer the objections raised by Derrida. Instead, he claims that "clarification of the relationship between deconstruction and apophatics is in the end nothing but an unfulfillable promise, and one that threatens to blur all necessary distinctions at that" (101). As I have demonstrated, this is not the case. Deconstruction can be clearly distinguished from negative theology if we proceed from the thinking of infinite finitude, which deconstruction articulates and negative theology denies. Negative theology rejects all descriptions of God in order to save God from finitude. For Derrida, on the contrary, finitude precedes and exceeds God.

The privilege that de Vries grants the name of God is thus untenable. For de Vries the name of God is "untouched and left intact" in Derrida's turn to religion: "As if the sacred name were not so much lacking (as Heidegger, misreading Hölderlin, believed) but to be found solely in the integrity—or absoluteness, safe and sound—of a host of idiomatic, singular, yet infinitely substitutable names of His name" (24).[56] In fact, Derrida consistently argues that there is no such integrity. The deconstruction of God is the deconstruction of the very idea of absolute immunity, which is the foundation of religion. There is nothing safe and sound, nothing holy and sacred, and the name of God is no exception. It is a name among other names and the common denominator for all names is that they spell out the mortality of whatever is named. As Derrida argues, "every case of naming involves announcing a death to come in the surviving of a ghost, the longevity of a name that survives whoever carries that name. Whoever receives a name feels mortal or dying precisely because the name seeks to save him, to call him and thus assure his survival."[57]

The desire to give or to receive a name is thus a desire for mortal survival. It seeks to remember what may be forgotten—to keep alive what may die. I want to demonstrate here how Derrida stages such desire for survival in his *Circumfession*. This autobiographical text is Derrida's own version of Augustine's *Confessions*, and he interlaces extensive quotes from the Latin text in his own narrative. As we will see, the literal duel with Augustine deconstructs the very desire for God and mobilizes the radically atheist desire for survival that is at work in Augustine's own confession.

Ironically, the reference to Augustine has served as the main evidence in the attempt to turn Derrida into a religious thinker. In *The Prayers and Tears of Jacques Derrida*, Caputo confesses that "all along I will have been clutching *Circumfession* close to my breast," with an audible sigh of relief that "at last Jacques fesses up that he has all along had religion" (xxviii). Caputo's avowed hero is Augustine, in whose conversion he sees an exemplary instance of the religious passion for the impossible.[58] It is such a passion Caputo also ascribes to Derrida.

For Caputo, the point of contact between Augustine and Derrida is the question, "What do I love when I love my God?"[59] Augustine raises this question in book 10 of the *Confessions*, and Derrida quotes it in *Circumfession*. Augustine's literal question is, "Quid ergo amo, cum deum amo?" (10.7), which Derrida in *Circumfession* misquotes as "Quid ergo amo, cum deum meum amo?" (122/117). Derrida inserts a "meum" that is not in Augustine's text, although the expression "deum meum" is employed in the preceding section of the *Confessions* (10.6). Derrida's misquotation is by all appearances deliberate, since he goes on to write: "Can I do anything other than translate this question by SA [Saint Augustine] into my language, into the same sentence, totally empty and huge at the same time, the change of meaning, or rather reference, defining the only difference of the 'meum': what do I love, whom do I love, that I love above all?" (122/117). The decisive question, then, is what the love of "my God" refers to in Augustine's and Derrida's respective confessions. Although Caputo repeatedly returns to this question, he never provides an account of Augustine's answer in the *Confessions* and fails to realize how Derrida undermines that answer in his *Circumfession*.

Augustine organizes his confession around the opposition between the mortal and the immortal. Before his conversion, Augustine's desire is directed toward mortal beings. This desire for mortal life is what he stigmatizes as the root of his sin. As he explains in the first book of the *Confessions*: "my sin was in this—that I looked for pleasures, exaltations, truths not in God Himself but in His creatures (myself and the rest), and so I fell straight into sorrows, confusions, and mistakes" (1.20). Augustine implores his soul not to be "foolish" (4.11) by clinging to the temporal that passes away. Rather, he urges his soul to turn toward God's eternal Word as "the place of peace that is imperturbable" (4.11). What is at stake is to convert the love for the mortal that always can be lost into a love for the immortal that never can be lost: "There fix your dwelling place . . . and you will lose nothing" (4.11). When Augustine declares what he loves when he loves his God, he thus emphasizes that it transcends the love for anything that is spatial and temporal; it is rather "a brilliance that space cannot contain, a sound that time cannot carry away" (10.6).

In *Circumfession* Derrida answers the question of what he loves in the opposite way. The purported love for the immortal (the passion for "my God" as the one I love above all) is reinscribed as a love for the mortal. The beloved "you" that Derrida addresses throughout *Circumfession* has a number of shifting references—himself, his mother, Geoffrey Bennington, and others—but their common denominator is that they are all mortal. As Derrida writes, "you stand in for anybody, my god" (166/156), and whoever is addressed as my god, as the one I love above all, is mortal: "you are a mortal god, that's why I write, I write you my god" in order "to save you from your own immortality" (264/244). Augustine's religious conception of the most desirable is thus radically inverted. Immortality is not the end that one desires and hopes for but the end that one fears and struggles against, since it would put an end to mortal life.

It is here instructive to consider the relation to the mother, which plays a crucial role in both Augustine's *Confessions* and Derrida's *Circumfession*.[60] Augustine's mother, Monica, is the driving force behind his conversion. As she declares shortly before her death, her goal in life has been to make sure that her son turn away from the pleasures of the world in favor of God: "There was only one reason why I wanted to stay a little longer in this life, and that was that I should see you a Catholic Christian before I died. Now God has granted me this beyond my hopes; for I see that you have despised the pleasures of this world and become his servant" (9.10). Even on her deathbed in a foreign country, Monica gives her son a lesson in true piety. When she regains consciousness after a severe fever and finds her sons grieving her imminent death, she declares: "'Here you will bury

your mother'" (9.11). While Augustine remains quiet and holds back his
tears, his brother expresses the hope that they will be able to bring her
back to her home country. Monica's reply is "a reproachful look for still
savoring of such earthly things" (9.11).

Thus, Monica imprints her religious lesson that "one must despise this
life and look forward to death" (9.11). But on her death Augustine is not
quite able to take Monica's lesson to heart. He confesses that "a great
flood of sorrow swept into my heart and would have overflowed in tears.
But my eyes obeyed the forcible dictate of my mind and seemed to drink
that fountain dry. Terrible indeed was my state as I struggled so" (9.12).
Although Augustine chastises himself "for being so feeble" (9.12), he cannot hold back the flood of sorrow and finally gives in to "weeping during the small portion of an hour for my mother" (9.12). He asks God to
forgive him for the sin of these tears and the "too carnal affection" (9.13)
that gave rise to them.

For all her piety, Monica herself displays the same carnal affection. In
retrospect Augustine reproaches her for having had "an affection that was
too much of the flesh" in her devotion to him: "For she loved having me
with her, as all mothers do, only she much more than most" (5.8). When
Augustine left her behind to go to Rome, "she wept and cried aloud and
by all this agony she showed in herself the heritage of Eve, seeking in sorrow what in sorrow she had brought forth" (5.8). It is such desire for mortal life that Augustine's conversion is meant to overcome. To receive the
embrace of the Lord, he must release himself from the bondage of women
and even from his mother, insofar as she represents the passion for birth
and the mourning of death for which the daughters of Eve are to blame
in Augustine's narrative.

Derrida's *Circumfession* stages an elaborate inversion of these motifs in
Augustine. Derrida's confession is not only pervaded by an unapologetic
sexual desire; his relation to his mother also reinforces the passion for
mortal survival that Augustine seeks to suppress and leave behind. The
point of departure for *Circumfession* is the imminent death of Derrida's
mother, Georgette, and his writing refutes every possible cure for the affliction of mourning. There is no reconciliation with death and no transcendent consolation, only a desperate and autoimmune struggle to prolong the life and preserve the memory of himself and his mother.

At the time of Derrida's writing (January 1989–April 1990), Georgette
is bound to a hospital bed in Nice, unable to recognize her son as a result

of her Alzheimer's disease. She does not die until December 5, 1991 (after *Circumfession* is published in March of the same year), but the fact that she is mortally ill and may die at any moment haunts Derrida's confession from beginning to end. Furthermore, the threat of Derrida's own death is accentuated while he writes *Circumfession*. In 1989 a viral infection paralyzes the left side of his face. The attack of the virus reinforces Derrida's fear of his own death—his internal struggle "against so many antibodies" (112/108) and his helpless exposure to "the decision deciding my life without me" (282/261). Indeed, Derrida is seized by a double fear. Either he will survive his mother and be left with the pain of mourning her death, or his mother will survive him and not even mourn his death since she no longer recognizes him.

The double bind of survival is thus reinforced. Derrida and his mother are caught in a "race against death" (112/108), where one cannot win without losing. The chance of survival is inseparable from the threat of facing the death of the beloved and being left to mourn. While such a double bind is at work in every moment of life—since there is no survival without the passing away of what has come before—it has marked the life of Derrida and his mother in a particularly poignant way. One year before Derrida was born, his brother Paul Moïse died while still an infant, and when Derrida was ten his two-year-old brother Norbert Pinhas died. Derrida is thus marked by his mother's experience of survival from the start. He is conceived as a replacement for his dead brother and is painfully aware of his mother's grief over the one whose ghost lives on in him. He perceives himself as "a precious but so vulnerable intruder, one mortal too many," who is "loved in the place of another" (51–52/52–53). When the second brother dies, Derrida is forced to watch his mother in mourning and once again function as "the sole replacement" (52/53). Derrida describes his position as that of "an excluded favorite" or more precisely as the one who is both "excluded *and* favorite" (279/258). He is excluded because he is a replacement for the dead, but for the same reason he is the favorite, since his mother's fear of losing him, too, makes her love him all the more. When he is sick, his mother weeps and worries that he will die "like her son before me, like her son after me" (117/113). Derrida in turn emphasizes that "my fear of death will only have reflected her own, I mean my death *for her* whose anxiety I perceived each time I was ill, and doubtless more subterraneously all the time" (211/196–97). Thus, when Derrida in 1989 finds himself in the inverse position—with his mother ill and him worrying that she will die—he also comes to mourn himself from the position of his mother. The response is inconsolable tears: "I weep for myself, I feel sorry for myself from my mother feeling sorry for me, I complain of my mother, I make myself unhappy, she weeps over me, who weeps over me" (128/122).

The story of Derrida's relation to his mother amounts to an affirmation of the desire that Augustine tries to negate in his relation to his mother. As we have seen, Monica wept in despair when Augustine left her for Rome, and the same attachment to the mortal beloved made Augustine cry after the death of Monica. The point for Augustine, however, is that these tears are sinful and misguided. What he claims to have learned from his mother is rather to devote himself to God and thus immunize himself from the pain of losing the mortal beloved.

In contrast, Derrida openly affirms that his mother's legacy is a desire for mortal life and an insurmountable fear of death, which Derrida describes as "the fear that has gripped me since always" (50/52). Far from leading him to God as a way out of such fear, Derrida's mother reveals to him that the name of God is subservient to the desire for mortal survival:

> I'm remembering God this morning, a quotation, something my mother said . . . the name of God as I heard it perhaps the first time, no doubt in my mother's mouth when she was praying, each time she saw me ill, no doubt dying like her son before me, like her son after me, and it was almost always otitis, the tympanum, I hear her say, "thanks to God, thank you God" when the temperature goes down, weeping in pronouncing your name, on a road in the "little wood," one summer, when a doctor had threatened me with a violent and dangerous operation, that serious operation that in those days left you with a hole behind your ear, and I'm mingling the name of God here with the origin of tears, the always puerile, weepy and pusillanimous son that I was, the adolescent who basically only liked reading writers quick to tears, Rousseau, Nietzsche, Ponge, SA, and a few others, that child whom the grown-ups amused themselves by making cry for nothing, who was always to weep over himself with the tears of his mother: "I'm sorry for myself," "I make myself unhappy," "I'm crying for myself," "I'm crying over myself"—but like another, another wept over by another weeper, I weep from my mother over the child whose substitute I am. . . . I'm more and more scared, like the scared child who up until puberty cried out "Mummy I'm scared" every night until they let him sleep on a divan near his parents, fear today of what just hap-

pened to me halfway through, just before I'm 59, with this facial paralysis or Lyme's disease. (117–20/112–15)

The prayer for survival—the prayer that he will not die, that she will not die—resounds throughout *Circumfession*. The prayer to God is not a prayer that he or she will be delivered from mortal life. On the contrary, it is a prayer that he or she will be saved from immortality by being allowed to live on as mortal. Whoever answers the prayer can in turn never master the survival that is asked for. Whoever is addressed as my God (as the one I love above all or as the one who has come to decide my fate) is mortal in itself. Every prayer is thus accompanied by tears of mourning, by hope, and by fear, which are all driven by a radically atheist desire for survival.[61]

Indeed, *Circumfession* is driven by the desire for survival even on the basic level of its composition. At the time of writing, Derrida is fifty-nine years old. *Circumfession* is accordingly divided into fifty-nine sections, described in the subtitle as "fifty-nine periods and periphrases." Each section runs as one long sentence that is only punctuated by "the comma of my breathing" (154/146) and serves to delay the termination that is marked by the final period. The termination of the sentence is not decided by Derrida but rather by the computer program in which he writes his sentence. *Circumfession* is composed according to a rule that prescribes that Derrida must stop writing his sentence as soon as the computer says that the paragraph will be too long.[62] Hence, Derrida writes in relation to a final period over which he has no command, just as he lives in relation to a death over which he has no command. The analogy between the final period and death is reinforced by the fact that Derrida writes in anticipation of his mother's death: "wondering at every moment if she will still be alive, having nonetheless stopped recognizing me, when I arrive at the end of this sentence which seems to bear the death that bears her, if she will live long enough to leave me time for all these confessions" (43/44). The writing of his life in an indefinite sentence can be interrupted not only by the computer command but also by the death of his mother or by his own death. In either case, it is "the unpredictable coming of an event" that "sculpts the writing from the outside, gives it its form and its rhythm from an incalculable interruption," so that the text depends "in its most essential inside on such a cutting, accidental and contingent outside, as though each syllable, and the very milieu of each periphrasis were preparing itself to receive a telephone call, the news of the death of one dying" (206–7/192–93).

Already on the level of syntax there is thus a drama of survival in *Circumfession*. Derrida's writing tries to imprint and prolong the rhythm of his breathing, in defiance of the death sentence that is being written at the same time. However, every breath that is supposed to postpone death, to give more time to live, is also marked by death from the start: "I posthume as I breathe" (26/28). Derrida strikingly describes himself as "the writer who is afraid of dying before the end of a long sentence, period" (51/52). His fifty-nine winding periphrases are figured as "59 periods, 59 respirations, 59 commotions, 59 four-stroke compulsions, each an Augustinian *cogito* which says *I am* on the basis of a *manduco bibo, already I am dead*, that's the origin of tears" (127–28/122). Derrida's confession, then, is driven by the desire to preserve traces of his successive selves across fifty-nine years, and he weeps in memory of what has already been eradicated. Indeed, *Circumfession* explicitly exhibits "the 59 widows or counterexemplarities of myself" (255/236–37), while making "59 prayer bands" (260/241) that inscribe the hope for survival and performing "59 conjurations without which I am nothing" (272/250–52).

Derrida maintains that he has always been inhabited by a "compulsion to overtake each second" (39/40)—to hold on to what passes away. At the time of writing *Circumfession* his desire to keep his temporal selves, to resist their disappearance, is intensified by at least three factors. First, the fact that his mother no longer recognizes him, that her memories of him are erased even before she has died, makes it all the more imperative for him to keep the traces of their life together. Second, his own illness also precipitates a greater desire to inscribe the memory of himself in opposition to the menace of death. Third, *Circumfession* is written in response to Geoffrey Bennington's *Derridabase*, which in Derrida's view erases the singularity of his life and writing. Bennington's *Derridabase* (named after the software dBase) seeks to provide access to the general system of Derrida's thought and thus make Derrida himself redundant in favor of the deconstruction that can operate without him. *Circumfession* and *Derridabase* were published together (with Derrida's text running below Bennington's text on every page) in the book *Jacques Derrida*. The book was produced according to a contract that is described in the preface and gives the framework for Derrida's text. The contract stipulated that Derrida, after having read Bennington's text, "would write something escaping the proposed systematization, surprising it" (1/3). This piece of writing is *Circumfession.*

Derrida does not argue against Bennington's reading of his work. Rather, he proceeds from the thought experiment that Bennington (mainly addressed as "G." in Derrida's text) would be in the position of an omniscient God, in command of everything "I might have written in the past but also of what I might think or write in the future, on any subject at all" (16/18). The question Derrida raises is why he would be driven to challenge and refute such a God. Thus, he alludes to Augustine's famous question concerning why he confesses to God when God already knows everything about him.[63] Augustine's answer is that we do not confess to God in order to inform Him about anything He does not know; we confess in order to repent for our sins and thus to transform ourselves rather than God. Confessing to God is what Augustine calls "making the truth" (*veritatem facere*). To make the truth is not simply to tell the truth but to make the truth come into being in oneself by turning toward God. Augustine's explicit motivation for writing his confession is to enable such making of truth in himself and in others: "Why then do I put before you in order the story of so many things? Not, certainly, so that you may come to know them through me, but to stir up my own and my reader's devotion toward you, so that we may all say: *Great is the Lord, and greatly to be praised*" (11.1).

In contrast, Derrida's motivation for writing *Circumfession* is to undermine G.'s "theologic program" by bearing witness to events that G. "will not have been able to recognize, name, foresee, produce, predict, *unpredictable things* to survive him" (31/32). The point is not to transcend temporal events but, on the contrary, to make them disrupt the theological program that tries to erase them. An omniscient God is not only unattainable but undesirable, since there would be "nothing left to say that might surprise him still and bring something about for him" (16/19). Derrida's inversion of Augustine's basic premise is brought to a head when he proposes that "Augustine still wanted, by force of love, to bring it about that in *arriving* at God, something should happen to God" (18/19). There could be no more radically atheist argument to be made against Augustine. For Augustine, the crucial point is that nothing happens to God and that such a timeless eternity is the most desirable. For Derrida, on the contrary, the eternal presence of an omniscient God is the most undesirable. If there were such a God, everything would be decided in advance, and Derrida would be "deprived of a future, no more event to come from me" (30/30).

Hence, *Circumfession* is written against "the theologic program of SA" (73/72). *SA* is both an abbreviation for Saint Augustine and for the idea of an absolute knowledge (*Savoir Absolu*) that would be able to comprehend everything and thus cancel out the unpredictable coming of time. For Derrida, such an absolute knowledge is not impossible because of our human limitations; it is impossible because it would cancel out the condition of temporality that is the possibility for anything to be. It is necessary that there be "the chance of events on which no program, no logical or textual machine will ever close, since it always in truth has operated only by not overcoming the flow of raw happenings, not even the theologic program elaborated by Geoff" (16/18). Derrida's point is not actually an objection to Bennington's formalization of the logical matrix of deconstruction, since the matrix accounts for why any purported totality is exceeded from within by events that it cannot master. Derrida himself reminds us that the matrix of deconstruction "remains by essence, by force, nonsaturable, nonsuturable" because it entails that there must be an opening to "the unanticipatable singularity of the event" (34/36).

Derrida's challenge to Bennington is thus not on the level of *saying* the truth of his work. It is rather on the level of *making* the truth in a radically atheist way. Making the truth is for Derrida not a matter of devotion to God but of a singular *testimony* that is always open to the possibility of perjury and lying.[64] Even in testifying to his singular life Derrida is liable to violate the truth of his life. He bears witness to what he has been, but he can do so only by speaking in the name of someone who is no longer and without guarantee that he remains faithful to his former self.[65] As Derrida writes in the last sentence of *Circumfession*: "you are less, you, less than yourself," and the testimony to "you alone whose life will have been so short" can only take place as "the crossing between these two phantoms of witnesses who will never come down to the same" (314–15/290–91).

Nevertheless, it is the divisibility of the instant—the fact that the moment passes away without ultimate witness—that induces the passion for testimony. To testify is to make truth by saying: "this happened to me, please believe me." Such a plea would be inconceivable without an interval that separates the past from the future. Without the disappearance of the past and the coming of the future, there would be no need to bear witness in the first place.[66] Due to the same interval of time, the one who testifies may always lie or perjure himself—since he testifies to an experience to which no one has direct access—but this possibility of deceit and distortion is not a privation of testimony. Rather, the possibility of deceit and distortion is a necessary condition for testimony. A testimony would be meaningless before an omniscient God. One testifies because something is *not* known and to prevent a finite event from being lost without a trace. It is the passion for such testimony that pervades Derrida's *Circumfession*. A recurring phrase declares that "it only happens to me" (305/282), and Derrida persistently returns to his desire to hold on to his irreplaceable life. He recounts the singular events that happen to him not only in order to "dismantle G.'s theologic program" (305/282) but also to make G. recognize and remember his unique existence.

The relation to G. as Geoffrey Bennington here crosses path with the relation to G. as Derrida's mother Georgette. At the time of writing *Circumfession*, Derrida's mother does not recognize his name and the indifference to his singular existence is also what troubles Derrida about *Derridabase*. While his mother never wanted "to read a single sentence" of his work (232–33/216), Bennington has made the choice not to quote Derrida at all in *Derridabase*. He has "decided to forget, to incinerate cold, carrying off with him, like my mother who doesn't speak my name, the uniqueness, literally, of my sentences" (28/30). Derrida is thus "fighting with him [Geoffrey Bennington] over the right to deprive me of my events" (32/33) and "to do without my body, the body of my writings" (28/30). Again, Derrida is not fighting against Bennington's reading of his work but against the obliteration of his name and unique signature. The aim of *Circumfession* is to "reinscribe" his name in order to oblige "the other, and first of all G., to recognize it, to pronounce it, no more than that, to call me finally beyond the owner's tour he has just done, forgetting me on the pretext of understanding me, and it is as if I were trying to oblige him to recognize me and come out of his amnesia of me which resembles my mother" (33/34).

It is certainly narcissistic to want one's philosophical commentator to pronounce one's name with the loving affection of a mother. But the narcissism is here the point. *Circumfession* is a reminder that Derrida writes not only to pronounce philosophical truth; he also writes to make truth and let his singular life live on in memory.[67] The desire for survival is of course already manifest in the desire to sign a text—to attach one's name to a corpus that can live on—and Derrida has often called attention to his own signature, along with the dates when he wrote a particular text. The common denominator for signatures and dates is that they preserve traces of the past for the future and thus operate in view of survival.[68] Derrida's desire to keep traces of his life in his writing is not only evident in the way he signs and dates his texts, however, but also in the way he lets autobiographical material invade his philosophical work. The most striking example before *Circumfession* is *The Post Card*, which opens with almost three hundred pages that are written as postcards to the beloved. These postal sendings (*envois*) are dated from June 3, 1977, to August 30, 1979, and record events in Derrida's life alongside philosophical arguments and polemics. It is certainly no accident that *The Post Card* is the one of his own books that Derrida quotes most frequently in *Circumfession*. These two works offer compelling testimony to the link between writing and the desire for survival, to which Derrida has often returned in the "confessional" mode of interviews. In an interview given at the time of writing *Circumfession* (April 1989), Derrida describes his "obsessive desire to save in uninterrupted inscription, in the form of memory" everything that happens to him.[69] What precipitated him to write "was first of all the adolescent dream of keeping a trace of all the voices which were traversing me," and Derrida confesses that "deep down this is still my most naïve desire" (35). He does not dream of "either a literary work, or a philosophical work" but rather of an autobiographical writing that proceeds from "the unique event whose trace one would like to keep alive" (35).

In an interview from 1983 Derrida elaborates the same notion of desire. He maintains that his desire to write is not primarily a desire to write philosophy or literature; it is rather a desire to keep everything that happens to him.[70] Derrida links this desire to "the dream of an idiomatic writing" (136/145). The question, however, is how such a dream should be understood. Derrida first describes it as the dream "of a purely idiomatic voice that would be what it is and would be in some way indivisible" (136/145–46). Such "unity remains inaccessible" so that the "dream is forever doomed to disappointment," but Derrida nevertheless holds that it is the impetus of desire: "there is the promise of unity and that is what sets desire in motion" (136/145–46). This account of desire adheres to a traditional logic, where differentiation is understood as the lack of unity. It is thus quite misleading as a deconstructive account of desire. Derrida himself goes on to say that "I do not believe desire has an essential relation to lack" (143/153), and on the basis of his own reasoning we can see why his initial account of desire is untenable.

Differentiation inhabits even the most immediate unity, and it is not a lack that prevents us from having access to the fullness we desire. Differentiation is not only a factual necessity but also the condition for everything that is thinkable and desirable. Derrida describes it as a "differential vibration" that is intrinsic to the very experience of enjoyment (*jouissance*). No enjoyment

> is thinkable that does not have the form of this pure difference; an enjoyment that would be that of a plenitude without vibration, without difference, seems to me to be both the myth of metaphysics—and death. If there is something that can be called living enjoyment or life, it can be given only in this form of painful enjoyment which is that of differential vibration. . . . This "differential vibration" is for me the only possible form of response to desire, the only form of enjoyment, and which can therefore only be an enjoyment divided within itself, that is, enjoyment for two or more, enjoyment in which the other is called; I cannot imagine a living enjoyment that is not plural, differential. This is marked in a minimal fashion by the fact that a timbre, a breath, a syllable is already a differential vibration. (137/146)

What is at stake, then, is to rethink enjoyment as essentially temporal. The temporality of enjoyment entails that it cannot repose in itself, but not because it has lost or aspires to reach a being-in-itself. On the contrary, enjoyment can only be enjoyment by not coinciding with itself. A full enjoyment would cancel itself out, since it would not give the time to enjoy anything at all. Consequently, the reason why there cannot be full enjoyment is not because there is an ontological lack of enjoyment but because the desired enjoyment is temporal. Even the most ideal enjoyment must be altered from within by the differentiation and deferral of time.[71]

For the same reason, the dream of an idiomatic writing cannot be the dream of an indivisible voice. The voice that one desires to keep is already divided within itself, just as every timbre, breath, or syllable is a differential vibration that passes away as soon as it comes to be. Moreover, it is the temporality of the singular that precipitates the dream of an idiomatic writing in the first place. If the singular were not passing away, there would be no desire to retain it in writing. The threat of losing the singular comes not only from the outside but also from within the singular itself. It is this intrinsic finitude that drives one to write:

> The suffering at the origin of writing for me is the suffering from the loss of memory, not only forgetting or amnesia, but the effacement of traces. I

would not need to write otherwise. My writing is not in the first place a philosophical writing or that of an artist, even if, in certain cases, it might look like that or take over from these other kinds of writing. My first desire is not to produce a philosophical work or a work of art: it is to preserve memory. Let's imagine a kind of machine, which by definition is an impossible one, that would be like a machine for ingramming [*engrammer*] everything that happens and such that the smallest thoughts, the smallest movements of the body, the least traces of desire, the ray of sunlight, the encounter with someone, a phrase heard in passing, are inscribed somewhere; imagine that a general electroencephalocardiosomatopsychogram were possible: at that moment my desire would be absolutely fulfilled—and finitude accepted (and by the same token denied). Thus, what pains me, over and above all the other possible kinds of suffering, is the fact that things get lost. (143–44/153)

Derrida here pushes the dream of an idiomatic writing to its logical extreme, which reveals the internal contradiction in the dream itself. The machine Derrida describes would produce an absolutely idiomatic writing: inscribing everything as it happens without loss or distortion. Such a machine is "by definition an impossible one" since the inscription must be susceptible to erasure. The machine can only record what happens by being open to events that may erase what has been inscribed. This impossibility of the machine is not a negative predicament, since nothing could happen without the possibility of loss and distortion. The temporality that makes it *impossible* for the machine to be closed in itself is what makes the machine *possible* in the first place. Without the succession of time there could be no repeatable inscriptions that retain what passes away. But the succession of time also exposes even the most ideal or the most idiomatic writing to eradication at every juncture.

We can discern the double bind of desire in Derrida's dream of the memory machine. If there were a machine that kept everything, his "desire would be absolutely fulfilled." But by the same token, it is clear that his desire cannot be absolutely fulfilled. Absolute fulfillment is not impossible because of any lack or negative limitation; it is impossible because absolute fulfillment would annul what is desired. In order to keep everything, the machine would have to cancel out the threat of anything that could come to erase what is kept and thus also cancel out the chance of anything that could come to receive what is kept. The reason why the machine cannot keep everything is not because it fails to capture the event as such but because there is no event as such. The event that Derrida wants to keep is temporal in itself and begins to erase itself as soon as it comes to be.

The dream of the memory machine stems from what Derrida calls the desire to keep (*désir de garder*). The French verb *garder* can mean both to keep something in the sense of guarding it and to keep off something in the sense of guarding against it. This double meaning answers to a double bind at the heart of the desire to keep. It is a desire to keep a finite life, but the life one wants to keep bears within itself the death one wants to keep off. The desire to keep is thus "at once an extremely protected, protective, protectionist attitude and the most threatened, exposed attitude" (146/155). It is utterly protectionist because it guards a life that may be lost, and it is utterly exposed because the death that it guards against is internal to the life that is guarded.[72] This double bind cannot even ideally be resolved, since the desire to keep cannot even in principle desire to be in complete possession of a given life. To keep something is by definition to keep it *for the future* and thus to breach any complete possession in advance. If one kept everything within oneself, in immutable possession, one would not keep anything. To keep something is rather an act directed toward the future: as a promise to guard the beloved, to affirm it anew. Accordingly, the desire to keep must expose itself to the possibility of death it tries to resist.

For the same reason, one cannot be cured from the fear of death and learn to "accept" finitude. As Derrida indicates in the passage above, *an acceptance of finitude would amount to a denial of finitude*. This is not a paradox but follows from the double bind inherent in the desire to keep a finite life. If one accepted finitude, one would accept death and thus deny the attachment to the finite life that is extinguished in death. Inversely, the desire to keep a finite life can never amount to an acceptance of death. On the contrary, the desire to keep a finite life amounts to a struggle against death. The desire to keep a finite life can never be reconciled with itself, since what it desires leads to death despite itself.[73]

It is such a drama of survival that is played out in *Circumfession*. According to Derrida, what G. "cannot let you understand or guess, and that no doubt my writings can manifest but as though illegibly" (37/39), is that the hope and fear of survival has haunted Derrida throughout his life: "I have lived in prayer, tears and the imminence at every moment of their survival, terminable survival from which 'I see myself live' translates 'I see myself die,' I see myself dead cut from you in your memories that I love and I weep like my own children at the edge of my grave" (39–40/41). Uncannily, Derrida associates these prayers and tears of survival with the sentence "I want to kill myself" (38–39/39–40). The point is not that Derrida wants to die but that the most intense affective attachment to his mortal life is produced through the fantasy where he is killed and yet survives to mourn his own death. The obsession with survival is the reason why Derrida in *Circumfession* keeps returning to "the scenes in which I see myself alone die, pray, weep" (43/44). He confesses that "the intense relation to survival that writing is, is not driven by the desire that something remain after me, since I shall not be *there* to enjoy it. . . . The point is, rather, in producing these remains and therefore the witnesses of my radical absence, to live today, here and now, this death of me" (191/178–79). The attempt to live his own death is not driven by a desire to be dead but reinforces his desire for the mortal life that will be lost. Derrida entertains the scenario of his own irrevocable death to "all the more intensely enjoy this light I am producing through the present experimentation of my possible survival, i.e. of absolute death, I tell myself this every time that I am walking in the streets of a city I love, in which I love, on whose walls I weep" (191–92/179). Hence, it is not a paradox that Derrida repeatedly confesses both to struggling for survival and to fantasizing about being killed. Derrida does not want to die, but he loves and guards his life precisely because he may lose everything in absolute death.

Moreover, even as Derrida resists absolute death, he has to kill himself—to leave behind or eradicate former selves—in order to live on. As he writes: "*I don't take my life, mais je me donne la mort*" (285/263). This formulation testifies to the autoimmunity of the desire for survival. On the one hand, to survive is to keep the memory of a past and thus to resist forgetting. On the other hand, to survive is to live on in a future that separates itself from the past and opens it to being forgotten. This division of time is inherent in every moment of survival, since one can only keep the memory of the past by leaving it as a trace for an unpredictable future. The tracing of time both constitutes and breaches the integrity of the self. I can only protect my past self by exposing it to the coming of a future self that may erase it but that also gives it the chance to live on. The immunity of survival is thus essentially autoimmune. No matter how much I try to protect the one I have been, I have to attack my own defense of the past, since the coming of the future opens my life to begin with.

We can thus understand the perhaps most striking passage in *Circumfession*. Derrida describes himself as incredibly happy and euphoric, "drunk with uninterrupted enjoyment," while at the same time being "the counterexample of myself, as constantly sad, deprived, destitute, disappointed, impatient, jealous, desperate, negative and neurotic" (268/248–49). According to Derrida, these opposed states of being "do not exclude one another for I am sure that they are as true as each other, simultaneously and from every angle" (268–70/249). If Derrida's assertion seems hyperbolic, it nevertheless testifies to the double bind we have traced across his work. Temporal finitude opens the chance for everything that is desirable *and* the threat of everything that is undesirable, so that it is the source of the most positive as well as the most negative affective responses.[74]

Hence, we can return to the experience of mourning with which I began this chapter. The double bind of temporal finitude is at work in every moment of life, but it becomes painfully poignant on the death of the beloved. To mourn the beloved is precisely to experience how the source of precious happiness always was to become the source of radical loss. Due to a constitutive finitude, every affirmation is inhabited by negation from the start, and even the most active embrace of life cannot be immune from the reactive mourning of death. In *Mémoires* Derrida describes the experience of mourning with bereaved clarity:

> Each time, we know our friend to be gone forever, irremediably absent, annulled to the point of knowing nothing or receiving nothing himself of what takes place in his memory. In this terrifying lucidity, in the light of this incinerating blaze where nothingness appears, we remain in *disbelief* itself. For never will we believe either in death or immortality; and we sustain the blaze of this terrible light through devotion, for it would be unfaithful to delude oneself into believing that the other living *in us* is living *in himself*. . . . If death comes to the other, and comes to us through the other, then the friend no longer exists except *in* us, *between* us. In himself, by himself, of himself, he is no more, nothing more. He lives only in us. But *we* are never *ourselves*, and between us, identical to us, a "self" is never in itself or identical to itself. This specular reflection never closes on itself; it does not appear *before* this *possibility* of mourning. . . . The "me" or the "us" of which we speak thus arise and are delimited in the way that they are only through this experience of the other, and of the other as other who can die, leaving in me or in us this memory of the other. This terrible solitude which is mine or ours at the death of the other is what constitutes that relationship to self which we call "me," "us,"

"between us," "subjectivity," "intersubjectivity," "memory." The possibility of death "happens," so to speak, "before" these different instances, and makes them possible. Or, more precisely, the possibility of the death of the other *as* mine or ours in-forms any relation to the other and the finitude of memory.

We weep *precisely* over what happens to us when everything is entrusted to the sole memory that is "in me" or "in us." But we must also recall, in another turn of memory, that the "within me" and the "within us" *do not* arise or appear *before* this terrible experience. Or at least not before its possibility, actually felt and inscribed in us, signed. The "within me" and the "within us" acquire their sense and their bearing only by carrying within themselves the death and the memory of the death of the other; of an other who is greater than them, greater than what they or we can bear, carry, or comprehend, since we then lament being no more than "memory," "in memory." Which is an-other way of remaining inconsolable before the finitude of memory. We know, we knew, *we remember*—before the death of the loved one—that being-in-me or being-in-us is constituted out of the possibility of mourning. We are only ourselves from the perspective of this knowledge that is older than ourselves; and this is why I say that we begin by *recalling* this to ourselves: we come to ourselves through this memory of *possible* mourning. (21, 28, 33–34/43, 49, 52–53)

Derrida's reflections on mourning always proceed from the absolute de-structibility of life; from the "incinerating blaze" and "terrible light" that reveals that the dead other is no longer and will never be again.[75] It is this radical finitude of the other that calls forth the desire to keep the memory of the other in ourselves. But the same finitude entails that the *possibility* of keeping the other is the *impossibility* of keeping the other unscathed. The death of the other reinforces this impossibility in the most agoniz-ing way, since it marks a violent alterity that cannot be overcome. All our memories of the other—all the traces we keep of him or her or it—are powerless to make the other come back to life. In Derrida's striking for-mulation, this is the reason we cry: "We weep *precisely* over what happens to us when everything is entrusted to the sole memory that is 'in me' or 'in us.'"

The origin of tears is thus the experience of mortal survival. The effects of such survival can be terrifying and unbearable. But this does not mean that the mortality of survival is a negative predicament that prevents us from having an ideal relation to the other. Rather, the mortality of sur-vival is the condition for every relation to the other. If the other could be fully incorporated in ourselves, there would be no other; and if the other were not mortal, there would be no desire to keep the other. Moreover, the self cannot even be given to itself before the possibility of mourning, as Derrida makes clear in the passage above. The *actual* mourning of the beloved testifies to a *possible* mourning that is operative in every relation from the beginning.

The experience of such mourning is the experience of radical atheism. Mourning stems from the attachment to a mortal other and from the desire to hold on to this mortal other. It is thus entirely consistent that the Christian Augustine condemns the mourning of his friend with which I began this chapter. While Augustine deplores the desire for mortal life that made his former self so vulnerable—"Mad and foolish I was at that time. I raged and sighed and wept and worried" (4.7)—his account of this desire testifies to an experience of radical atheism that remains legible in the *Confessions*. I want to conclude this chapter by quoting a remarkable example of such radical atheism. The passage in question recounts how the bereaved Augustine refused to seek comfort in God, since God could not replace his mortal friend. Augustine's official narrative would maintain that the God he refused was just a Manichean phantasm and not the true Christian God he discovered later in his life. But his writing also tells another story. The reason why Augustine refused to seek comfort in God was not because he had an inadequate understanding of God's immortality but because his desire for his mortal friend was incompatible with a desire for the immortality of God. If one wants a mortal friend *one cannot want* an immortal God for a friend, since immortality would cancel out the possibility of having mortal friends. It follows that there cannot even in principle be a transcendent consolation for the loss of mortal friends and no final cure for the affliction of mourning. Here is Augustine, living in the terrible light of irrevocable death and yet maintaining the memory of his friend in an indefinite struggle for survival:

> My heart was darkened over with sorrow, and whatever I looked at was death. My own country was a strange torment to me, my own home was a strange unhappiness. All those things which we had done and said together became, now that he was gone, sheer torture to me. . . . I had become a great riddle to myself and I used to ask my soul why it was sad and why it disquieted me so sorely. And my soul did not know what to answer. If I said "Trust in God," it very rightly did not obey me, because the man whom I had lost, my dearest friend, was more real and better than the fantastic god in whom my soul was asked to trust. (4.4)

§ 5 Autoimmunity of Democracy: Derrida and Laclau

> I never stop analyzing the phenomenon of "survival" as the structure of sur-
> viving, it is really the only thing that interests me, but precisely insofar as I do
> not believe that one lives on *post mortem*. And at bottom it is what commands
> everything—what I do, what I am, what I write, what I say.
>
> —Derrida, *A Taste for the Secret* (88)

In the preceding chapters I have demonstrated how Derrida's work offers powerful resources to think life as survival and the desire for life as a desire for survival. I have argued that every moment of life is a matter of survival because it depends on what Derrida calls the structure of the trace. The structure of the trace follows from the constitutive division of time. Given that every moment of life passes away as soon as it comes to be, it must be inscribed as a trace in order to be at all. The tracing of time enables the past to be retained and thus to resist death in a movement of survival. However, the survival of the trace that makes life possible must be left for a future that may erase it. The movement of survival protects life, but it also exposes life to death, since every trace is absolutely destructible. I have argued that such radical finitude is not a lack of being that it is desirable to overcome. Rather, the finitude of survival opens the possibility of everything we desire *and* the peril of everything we fear. The affirmation of survival is thus not a value in itself; it is rather the unconditional condition for all values. Whatever one may posit as a value, one has to affirm the time of survival, since without the time of survival the value could never live on and be posited as a value in the first place.

In this final chapter I want to elaborate how the unconditional affirmation of survival allows us to rethink the condition of political responsibility and especially the desire that drives political struggle. I will argue that the radical finitude of survival is not something that inhibits responsibility and political struggle; it is rather what gives rise to them. If we were not exposed to the coming of a future that could violate and erase us, there would be nothing to take responsibility for, since nothing could happen to us. It is thus the finitude of survival—and the affirmation of such survival—that raises the demand of responsibility. If I did not desire the survival of someone or something, there would be nothing that precipitated me to take action. Even if I sacrifice my own life for another, this act is still motivated by the desire for survival, since I would not do anything for the other if I did not desire the survival of him or her or it.

The unconditional affirmation of survival, however, does not have a moral value in itself. No given ethical stance can be derived from it. Finitude is certainly the reason for all compassion and care, but also for all fear and hatred. Without the desire for survival I would not commit myself to anything, but I would also not be hostile to anything, since I would not be threatened by anything. The affirmation of survival can thus lead me to attack the other just as well as it can lead me to defend the other.

The same undecidable force is operative in my self-relation. The unconditional affirmation of survival can lead me to attack myself just as well as it can lead me to defend myself. Even the act of suicide presupposes the affirmation of survival, for at least two reasons. First, to commit suicide, one has to affirm the time of survival, since it gives the time for any act to be executed. Second, without the affirmation of survival one would not experience any suffering that could motivate suicide, since one would not care about what happened to oneself. The affirmation of survival is not only the source of all joy in life but also the source of all suffering in life and can thus turn against itself. The unconditional affirmation of survival has therefore nothing to do with an a priori ethical stance against suicide; it is an essential possibility of the condition of survival that it can become unbearable and the response to suffering cannot be given in advance.

Moreover, the violation of integrity is inscribed in the movement of survival as such. If I survived wholly intact—unscathed by the alteration of time—I would not be surviving; I would be reposing in absolute presence. When I live on, it is always at the expense of what does *not* live on, of those past selves that are obliterated or eradicated in the movement of survival.

For the same reason, whenever I affirm the survival of another, it is at the expense of another other. It will always be necessary to make discriminatory decisions, which can never avoid being violent. To maintain the memory and life of certain others is necessarily to violate other others—whether the violence consists in ignoring, subordinating, or destroying those others. The affirmation of survival that precipitates responsibility is thus inherently violent. Indeed, the value of survival is essentially violent and autoimmune, since one can protect the value of survival only by compromising it. To defend the survival of something is necessarily to attack the survival of something else.

The necessity of discrimination, of struggling for the survival of some at the expense of others, is what Derrida calls the "law of finitude, law of decision and responsibility for finite existences, the only living-mortals for whom a decision, a choice, a responsibility has meaning and a meaning that will have to pass through the ordeal of the undecidable."[1] The law of finitude is not something that one can accept or refuse, since it precedes every decision and exceeds all mastery. There can be no taking of responsibility and no making of decisions without the temporal finitude of survival, which always entails a violent discrimination. This does not mean, however, that Derrida tries to *justify* discrimination. Discriminatory decisions are necessary, but they cannot be grounded or justified as such. If a final justification were possible, there would be an origin or end to justice, which is precisely what Derrida contests. Furthermore, deconstructive reason demonstrates that a final justification is neither thinkable nor desirable. If a decision was justified as such, it would abolish the undecidable time of justice, since the decision could not be criticized or questioned. There would be nothing to come in relation to the decision, which would be unquestionably just, and by the same token there would be no justice.

The reason why there cannot be absolute justice is thus not because it is an unattainable Idea, but because the struggle for justice is not oriented toward absolute justice in the first place. Rather, the struggle for justice is always a struggle for survival, which makes it essentially dependent on the negative infinity of time. In the "Exordium" to *Specters of Marx*, Derrida outlines such an argument. His formulation of the matter is admittedly oblique, but given the framework I have established we can unpack the implications:

> No justice . . . seems possible or thinkable without the principle of some *responsibility*, beyond all living present, within that which disjoins the living present, before the ghosts of those who are not yet born or who are already dead, be they victims of wars, of political or other kinds of violence, nationalist, racist, colonialist, sexist, or other kinds of exterminations, victims of the oppressions of capitalist imperialism or any of the forms of totalitarianism.

Without this *non-contemporaneity with itself of the living present*, without that which secretly unhinges it, without this responsibility and this respect for justice concerning those who *are not there*, those who are no longer or who are not yet *present and living*, what sense would there be to ask the question "where?" "where tomorrow?" "whither?"

This question *comes*, if it comes, it questions with regard to what will come in the future-to-come. Turned toward the future, going toward it, it also comes from the future, it proceeds *from* [*provient* de] the future. It must therefore exceed any presence as presence to itself. At least it has to make this presence possible only on the basis of the movement of some disjointing, disjunction, or disproportion: in the inadequation to itself. Now, if this question, from the moment it comes to us, can clearly come only from the future (whither? where will we go tomorrow? where, for example, is Marxism going? where are we going with it?), what stands *in front of* it must also precede it like its origin: *before* it. Even if the future is its provenance, it must be, like any provenance, absolutely and irreversibly past. "Experience" of the past as to come, the one and the other absolutely absolute, beyond all modification of any present whatever. If it is possible, and if we must take it seriously, the possibility of the question, which is perhaps no longer a question and which we are calling here *justice*, must carry beyond *present* life, life as *my* life or *our* life. *In general*. For it will be the same thing for the "my life" or "our life" tomorrow, that is, for the life of others, as it was yesterday for other others: *beyond therefore the living present in general*. . . .

. . . This axiom may be shocking to some. And one does not have to wait for the objection: To whom, finally, would an obligation of justice ever entail a commitment, one will say, and even be it beyond law and beyond the norm, to whom and to what if not to the life of a living being? Is there ever justice, commitment of justice, or responsibility in general which has to answer for itself (for the living self) before anything other, in the last resort, than the life of a living being, whether one means by that natural life or the life of the spirit? Indeed. The objection seems irrefutable. But the irrefutable itself supposes that this justice carries life beyond present life . . . not toward death but toward a *living-on* [*sur-vie*], namely, a trace of which life and death would themselves be but traces and traces of traces, a survival whose possibility in advance comes to disjoin or dis-adjust the identity to itself of the living present. (xix–xx/15–18)

This passage derives responsibility and the concern for justice from the negative infinity of time. In the positive infinity of eternity there would be no question of justice, since everything would be given in an absolute presence that annuls the past and the future. There would be nothing to take responsibility for, since nothing can have happened and nothing can come to happen in a positive infinity. Moreover, there would be no others to take responsibility for or to demand responsibility from, since the absolute here and now of a positive infinity annuls the spatial exteriority of others.

Responsibility and justice, then, require the negative infinity of finitude. Even if I only take responsibility for myself, this act of responsibility presupposes that I am not fully present to myself. If I were fully present to myself, there would be no past and no future for which I could be held responsible. For the same reason, there can be no commitment to justice without the movement of survival that "in advance comes to disjoin or dis-adjust the identity to itself of the living present." Even my most immediate commitment to myself or to a living being right in front of me presupposes that we are already marked by temporal finitude. If we were not marked by temporal finitude, if we were immutable, nothing could happen to cause the concern for and the commitment to justice.

Consequently, the present must be divided within itself—it must be disjoined between the past and the future—for there to be responsibility and justice. The deepest reason for this division is the constitution of time, which is here epitomized by what Derrida calls the "absolute past" and the "absolute future." The past is absolute because it has *never* been present, and the future is absolute because it will *never* be present. The absolute past and the absolute future are thus by no means mythic instances or utopian ideas. On the contrary, they designate that the movement of temporalization has always been and will always be the condition for experience and life in general. That is why Derrida glosses *experience* as the experience of an absolute past and an absolute future, namely, of an originary division between being no longer and being not yet.

When Derrida speaks of "infinite responsibility" or "infinite justice," he is not referring to an ideal beyond the limitations of finite responsibility or finite justice. On the contrary, the terms in question designate that responsibility and justice always take place in relation to an infinite finitude of others. I will here focus on the infinite finitude of justice, since I addressed the parallel example of infinite responsibility in Chapter 3. The infinite finitude of justice entails that justice never can be consummated; it is always open to innumerable times past and to come. As Derrida writes in the passage above, justice can in principle be demanded for all "those who are not yet born or who are already dead, be they victims of wars, of political or other kinds of violence, nationalist, racist, colonialist, sexist, or other kinds of exterminations, victims of the oppressions of capitalist imperialism or any of the forms of totalitarianism." The point is not that there ought to be an ideal justice that can encompass and do justice to all these others. Such a totalizing justice would annul the victims and everything else, since it would annul the irreversible past and the unpredictable future. Derrida's argument is rather that any given decision or definition of justice can be called into question, since it is preceded and exceeded by innumerable finite others that it excludes. Accordingly, Derrida connects his use of the term *justice* to a principally endless questioning by defining "the possibility of the question" as what "we are calling here *justice*." If justice is inseparable from *the coming*, it is not because anything or anyone will come and ordain a final justice. On the contrary, it is the possibility of the question that always comes, the possibility of yet another question that always opens anew and "questions with regard to what will come in the future-to-come. Turned toward the future, going toward it, it also comes from the future, it proceeds *from* the future. It must therefore exceed any presence as presence to itself."

What I want to emphasize is that the deconstructive analysis of justice makes it possible to reconceptualize the desire for justice. The desire for justice is traditionally derived from a *lack* of absolute justice. Absolute justice is thus figured as an Idea that remains out of reach but that propels the desire for justice. Such an Idea of absolute justice is necessarily the Idea of a *positive infinity* that would be sealed against corruption, alteration, and error. In contrast, the deconstructive idea of justice is the idea of the *negative infinity* of time, which will always disjoin the present from itself and expose it to the unpredictable coming of other circumstances.[2] The coming of time is the possibility of justice, since it opens the chance to challenge laws, transform rights, and question decisions. The concomitant impossibility of absolute justice is not a lack of justice, since it does not testify to the absence of an ideal justice. Derrida describes the negative infinity of justice as an *infinite perfectibility*, which is the same as an *infinite corruptibility* and undercuts the regulative Idea of final perfection. The impossibility of such an absolute state is not a privation but the possibility of change at any juncture, for better and for worse.[3]

Every call for justice must affirm the coming of time, which opens the chance of justice and the threat of injustice in the same stroke. The desire for justice has thus *never* been a desire for absolute justice. The desire for justice is always a desire for the survival of finite singularities, which violates the survival of other finite singularities. Every ideal of justice is therefore inscribed in what Derrida calls an "economy of violence." To be sure, struggles for justice are often perpetrated in the name of absolute justice, but these claims can always be shown to be incoherent and hypocritical. There is no call for justice that does not call for the exclusion of others, which means that every call for justice can be challenged and criticized. The point of this argument is not to discredit calls for justice but to recognize that these calls are always already inscribed in an economy of violence.

There cannot be any equilibrium in the economy of violence. Violence is absolutely irreducible, but the amount of violence is never stable. If the amount of violence was stable, there would be no reason to struggle for justice, since nothing could ever be changed. The struggle for justice is thus not a struggle for peace, but a struggle for "lesser violence." As I argued in Chapter 3, all decisions made in the name of justice are made in view of what is judged to be the lesser violence. If there is always an economy of violence, decisions of justice cannot be a matter of choosing what is nonviolent. To justify something is rather to contend that it is less violent than something else. It is important to note, however, that there can be no given measure for the calculation of the lesser violence. The act of calculation is itself subjected to a temporality that cannot finally be calculated. Consequently, there can be no guarantee that a struggle for "lesser violence" is legitimate, and it may always exercise more rather than less violence.

The first commentator to elaborate the notion of "lesser violence" was Richard Beardsworth in his valuable book *Derrida and the Political*. Beardsworth's understanding of lesser violence is considerably different from mine, however, since he holds that deconstructive thinking makes us better at judging what is less violent. Beardsworth rightly observes that "it is in fact only through the experience of the economy of violence that judgments of lesser violence can be made" (24), but he wants to distinguish between political judgments that manage to "endure" the economy of violence and those that do not. Thus, Beardsworth claims that "political judgments which recognize difference according to the lesser violence are those that have endured this experience" (xvi–xvii). This argument is untenable, since *all* judgments must endure the experience of a violent economy, and there can be no given criteria for how to deal with this experience. On the contrary, the experience of a violent economy precipitates judgments of greater violence just as well as judgments of lesser violence for the simple reason that it precipitates *all* judgments. Furthermore, the logic of deconstruction spells out that one cannot finally learn how to negotiate the economy of violence and make less violent judgments. Deconstructive thinking enables a new understanding of the inherent contradictions and the mortal desire that has haunted politics from the beginning. But it does not necessarily make us better at dealing with the political problems that constantly emerge as a result of these inherent contradictions and this mortal desire.[4]

We can thus begin to articulate the link between deconstruction and what Derrida calls democracy to come (*démocratie à venir*). Democracy to come does not designate a utopian hope for a democracy that will come one day and bring about a just society. It is not an ideal, and it cannot serve to *justify* any political commitment. If the commitment to democracy was justified by deconstruction, we would no longer have to make any decision or take any responsibility for this commitment, since we would know that it was justified. Rather, all aspects of democracy require political negotiations that cannot be grounded in deconstruction or anything else. There is no given concept, constitution, or regime of democracy, which means that a commitment to "democracy" cannot be justified in itself. To look for such justification in Derrida's work is to misunderstand the level on which his analyses operate. Derrida does not offer solutions to political problems or normative guidelines for how to approach them. On the contrary, he argues that solutions and norms cannot be justified once and for all, since they are instituted in relation to the undecidable coming of time that precedes and exceeds them. Far from absolving us from politics, it is the undecidable coming of time that makes politics necessary in the first place, since it precipitates the negotiation of unpredictable events. The undecidable coming of time makes it *possible* to justify decisions but at the same time makes it *impossible* for any justifications to be final or sheltered from critique.

If Derrida privileges the concept of democracy, it is not because he thinks it can guarantee a good or just society but because the concept of democracy more evidently than other concepts takes into account the undecidable future. Strictly speaking, one cannot posit an absolute democracy even as a theoretical fiction. The very concept of democracy inscribes the relentless coming of other circumstances that one will have to negotiate. The coming of the future presupposes an intrinsic alteration that gives the space and time for change in any circumstance. Such spacing opens the chance for critique but simultaneously opens the risk that any critique will have been inadequate and thus needs to be scrutinized in its turn. Because the ever-possible revision is inscribed in the concept of democracy, it undermines the idea of a final goal for the work of politics and marks the undecidable future as a constitutive condition. The undecidable future makes it possible to enforce laws and rights but at the same time makes it impossible to eliminate incalculable forces that may break the laws or transform the rights.

Consequently, Derrida's analysis of democracy does not propose either a theory or a practice of democracy that can be safely distinguished from the nondemocratic. Rather, he claims that democracy is autoimmune on every level of its constitution:

> There is no absolute paradigm, whether constitutive or constitutional, no absolutely intelligible idea, no *eidos*, no *idea* of democracy. And so, in the final analysis, no democratic ideal. For, even if there were one, and wherever there would be one, this 'there is' would remain aporetic, under a double or autoimmune constraint.[5]

To consolidate this claim, it is instructive to begin with the Greek root of the word *democracy*. It indicates that democracy is a regime in which the people (*dēmos*) have the power (*kratos*) to govern themselves. From this basic definition of democracy ensues the problem regarding the relation between freedom and equality, which haunts the entire democratic tradition and is central to Derrida's argument in *Rogues*. If the people have the power to govern themselves, it follows that they are free to do whatever they want. But this freedom is immediately restricted within itself, since there is always more than one member of the people, which forces each one to act in relation to others that limit his or her freedom. The freedom of the people is thus unthinkable without equality, since the plurality of people only can constitute themselves as an entity if everyone is equally free.

The clearest example is the system of democratic voting, where each member of the people has the freedom to choose by submitting a vote that is equally counted. As is well known, such democratic sharing of power is compromised by social and economic forces that give some a greater freedom to set the agenda or maintain their position and thus introduce inequality among the members of the people. Derrida, however, does not primarily address these "exterior" threats to freedom and equality. Rather, he aims at showing that the relation between freedom and equality necessarily is an autoimmune relation, which means that the threats to freedom and equality are "interior" to the concepts themselves.

Derrida's first move is to align equality with the calculable and freedom with the incalculable. The two principles have often been recognized as conflicting or even as mutually exclusive. Equality reduces each member of the people to a calculable unit that is homogeneous with other units, whereas freedom marks that each member of the people has an incalculable power to act that makes him or her heterogeneous to the others. Derrida does not deny that the two principles are contradictory, but he emphasizes that the contradiction is irresolvable and constitutive of democracy. Freedom is compromised by equality, and equality is compromised by freedom, but without such compromise there can be no democracy.

Thus, Derrida argues that the calculation of equality is not something that befalls an ideal democratic freedom. Without the measure of equality there would be no concept of everyone's immeasurable freedom, since there would be no "chance to neutralize all sorts of differences of force, of properties (natural and otherwise) and hegemonies, so as to gain access precisely to the *whoever* or the *no matter who* of singularity in its very immeasurability" (52/80). However, the calculation of equality that gives the chance of democratic freedom simultaneously poses a threat to democratic freedom. Derrida describes the problem as follows:

> By effacing the difference of singularity through calculation, by no longer counting on it, measure risks putting an end to singularity itself, to its quality or its nonquantifiable intensity. And yet the concept of measurable equality is not opposed to the immeasurable. . . .
>
> . . . This "technical measure of equality" is not some accident or fall, some mishap or misfortune for the incalculable or the incommensurable (and I insist here on "technique" because the politico-juridico-ethical, as we understand it, presupposes such a calculating technique, a seriality or circularity that is not simply secondary or auxiliary). This technique is also the chance for the incommensurable; *it is what gives access to it.* A chance given by the political, the juridical, the ethical and their invention, wherever it takes place.
>
> . . . This chance is always given as an autoimmune threat. For calculating technique obviously destroys or neutralizes the incommensurable singularity to which it gives effective access. (52–53/80)

The concept of democratic freedom is thus autoimmune, since the equality that protects it also attacks it from within and compromises its integrity. Inversely, the same autoimmunity is at work in the concept of democratic equality. If everyone is equally free, it follows that freedom is intrinsic to equality and threatens it from within.[6] The calculation of equality is always the calculation of an incalculable freedom that opens the possibility of inequality.

Hence, already at the root of democracy we find a violent economy between two principles that cannot be reconciled but are indispensable to one another. This problem cannot be resolved through a "happy medium" between the two principles. A happy medium requires that one can establish *the right measure*. It thus requires that freedom and equality are calculable, which is impossible since both freedom and equality entail the incalculable even as they lend themselves to calculation. The compromise between freedom and equality can therefore never be a final peace agreement but is maintained in a more or less violent economy that does not have a given measure.[7]

We can here return to the example of the Algerian elections with which I began the first chapter of this book. The Algerian example clearly reinforces the autoimmunity of democratic freedom and equality. A numerical majority (calculated according to the principle of equality) may always use its freedom to elect a government that attacks the same freedom and equality. Democracy can only protect itself from such a threat by in turn attacking itself, which is what happened in Algeria when the elections were suspended. The state that defended democracy was at the same time assaulting the democratic freedom to vote and the democratic right to equality before the law.

The Algerian elections may appear to be an extreme example, but for Derrida only a difference of degree separates them from so-called normal democratic practice. Derrida pursues this point by arguing that democracy is always a process of *renvoi*, in which the violence of exclusion necessarily is operative. The French verb *renvoyer* has both spatial connotations (to dismiss, to send off) and temporal connotations (to postpone, to put off). These connotations come together in the sense of *renvoi* as a referral or deferral that requires the general condition of spacing. Following Derrida's schema in *Rogues*, we can begin by distinguishing between the spatial and the temporal *renvoi* of democracy, even though they are ultimately inseparable, since becoming-space is inherent in time and becoming-time is inherent in space.

The spatial *renvoi* of democracy operates by dismissing those who are judged to be foreign to democracy or by sending off those who are perceived to threaten it from within. This happened in Algeria when the supposed enemies of democracy were excluded from the democratic process, but the same movement of discrimination is at work to a greater or lesser degree in every democracy. The power of the people can only constitute itself by drawing a border that defines who does and who does not belong to "the people." The border that defines the people as white men, while excluding women and other races, has begun to be perforated, but this does not prevent other borders from being operative. The most apparent ones are perhaps the national borders that restrict democratic rights to citizenship, which is a problem to which Derrida has devoted much attention. The problem concerning the restriction of democracy is in principle infinite, however, since there is no natural or justified limit to the equality prescribed by democracy. As Derrida underscores, one can demand that democratic equality be extended not only to all human beings but also "to all nonhuman living beings" and furthermore "to all the nonliving, to their memory, spectral or otherwise, to their to-come or to their indifference with regard to what we think we can identify, in an always precipitous, dogmatic, and obscure way, as the life or the living present of living [*la vivance*] in general" (53/81). The violent exclusion of democracy is thus not only at work in relation to other "humans assumed to be like me" (53/81) but also in relation to "the dead, to animals, to trees and rocks" (54/82). Derrida is not advocating that we should include all these others in democracy and abandon hierarchies. Rather, he aims to show that democracy must violate the principle of equality that it defends. There can be no democracy without the institution of discriminating criteria, but by the same token the given limits of democracy will always be contestable by other calls for democratic equality, for better and for worse.

The temporal *renvoi* of democracy operates by postponing democracy in the name of democracy itself. The Algerian elections are once again a clear example, since the elections were put off under the pretext of protecting democracy. Such deferral of democracy is at work to a greater or lesser degree in every moment of democracy. Democracy can never be absolutely present, since it must defer to the result of past elections or to the outcome of future elections. However, it is misleading to say that democracy is "always deferred" insofar as this implies that there is a democracy (or an Idea of democracy) that remains out of reach. The point is not that democracy is deferred but that democracy *is* deferral and cannot overcome the movement of deferral without ceasing to be democracy.

The deferral of democracy is both temporal (deferring to past or future elections) and spatial (deferring to other members of democracy). This deferral is never a simple respect for democratic freedom and equality; it is also a violation of these principles. As Derrida points out, the spatial *renvoi* of democracy signifies both an invitation to the other ("the sending off or referral *to* the other, respect for the foreigner or for the alterity of the other") and a deportation of the other ("a sending off *of* the other through exclusion").[8] Similarly, the temporal *renvoi* of democracy is both what gives the chance for democratic processes and what threatens to eliminate those whose democratic needs cannot wait.

The violent spacing of *renvoi* is "an autoimmune necessity" (36/61) that is inscribed in the idea of democracy as such. Democracy is necessarily autoimmune, since it must attack the principles of freedom and equality that it defends. The principle of democratic freedom grants the right to criticize democracy in the most damaging ways and to mobilize forces that overturn democracy. To protect itself from these threats, democracy must restrict its own principle of freedom, but by the same token it compromises itself. There is no happy medium that could guide us with regard to *how much* democracy should restrict the principle of freedom. To attack democracy with greater force (by further restricting the principle of freedom) may be to defend democracy with greater force (by preventing it from further corruption). Inversely, what is presented as a greater defense of democracy may be a greater attack on democracy.

The same autoimmune undecidability haunts the principle of democratic equality. The violation of equality is at work not only in relation to those that democracy excludes from without but also *within* a given democracy, where the calculation of the *dēmos* is never a neutral operation. The majority that rules over a minority is calculated according to certain criteria that exclude other criteria. There is thus always an economy of violence in the calculation of democratic equality, but how it should be negotiated can never be given in advance or decided on the basis of a priori criteria. As Derrida maintains, one electoral law is "at the same time more and less democratic than another" since "one will never actually be able to 'prove' that there is more democracy in granting or in refusing the right to vote to immigrants . . . nor that there is more or less democracy in a straight majority vote as opposed to proportional voting; both forms of voting are democratic, and yet both also protect their democratic character through exclusion, through some *renvoi*" (36/61).

The democratic *renvoi* sends us back to the definition of *différance* as the becoming-space of time and the becoming-time of space. Given that such spacing is the condition for life in general, democracy cannot simply be *opposed* to other regimes and other political ideals. Because of the trace structure of time, the problem of democracy is at work in every moment and every political regime. As Derrida puts it in *Rogues*: "there is always some trace of democracy; indeed every trace is a trace of democracy" (39/64).[9] The exercise of power cannot be an act of indivisible sovereignty; it has to remain more or less open to alteration and critique. Even the most despotic monarch or totalitarian dictator is engaged in a "democratic" relation, since he must negotiate with past and future selves that may overturn his rule.

For the same reason, there can be no essential demarcation of democracy from dictatorship; such demarcation is always a matter of precarious negotiations and more or less violent decisions. The conceptual borders that serve to distinguish one regime as "democratic" in contradistinction to another are essentially permeable and can always be manipulated for the sake of other interests, since democracy is autoimmune and cannot be protected in itself. This may seem disconcerting, but without autoimmunity there can be no democracy. The possibility of attacking itself is inscribed in democracy itself, since the democratic site of power is inherently mutable and open to whoever or whatever may come to take power. Moreover, without the threat of democracy becoming totalitarian (and without the chance of the totalitarian becoming democratic) there would be no reason to engage in the struggle for democracy.

Derrida's thinking of the political can thus be described in accordance with the logic of *essential corruptibility*. This logic seeks to account for why the integrity of every "pure" concept necessarily is compromised by what is "other" than itself and thus liable to corruption. I will here focus on how Derrida pursues the logic of essential corruptibility with regard to the political, but it is instructive to first consider the logic in more general terms. In his afterword to *Limited Inc* Derrida makes the following remark concerning the demands of conceptual logic:

Every concept that lays claim to any rigor whatsoever implies the alternative of "all or nothing." Even if in "reality" or in "experience" everyone believes he knows that there is never "all or nothing," a concept determines itself only according to "all or nothing." Even the concept of "difference of degree," the concept of relativity is, qua concept, determined according to the logic of all or nothing, of yes or no: differences of degree *or* nondifference of degree. It is impossible or illegitimate to form a *philosophical concept* outside this logic of all or nothing. . . . When a concept is to be treated as a concept I believe that one has to accept the logic of all or nothing. I always try to do this and I believe that it always has to be done, at any rate, in a theoretical-philosophical discussion of concepts or of things conceptualizable. Whenever one feels obliged to stop doing this (as happens to me when I speak of *différance*, of mark, of supplement, of iterability and of all they entail), it *is better* to make explicit in the most conceptual, rigorous, formalizing, and pedagogical manner possible the reasons one has for doing so, for thus changing the rules and the context of discourse. (116–17/211–12)

The deconstruction of conceptual logic that Derrida describes can be formalized as a three-step operation, which recurs in different variations in his readings of other philosophers. First, Derrida locates a conceptual distinction that serves as the ground for the given discourse with which he is engaged. Following the logic of all or nothing, Derrida reinforces that the distinction in question must be absolutely pure and that the entire edifice for the discourse otherwise would crumble. Second, Derrida demonstrates that the distinction in question cannot be absolutely pure—not for empirical reasons but due to an essential necessity of contamination—so that the construction of the edifice already implied its own ruin. Third, Derrida argues that this principle of ruin is not simply negative or destructive and does not authorize any imprecision in the treatment of concepts. Rather, it calls for a new conceptual logic, which must be developed "in the most conceptual, rigorous, formalizing, and pedagogical manner."

With regard to the concept of the political, it is helpful to consider Derrida's reading of Carl Schmitt in *Politics of Friendship*. In accordance with the schema delineated above, Derrida's reading can be seen to follow three steps. First, Derrida focuses on Schmitt's ambition to provide a *pure* concept of the political. Although Derrida is highly critical of Schmitt—whose theses, according to Derrida, are "as ragingly conservative in their political content as they are reactive and traditionalist in their philosophical logic" (83–84/101–2)—Derrida takes great interest in Schmitt because he "offers a *pure and rigorous* conceptual theory of the political, of the specific region of that which is properly and without polemical rhetoric called the 'political,' the politicity of the political" (117/137; my emphasis). Second, Derrida reads this pure concept of the political against itself in order to formalize what he calls "a principle of ruin or spectrality" (130/153) at the core of Schmitt's discourse on the political. Third, the logic of decision that informs this deconstruction leads to a new logic of the political, which can be described in terms of essential corruptibility.

Now, Schmitt builds his theory of the political on the distinction between friend and enemy. The purity of this distinction is for Schmitt what allows the political to have a proper domain that in principle is independent from other domains.[10] Thus, Schmitt argues that the political identification of friend and enemy is not de jure tied to moral, aesthetic, or economic values, even though the political de facto is bound up with these domains. For example, a proper political identification of the enemy should not rely on the idea that the enemy is evil or worthy of hatred. Neither should it rely on racial, ethnic, or religious criteria. Such sentiments and valuations belong to the "private" sphere, which should not contaminate the "public" sphere of the political.

The opposition between private and public organizes not only Schmitt's conceptual moves but also his historical schema. In the epoch that is coming to an end with the decline of the sovereign state system, the enemy was (according to Schmitt) respected as a "clean" enemy, namely, as a "public enemy" with recognized rights, including the right to extinguish oneself in battle. As Schmitt argues in his 1963 preface to *The Concept of the Political*, this proper concept of the enemy has been perverted into the concept of the enemy as a despised "foe" that has to be eliminated at all costs.[11] The transition from the proper concept of the enemy to the perverted concept of the foe answers to the transition from "absolute war"—which heeds the distinctions between soldiers and civilians, respected enemies and criminalized foes—to "total war" that does not heed these distinctions.

The coming to an end of these "clear distinctions" is what Schmitt deplores as "depoliticization," in contrast to the proper political relation that has been lost. As Derrida emphasizes, Schmitt's concept of the proper political relation hinges on the possibility that the enemy can be *identified as such*. When it is not possible to identify the enemy as such—when one cannot definitely decide *what* "enemy" means or *who* the enemy is—the

political field loses its specificity and autonomy. In short, it is "depoliti-
cized." Derrida's argument against Schmitt is that such depoliticization
does not supervene on, and cannot be placed in opposition to, a proper
politics or politicization. Rather, the conceptual purity that Schmitt's
theory requires is *in principle* impossible. As Derrida writes, Schmitt's essential distinctions between friend and enemy are "a priori doomed to
failure" (*Politics of Friendship*, 116/135) since "every time, a concept bears
the phantom of the other. The enemy the friend, the friend the enemy"
(ibid., 72/92).

Derrida pursues his argument on two levels in *Politics of Friendship*.
On one level he takes issue with Schmitt's historical and philological assumptions concerning what the concept of "enemy" has signified in the
history of Western thought from the Greeks onward. While this debate
is certainly interesting, I will not address it here. Instead, I will focus
on the other level of Derrida's argument, where he takes issue with the
conceptual logic that informs Schmitt's articulation of the friend-enemy
distinction.

As Schmitt makes clear, there are no external, objective criteria that
can determine who is the enemy. Rather, the enemy is an enemy because he or she poses an "existential" threat to the state. Only such an
existential threat—what Schmitt calls "the extreme case" or "the state
of exception"—can justify the attack on another people, and justify the
demand on one's own citizens to sacrifice their lives in combating the
enemy. The problem, then, is how to decide when there is an existential threat that can legitimate an attack. According to Schmitt, there is a
concrete knowledge that grounds such decisions: "the actual participants
can correctly recognize, understand, and judge the concrete situation and
settle the extreme case of conflict. Each participant is in a position to
judge whether the adversary intends to negate his opponent's way of life
and therefore must be repulsed or fought in order to preserve one's own
form of existence."[12] Following the same logic, Schmitt argues that there
must be an ultimate instance in the state—"the sovereign"—who decides
when there is a state of exception. This sovereign decision should not be
possible to question; its power should be unconditional and indivisible.
As Schmitt underscores in *Political Theology*, the decision of the sovereign
"frees itself from all normative ties and becomes in the true sense abso-

lute" (12). This is necessary for the sovereign to be the one who "definitely decides" (13) beyond the division of power.

To be sure, Schmitt has good reasons to insist on the indivisible sovereignty of the political decision. If the decision is not sovereign, it is dependent on something other than itself and thus always open to corruption. For the same reason, if the one who makes the decision can always be questioned—namely, if it is *always possible* that he can be wrong—there is nothing that can safeguard Schmitt's essential distinctions. For example, the attack on a purported enemy can always turn out to be an attack on someone who did not in fact threaten the state, and the allegedly "political" killing can never be safely distinguished from a criminal murder. Indeed, the very possibility of questioning the decision of the sovereign divides its power in advance. Schmitt insists that to prevent such consequences, the sovereign must be the one who "definitely" decides on the state of exception.

In contrast, Derrida argues that the structure of decision undercuts the possibility of a "definitive" decision, as well as the possibility of an indivisible sovereignty. If the sovereign is to be authoritative in the sense that Schmitt's theory requires, he has to know who his enemy is and who he himself is in relation to his enemy. But if there were such knowledge, there would be no decision concerning these issues. Rather, the positions of friend and enemy would already be determined by a program and would not require any decision. Inversely, if decisions are necessary, it is because there is no given knowledge, not even the "concrete knowledge" or "concrete identification" of the enemy to which Schmitt appeals. While decisions are necessary, they cannot be grounded in the indivisible sovereignty that is required for a "proper" political decision in Schmitt's sense. Rather, Derrida is "confirming—but not by way of deploring the fact, as Schmitt does—an essential and necessary depoliticization" (104/127).

It is important to understand that Derrida's insistence on a necessary depoliticization does not entail any relativism or nihilism with regard to the political. On the contrary, Derrida argues that what Schmitt denounces as depoliticization—namely, the absence of an autonomous domain for the political—answers to a "hyperpoliticization" (133/157) that marks the political from its beginning. In other words, there has *never* been an autonomous domain for the political. The impossibility of a definitive delimitation of the political is both the reason why there is politics in the first place and why politics has no end. The delimitation of the political is itself a political act that is inherently unstable and always can be called into question. While Schmitt wants to short-circuit the possibility of such questioning with reference to a sovereign decision, Derrida argues that the possibility of the political stems from the impossibility of a sovereign decision. As Derrida writes, "the antithesis of the political" (in Schmitt's sense) "dwells within, and *politicizes*, the political" (138/160; my emphasis).

It is here instructive to compare Derrida's distinction between law and justice with Schmitt's distinction between norm and decision, which is clearly outlined in the first two chapters of *Political Theology*. Schmitt forcefully argues that the legal order ultimately rests on a decision and not on a norm. The norm is the instituted laws and regulations, whereas the decision is the application of the law to a particular case. Similarly, Derrida distinguishes between law as the given rules and justice as the making of decisions that relates these rules to singular cases. There is thus a clear structural parallel between Schmitt's and Derrida's respective accounts. For both thinkers the decision is external to the law, but at the same time its indispensable condition of possibility, its very execution, which can never be reduced to what is given in the law itself. The pivotal difference between Schmitt and Derrida, however, concerns the "exceptional" status of the decision. For Schmitt the decision is exceptional because it is an act of indivisible sovereignty that suspends the law and puts an end to debate. For Derrida, on the contrary, the sovereign decision is impossible as such; it can never be *in itself* but is haunted by a structural opening to the undecidable future.

Consequently, Derrida refers to "the unstable and unlocatable border between law and justice" as the border "between the political and the ultrapolitical" (*Rogues*, 39/63). The ultrapolitical notion of justice answers to what Derrida calls the hyperpolitical in his reading of Schmitt. Derrida's notion of justice spells out that decisions must be made from time to time, without any final assurance concerning what is just or unjust. This notion of justice is ultrapolitical because it breaches the integrity of any political border and opens it to transformation. The precarious relation between law and justice is therefore at the heart of political struggle. The force of any call for justice resides in its ability to demonstrate that the legal system of laws and rights, while laying claim to a solid foundation in the community, is in fact ungrounded and violently exclusive. The deconstructibility of law is thus what enables the demands for a justice beyond the prevalent structures of power. But for the same reason the demands for justice cannot be oriented toward a society that would finally be liberated from violence and antagonistic interests. Those who succeed with their reforms or revolutions must in turn enforce a legal system that is more or less discriminating and open to new attacks or conflicting demands.[13]

The violent economy of law and justice is central for Derrida's articulation of the problem of sovereignty. In accordance with Derrida's hyperpolitical logic, the principle of sovereignty cannot simply be stigmatized as "bad." On the contrary, the temporality of responsibility entails that it is sometimes better to be *for* the principle of sovereignty rather than *against* the principle of sovereignty (and vice versa). As Derrida puts it: "according to the situations, I am an antisovereignist *or* a sovereignist—and I vindicate the right to be antisovereignist at certain times and a sovereignist at others."[14] Derrida's logic does not provide a rule for how to make these decisions concerning sovereignty (for example, it does not dictate that it is better to be *less* sovereign rather than *more* sovereign), but it does account for *why* the principle of sovereignty must remain undecidable.

On the one hand, Derrida emphasizes that the principle of sovereignty cannot unilaterally be denounced or done away with. Without the right to sovereignty, there would be nothing to protect the integrity of the state, the individual, or any other legal subject. On the other hand, sovereignty has never been possible as such, since it cannot be indivisible and given in itself.[15] The sovereign is not only threatened by *external* others but also by an *internal* division that makes the sovereign liable to turn against itself at every moment. This autoimmunity of sovereignty is not something that could or should be overcome; it is an *unconditional* necessity that gives the chance for both positive change and negative corruption.

The traditional notion of the unconditional as a sovereign instance (which is the foundation of Schmitt's decisionism) is therefore quite incompatible with Derrida's thinking of the unconditional. For Derrida, what is unconditional is the exposure to the undecidable coming of time, which compromises the sovereignty of every instance a priori. This unconditional openness to unpredictable events is not a new ethical ideal that can replace the ideal of unconditional sovereignty. Rather, the unconditional coming of time deconstructs the ideal of sovereignty from within. What Derrida calls the "unconditional renunciation of sovereignty" is not a matter of a choice that some people make and others do not. On the contrary, Derrida maintains that the renunciation of sovereignty is "required a priori" and takes place whatever you do, "even before the act of a decision," since nothing can happen without the coming of time that undercuts sovereignty in advance.[16] Far from being an ethical ideal, this unconditional renunciation of sovereignty accounts for why every sovereign power has always been and will always be essentially corruptible.

When Derrida claims that "the passive decision" is "the condition of the event," he is thus *not* proposing an opposition between two kinds of decision, one active and one passive.[17] Rather, the structure of temporality requires one to rethink the relation between activity and passivity in a nonoppositional way. A facile misreading would be to understand the passive decision as "good" because it welcomes the other and the active decision as "bad" because it places restrictions on welcoming the other. The same type of reading would understand "the condition of the event" as normative in some sense, so that the condition for a "genuine" event is that we remain passive, whereas an active attitude compromises the "genuine" event. However, what Derrida calls "the condition of the event" is radically descriptive, since it designates the condition for anything to happen and for everything that happens. Even the most active and sovereign decision is passive, for the same reason that even the most immediate autoaffection is inhabited by a heteroaffection. Whoever makes a decision is passively affected by his own decision because the decision *takes time* and has effects that cannot finally be mastered by the one who makes the decision. This condition of the event is the possibility for everything good and everything bad, since without it nothing could happen. A form of government that would be able to guarantee its own legitimacy—exempted from the risk of powers being misused or principles corrupted—would short-circuit the possibility of politics and of life in general.[18]

To develop the above conception of politics, I want to engage in a dialogue with Ernesto Laclau's theory of hegemony. For more than two decades Laclau has pursued a thinking of democracy that can be described in terms of the logic of "hyperpoliticization" that I have delineated. For a hyperpolitical thinking, nothing (no set of values, no principle, no demand or political struggle) can be posited as good in itself. Rather, everything is liable to corruption and to appropriation for other ends, which also means that no instance can have an a priori immunity against interrogation and critique. As Laclau has demonstrated, the deconstructive notion of undecidability is crucial for thinking such a radical politicization.[19] Given that there is a structural undecidability, to make a decision is necessarily to repress other possible decisions. Every political order is thus founded on exclusion and an exercise of power. Rather than having an ultimate legitimacy, it can be challenged on the basis of what it does not include and must remain open to contestation because of its temporal constitution.

To assert such a condition is not to give in to relativism or irrationalism. As Laclau emphasizes, undecidability does not preclude that a decision can be *reasonable*, in the sense that "an accumulated set of motives, none of which has the value of an apodictic foundation, make it preferable to other decisions."[20] What undecidability does preclude is a decision that would be *rational* in the sense that it could not in principle be challenged or reasoned with. Derrida develops a similar argument in the last part of *Rogues*, where he uses the term *reasonable* to designate that every given reason is related to unpredictable events that may call it into question. To make a decision is "an always perilous transaction" (151/208) between the calculation of reason and the incalculable coming of time. It is therefore part of deconstructive reason to recognize that no value has an inherent value, and that any value can be used for better and for worse. The thought of essential corruptibility answers to a radical politicization, since it spells out the necessity of political vigilance concerning every position.[21]

Laclau's theory of the political proceeds from such a thinking of undecidability. If there were not undecidability—that is, if decisions were determined by the structure that makes them possible—there would be no possibility for politics, since a decision or strategic intervention could never make a difference. Rather, everything would be determined in advance, and there would be no space and time for the transformative effects of political struggle. Inversely, if there is a constitutive undecidability, nothing can be given as positive in itself but will depend for its effects on a context that is essentially vulnerable to change. Consequently, Laclau maintains that "undecidability should literally be taken as that condition from which no course of action necessarily follows. This means that we should not make it the necessary source of *any* concrete decision in the ethical or political sphere."[22] Rather than providing a ground for decisions, undecidability opens the possibility of politicizing even the apparently most nonpolitical institutions or norms, by recalling that they rely on decisions that are not derived from an incontestable ground. For

Laclau, undecidability goes *all the way down* and does not leave room for anything that would be exempt from the condition of politics understood as a contingent historicity.

It is therefore misguided to claim—as Simon Critchley does—that Laclau's thinking of the political needs to be grounded in a Levinasian ethical injunction. According to Critchley, there is an ethical injunction "which *governs* the whole field of undecidability opened by deconstruction."[23] This is a startling statement, to say the least, since undecidability cannot be delimited as a "field" and is quite impossible to "govern."[24] For Critchley, however, there must be something that governs undecidability in order to secure the distinction between the democratic and the nondemocratic. Critchley's critical question to Laclau is thus the following: "if all decisions are political, then in virtue of what is there a difference between democratizing and non-democratizing forms of decisions?"[25] Now, the deconstructive point is precisely that there is *no such guarantee* for what is democratic and nondemocratic. If there were a stable criteria for what is democratic and nondemocratic, there would be no democracy. It belongs to the essence of democracy that even the criteria for what counts as democratic can be overturned by the power of the people. To impose an incontestable criteria for what counts as democratic—even if the criteria only concerns formal procedures—is therefore to preclude a radical thinking of democracy. Critchley asserts that "democratic political forms are simply *better* than non-democratic ones—more inclusive, more capacious, more just."[26] This argument presupposes that there are given *forms* of democracy, which in all situations are preferable to supposedly nondemocratic forms of politics. A basic question of democracy—namely, the question of its *form*—is thus withdrawn from any possible debate and instead becomes a matter of authoritarian assertion. As Laclau points out in response to Critchley, "if the ethical from the beginning has a content necessarily attached to it, all other conceptions have to be rejected offhand as unethical. It is not difficult to realize the authoritarian and ethnocentric consequences which follow potentially from such an approach."[27] The challenge of democratic politics is rather that it cannot be reduced to given norms or institutions. For example, Laclau argues that in Latin America during the 1930s and 1940s "the nationalist military regimes which incorporated the masses to the public sphere were far more democratic than the corrupt and clientelistically-based parliamentary regimes that preceded them, although the latter respected the formal liberal rules."[28]

The undecidability of democracy does not only apply to empirical political regimes but also to the principle of being open to the other, which Critchley posits as the ethical injunction of democracy. As I argued in Chapter 3, the openness to the other cannot be an ethical principle since it is not a matter of choice. Openness to the other answers to the openness to the unpredictable coming of time and is thus the condition for whatever there is (whether it is called fascism or democracy or something else). Furthermore, nothing can guarantee that it is better to be *more* open than to be *less* open to the other (or vice versa). More openness to the other may entail more openness to "bad" events and less openness to the other may entail less openness to "good" events. The decision concerning how one should relate to the other can therefore not be dictated by an ethical injunction, but must be reinvented from time to time. Far from providing an ethical ground, the deconstructive thinking of alterity thus politicizes even the most elementary relation to the other.

Laclau has pursued such a hyperpolitical thinking in a series of critical engagements with contemporary theorists, including Michael Hardt and Antonio Negri, Giorgio Agamben, Alain Badiou, and Richard Rorty.[29] While taking into account the wide-ranging differences between these thinkers, Laclau's critique is always directed at the ways in which they fail to think the radical undecidability of politics. A clear example is his critique of Hardt and Negri's *Empire*. The crucial question here concerns how diverse political struggles can come together in opposition to an oppressive power. For Hardt and Negri, the emancipatory subject is "the multitude" in its resistance to the repressive operations of Empire. The multitude is thus supposedly what unites the particular struggles against global capitalism. As Laclau points out, however, there is no account in Hardt and Negri of how the multitude is politically constructed and mediated as a unity. Rather, for Hardt and Negri "the unity of the multitude results from the *spontaneous* aggregation of a plurality of actions, which do not need to be articulated with one another."[30] For there to be such a spontaneous unity, the diverse struggles would have to converge automatically in an assault on the same enemy and their particular aims could never be incompatible with each other, since the latter situation would require negotiations and mediations that contradict the spontaneous unity. As Laclau maintains, these premises are not only highly unrealistic but also cancel out the need for politics in the first place. If there is a spontaneous identification of the enemy and a spontaneous unity of the particular aims, there is no need for a political articulation of these matters, since they are already settled.

In contrast, Laclau argues that the moment of political articulation is absolutely irreducible. In *Hegemony and Socialist Strategy* Laclau and Chantal Mouffe define "articulation" as "any practice establishing a relation among elements such that their identity is modified as a result of the articulatory practice" (105). The reason why there must be articulation is because there is no necessary link between the elements of a political struggle; their alliance is rather a *contingent* relation that must be established in a historical terrain where it may be transformed or undone. To think politics in terms of articulation is therefore to think it without reference to an underlying essence that would provide unity, power, or privilege to a certain political agent. Any unity, power, or privilege depends on strategic articulations that are contingent, both because they must discriminate between alternative actions and because nothing determines their outcome in advance. Consequently, the constitution of an emancipatory subject (such as "the multitude") depends on a precarious historical construction rather than on a spontaneous upsurge of resistance. As Laclau argues, even the most immediate *will to be against* (which plays an important role in *Empire*) is a matter of contingent historical mobilization: "the ability and the will to resist are not a gift from heaven but require a set of subjective transformations that are only the product of the struggles themselves *and that can fail to take place*."[31] Furthermore, "all struggle is the struggle of concrete social actors for particular objectives, and nothing guarantees that these struggles will not clash with each other."[32]

Political power is thus a matter of *hegemony*. As Laclau and Mouffe explain: "in order to have hegemony, the requirement is that elements whose own nature does not predetermine them to enter into one type of arrangement rather than another, nevertheless coalesce, as a result of an external or articulating practice."[33] The concept of hegemony reinforces that political power is never wholly sovereign; it can only be established by bringing together heterogeneous elements and by suppressing elements that are antagonistic to the hegemonic articulation. This act of suppression already testifies to a limitation of sovereignty, since a wholly sovereign power would never have to suppress or be antagonistic to anything.

What Laclau and Mouffe call "the democratic revolution" is a historic process that reinforces the impossibility of absolute sovereignty. A key moment for Laclau and Mouffe is the French Revolution, with its opposition to "a society of a hierarchic and inegalitarian type, ruled by a theological-political logic in which the social order had its foundation in divine will" (155). The idea of democratic equality challenges such a theological alibi for the social order. Given the idea of democratic equality, relations of subordination can be regarded as forms of unjust oppression rather than as hierarchical positions that have been sanctioned by God or nature.[34] Laclau and Mouffe here take the example of feminism:

> If throughout the centuries there have been multiple forms of resistance by women against male domination, it is only under certain conditions and specific forms that a feminist movement which demands equality (equality before the law in the first place, and subsequently in other areas) has been able to emerge. Clearly, when we speak here of the "political" character of these struggles, we do not do so in the restricted sense of demands which are situated at the level of parties and the State. What we are referring to is a type of action whose objective is the transformation of a social relation which constructs a subject in a relationship of subordination. . . .
> . . . If, as was the case with women until the seventeenth century, the ensemble of discourses which constructed them as subjects fixed them purely and simply in a subordinated position, feminism as a movement of struggle against women's subordination could not emerge. Our thesis is that it is only from the moment when the democratic discourse becomes available to articulate the different forms of resistance to subordination that the conditions will exist to make possible the struggle against different types of inequality. . . .
> . . . It is because women as women are denied a right which the democratic ideology recognizes in principle for all citizens that there appears a fissure in the construction of the subordinated feminine subject from which an antagonism *may* arise. It is also the case with the ethnic minorities who demand their civil rights. (153, 154, 159)

A crucial feature of the democratic revolution is thus the ability to recognize relations of subordination as relations of oppression. Visions of possible political transformation are thereby strengthened, but Laclau and Mouffe are careful to emphasize that there is nothing inherently progressive about the democratic revolution. Rather, the specific outcomes and consequences of the democratic revolution will always be a matter of hegemonic struggle:

At this point it is necessary, nevertheless, to make it clear that the democratic revolution is simply the terrain upon which there operates a logic of displacement supported by an egalitarian imaginary, but that it does not predetermine the *direction* in which this imaginary will operate. If this direction were predetermined we should simply have constructed a new teleology—we would be on a terrain similar to that of Bernstein's *Entwicklung*. But in that case there would be no room at all for a hegemonic practice. The reason why it is not thus, and why no teleology can account for social articulations, is that the discursive compass of the democratic revolution opens the way for political logics as diverse as right-wing populism and totalitarianism on the one hand, and a radical democracy on the other. Therefore, if we wish to construct the hegemonic articulations which allow us to set ourselves in the direction of the latter, we must understand in all their radical heterogeneity the range of possibilities which are opened in the terrain of democracy itself. (168)

The meaning of a political struggle is not given in itself but depends on its discursive articulation and its relation to other struggles. The "same" political struggle can lend itself to radically different agendas depending on the circumstances. This is not an argument for relativism but one that highlights the need for hegemonic articulations. The fact that a political struggle does not have an immutable significance means that it may be appropriated by right-wing discourses just as well as by left-wing discourses. Indeed, Laclau underscores that "a Fascist regime can absorb and articulate democratic demands as much as a liberal one."[35] It is precisely because of this undecidability that politics is a matter of hegemony. To hegemonize is to appropriate elements that do not have a necessary connection in order to form an alliance that could not exist without the hegemonic articulation. The task of democratic politics is therefore not to find a privileged political subject which is destined for emancipation (such as the working class in traditional Marxism) but to create a hegemonic articulation that can empower a number of heterogeneous demands and counter other hegemonic articulations of the same demands. Accordingly, even the most ideal democracy must exercise violence. In Laclau's formulation "even the most democratic of societies is a system of power and is partly based on force and exclusion."[36] This is not because actual democracies fall short of being ideal democracies, but because there can be no politics without a hegemonic articulation.

By developing the concept of hegemony, Laclau provides an account of how political decisions are made and how political identities are constructed in the historical terrain of undecidability. As such, his theory of hegemony is an important contribution to a deconstructive thinking of the political. The issue I want to raise, however, concerns the notion of *desire* that informs Laclau's theory. While the concept of hegemony makes clear that there cannot be a sovereign order, Laclau does not call into question that we desire such an order. Rather, he maintains that the struggle for hegemony is driven by a desire for the absolute fullness of sovereign being. His theory of hegemony thereby remains within the bounds of traditional atheism, where mortal being is still conceived as a *lack* of being that we desire to transcend. I will attempt to show how this conception of desire leads to a number of symptomatic contradictions in Laclau's work and to an impasse for his thinking of democracy. My argument is that the possibility of democracy hinges rather on the radically atheist conception of desire that I have developed.

Let us begin by considering the role of desire in Laclau's account of hegemonic construction. According to Laclau, a hegemony is constructed through a *chain of equivalence* between a number of particular demands. One of his basic examples is the collective resistance to a repressive regime. When workers begin to strike for higher wages, their particular demand can also be linked to other demands that are directed against the repressive regime (e.g., the demand for freedom of the press and for reformation of the educational system). As Laclau points out, "each of these demands is, in its particularity, unrelated to the others; what unites them is that they constitute between themselves a chain of equivalences in so far as all of them are bearers of an anti-system meaning."[37] However, for the chain of equivalence to be constituted as such and acquire a hegemonic force something must represent the term to which every other term is equivalent. A particular term (e.g., a particular social body, a particular cause, or a particular idea) must assume the representation of the more universal struggle against repression. Laclau emphasizes that there is no term that in itself has a universal significance; every term is itself subject to the play of difference. The privileged term can therefore not relieve its particularity in a pure universality; it is rather a *hegemonic universality* that relies on an *antagonistic* relation, where the different elements of the struggle are posited as equivalent by all being opposed to an antagonistic pole.

The body that assumes the representation of universality is therefore not a sovereign body; it is by necessity partial and threatened, since it is predicated on exclusion and never acquired for good but liable to being subverted. For Laclau, however, the hegemonic body is supported by what he calls a *radical investment* that transforms it into "the embodiment of a fullness totally transcending it."[38] A radical investment is the investment of the desire for absolute fullness in a contingent and particular body. Although the hegemonic body is finite, we support it because we believe that it will restore an infinite fullness to society. Indeed, Laclau maintains that the desire for an absent fullness is constitutive of experience in general: "finitude involves the experience of fullness, of the sublime, as that which is radically lacking . . . so the life of the individual will be the vain search for a fullness from which he/she is going to be systematically deprived."[39]

Laclau's explicit model here is the psychoanalytic theory of desire formulated by Jacques Lacan. While Lacan clearly recognizes that there is no fullness of being, he holds that we *desire* to reach such fullness and that our mortal being is a lack of being. For Lacan the lack of being is not derived from an object we once had and subsequently lost. As he explains in *Seminar II*, "It is not the lack of this or that, but the lack of being whereby being exists" (223). Even though Lacan often describes the lacking fullness in terms that may seem to invoke a lost object (such as "the Thing"), it is important to understand that the desired fullness cannot be equated with any object whatsoever. What is desired under the heading of "the Thing" is a state of absolute fullness to which no object can ever be adequate.[40] The lack of such fullness is for Lacan the *cause* of desire, since it is precisely because desire cannot be fulfilled that there is desire.

Hence, in the register of desire there can be no satisfaction. Every actual object of desire is an insufficient substitute for the fullness of being (the Thing) that the subject desires. The failure of the actual object to be the Thing propels the subject to search for new objects that in turn will betray its ideal, in a chain of metonymic displacements that for Lacan testifies to the subject's fundamental lack of being. In his late work, however, Lacan introduces the register of *the drive* to explain how there can be satisfaction despite the fundamental lack of being.[41] In the register of the drive, the desire for fullness is not displaced from one object to another but invested in a particular object. As Joan Copjec has argued, the operation of the drive should thus be understood in accordance with Lacan's definition of sublimation as "the elevation of an ordinary object to the dignity of the Thing."[42] While this establishes a distinction between desire and drive, the founding assumption in both cases is that the subject aspires to an absent fullness. The difference is that desire rejects all objects as inadequate in comparison to the Thing that would satisfy it once and for all, whereas the drive satisfies itself with a substitute. It is clear from this schema, however, that the lack of fullness is not called into question but is located at the root of both desire and drive. The object of the drive is explicitly posited as an object of lack, from which the subject can derive satisfaction only by regarding it as the incarnation of fullness. Consequently, Copjec maintains that the object of the drive "emerges *out of the lack*, the void, opened by the loss of the original plenum or *das Ding*. In place of the mythical satisfaction derived from being at one with the maternal Thing, the subject now experiences satisfaction in this partial object."[43]

Laclau directly translates the operation of the drive into his own notion of radical investment. Drawing on the work of Copjec, he describes radical investment as the act of "making an object the embodiment of a mythical fullness."[44] Furthermore, he goes on to emphasize that the Lacanian notion of the drive and his own logic of hegemony answer to the same ontological structure: "No social fullness is achievable except through hegemony; and hegemony is nothing more than the investment, in a partial object, of a fullness which will always evade us."[45]

For Laclau, the Lacanian notion of lack is not a theory among others but the ontological truth of human existence. As he asserts: "I do not think that the *objet petit a* or the subject of lack are ontic categories limited to a particular region of human reality. When one realizes their full ontological implications they transform *any* field, the political field included."[46] Consequently, Laclau argues that all political struggle ultimately should be understood in terms of ontological lack and radical investment. Laclau's favorite example (repeated numerous times in his writings) is the following:

> Let us suppose a situation of generalized social disorder: in such a situation "order" becomes the name of an absent fullness, and if that fullness is constitutively unachievable, it cannot have any content of its own, any form of self-presentation. "Order" thus becomes autonomous *vis-à-vis* any particular order in so far as it is the name of an absent fullness that no concrete social order can achieve (the same can be said of similar terms such as "revolution," "unity of the people," etcetera). That fullness is present, however, as that which is absent and needs, as a result, to be represented in some way. Now,

its means of representation will be constitutively inadequate, for they can only be particular contents that assume, in certain circumstances, a function of representation of the impossible universality of the community. This relation, by which a certain particular content overflows its own particularity and becomes the incarnation of the absent fullness of society, is exactly what I call a hegemonic relation.[47]

While the example of a general social disorder may seem extreme, Laclau extends the same logic to the investment in all political ideals. To call for "justice" or "equality" or "freedom" is ultimately to express the desire for an absent fullness:

> In a situation of radical disorder, the demand is for *some kind* of order, and the *concrete* social arrangement that will meet that request is a secondary consideration (the same can also be said of similar terms such as "justice," "equality," "freedom," etc.). It would be a waste of time trying to give a positive definition of "order" or "justice"—that is, to ascribe to them a conceptual content, however minimal it might be. The semantic role of these terms is not to express *any* positive content but, as we have seen, to function as the names of a fullness which is constitutively absent. It is because there is no human situation in which injustice of some kind or another does not exist that "justice," as a term, makes sense. Since it names an undifferentiated fullness, it has no conceptual content whatsoever: it is not an abstract term but, in the strictest sense, *empty.*[48]

The premise of Laclau's argument is that the ideal justice would be an undifferentiated fullness. Such an absolute fullness is inseparable from absolute emptiness, since everything that is finite (which is to say everything) must be eliminated for there to be absolute fullness. Laclau is well aware of this paradox, but it does not lead him to question that absolute fullness is desirable. Rather, he derives the struggle for justice from a lack of absolute justice. Given that no content can be adequate to the fullness of absolute justice, the term *justice* is in itself empty of normative content and can in principle be hegemonized by any political order or hegemony.[49] The same desire for fullness thus informs both democratic and totalitarian struggles for "justice." In both cases a radical investment will posit a particular social body as the incarnation of the desired fullness of justice.

Now, I want to argue that the above conception of desire is incompatible with the desire for democracy. The desire for democracy cannot be a desire for absolute fullness, since the very idea of democracy undercuts the idea of absolute fullness. If the idea of democracy were an idea of absolute fullness, it would be possible to think a perfect democracy that we strive toward, even though it is impossible to reach for us as temporal beings. However, if one strives toward democracy, one cannot strive toward a perfect democracy. A perfect democracy would cancel out democracy, since democracy must be perfectible and corruptible in order to be democratic. The impossibility of a perfect democracy is thus *not* a lack of fullness. On the contrary, the impossibility of a perfect democracy is what opens the possibility of democracy.

The infinite perfectibility of democracy is essentially a negative infinity, which cannot be oriented toward the immutable ideal of a positive infinity. If there is an immutable ideal, then perfectibility is not infinite, since the ideal itself cannot be perfected. In contrast, the infinite perfectibility of democracy entails that *the ideal itself* is temporal and alterable. As I have argued throughout this book, the same condition is constitutive of life and the desire for life in general. To desire life (in whatever form) is to desire something temporal, since life must remain open to its own alteration in order to live on.

It is the opening to an undecidable future that Derrida seeks to emphasize with his expression "democracy to come." The point is not that there is an ideal democracy that will come, but that the coming of time is necessarily inscribed in the idea of democracy itself:

> The expression "democracy to come" takes into account the absolute and intrinsic historicity of the only system that welcomes in itself, in its very concept, that expression of autoimmunity called the right to self-critique and perfectibility. Democracy is the only system, the only constitutional paradigm, in which, in principle, one has or assumes the right to criticize everything publicly, including the idea of democracy, its concept, its history, and its name. Including the idea of the constitutional paradigm and the absolute authority of law. It is thus the only paradigm that is universalizable, whence its chance and its fragility. But in order for this historicity—unique among all political systems—to be complete, it must be freed not only from the Idea in the Kantian sense but from all teleology, all onto-theo-teleology. (*Rogues*, 86–87/126–27)

We can thus specify why Derrida privileges the concept of democracy. More forcefully than any other political concept, democracy brings out the autoimmunity that is the condition for life in general. In the name of democratic freedom one can assault the given delimitation of democratic freedom, and in the name of democratic equality one can assault the given delimitation of democratic equality. This does not mean that democracy can avoid the violence of exclusion or that it necessarily is less violent than other political systems. What distinguishes the concept of democracy, however, is that it explicitly takes into account that the violence of exclusion does not have an ultimate justification. The principle of democratic equality spells out that the power of some to decide over others is not given by God or nature; it is rather contingent on political practices that can be revised. Similarly, the principle of democratic freedom spells out that nothing is holy or untouchable, but everything is subject to possible critique. The common denominator between these principles is that they reinforce the openness to contestation and transformation at every juncture of democracy. This openness is both what makes democracy *infinitely perfectible* (it can always become better) and *infinitely corruptible* (it can always become worse).

Thus, the concept of democracy testifies to an "absolute and intrinsic historicity" where nothing is immune from its own destructibility. As Derrida points out in the passage quoted above, to think this radical historicity we must dissociate democracy from the structure of the Kantian Idea and indeed from any form of regulative teleology. Laclau himself takes us a long way toward such a thinking of democracy. He emphasizes that democracy entails the recognition that no ground, value, or normative content can have an ultimate foundation but is radically historical and contingent. Moreover, Laclau holds that the radical historicity and contingency of being is not a reason for pessimism; it is rather the chance for any kind of optimism, since without it nothing could happen. As he puts it with a memorable formulation: "The future is indeterminate and certainly not guaranteed for us; but that is precisely why it is not lost either."[50]

Accordingly, Laclau argues against those who think that if we abandon the appeal to an ultimate foundation, we will lose the sense of community and the source of our engagement in the world. Laclau here formulates two crucial arguments. First, he reiterates that the sense of contingency is not simply negative but also the source of any sense of freedom: "If people think that God or nature have made the world as it is, they will tend to consider their fate inevitable. But if the being of the world which they inhabit is only the result of the contingent discourses and vocabularies that constitute it, they will tolerate their fate with less patience" and rather consider it as subject to possible transformation through political struggle.[51] Second, he argues that "the perception of the contingent character of universalist values will make us all the more conscious of the dangers which threaten them and of their possible extinction. If we happen to believe in those values, the consciousness of their historicity will not make us more indifferent to them but, on the contrary, will make us more responsible citizens, more ready to engage in their defense."[52]

These arguments, however, are in direct contradiction with the conception of desire Laclau advocates under the heading of radical investment. According to the theory of radical investment, I engage in the defense of a hegemonic body because I regard it as the incarnation of an absolute fullness. The awareness that the hegemonic body is in fact *not* an incarnation of absolute fullness, but only a finite and contingent historical construct, would then certainly lead me to withdraw my investment. Laclau's argument that the awareness of finitude leads us to *increase* our investment in the hegemonic body presupposes a different conception of desire that he never develops, namely, the radically atheist desire for survival. Only if I desire the finite and want it to *live on as finite* will the threat of death make me more liable to engage in its defense. Indeed, if I did not want the hegemonic body to live on as finite, the threat of death would not be a problem in the first place, since only finite existence can be threatened by death.

The constitutive drive for survival is quite incompatible with the constitutive drive for fullness that Laclau assumes as the foundation for his theory. Laclau wants us to recognize that "freedom and consciousness of our own contingency go together."[53] However, if we really desire an absolute fullness, such a recognition is unthinkable. If the freedom I desire is an absent fullness, the freedom of contingency can only be disappointing. Indeed, if I desire fullness and receive Laclau's insight that fullness is incompatible with freedom, the result can only be resignation with regard to the issue of freedom. The freedom I have cannot be the fullness I want (so I will never have a reason to defend it), and the freedom I can obtain cannot be the fullness I want (so I will never have a reason to struggle for it).

Laclau himself explicitly denies that a radical investment would lead to resignation or disappointment. On the contrary, the theory of radical investment is supposed to account for how we engage in political struggle despite the absence of fullness. According to this account, however, we invest in a political cause because we think it incarnates the fullness of being. The theory of radical investment is thus ultimately at odds with Laclau's theory of democracy. The distinctive feature of democracy is for Laclau the recognition that a political cause cannot be fully universal but remains particular and open to contestation. A radical investment is, on the contrary, predicated on the illusion that the political cause is fully universal:

> Since society as fullness has no proper meaning beyond the ontic contents that embody it, those contents are, for the subjects attached to them, *all there is*. They are thus not an empirically achievable second best *vis-à-vis* an unattainable ultimate fullness for which we wait in vain. This, as we have seen, is the logic of hegemony. This moment of fusion between partial object and totality represents, at one point in time, the ultimate historical horizon, which cannot be split into its two dimensions, universal and particular.[54]

What Laclau here describes as the general structure of political investment is exactly the structure he elsewhere denounces as totalitarian. In his formulation, "the best prescription for totalitarianism" is the conflation of justice with "what a certain society considers as just at some point in time."[55] Given the structure of radical investment, however, such a conflation is unavoidable. To make a radical investment is to identify a particular content with the fullness of absolute justice. To make such a radical investment, I must necessarily be deaf to Laclau's democratic argument that there is no fullness of being. The hegemonic body I support is certainly finite and contingent, but as a radical investor I am necessarily blind to this fact, since I believe that it incarnates an infinite fullness. Given that for me the hegemonic body is *all there is*, I cannot listen to any arguments saying that it exercises illegitimate exclusions or is in need of revision.

If there is a constitutive drive for fullness, we are thus left with only two alternatives when faced with Laclau's arguments concerning democracy and the impossibility of a universal hegemonic body. On the one hand, to make a radical investment, we must ignore his arguments and believe that the hegemonic body is fully universal, but in that case we are committed to what Laclau calls totalitarianism rather than democracy. On the other hand, if we heed his arguments and realize that nothing can answer to the desire for fullness, we will be fatally disappointed and not commit ourselves to anything, since we know that we will never get what we want.

In neither case, then, does the drive for fullness allow for the recognition that the impossibility of the absolute is *not* a negative limitation, not an ontological lack, but the possibility of the temporal being we desire. Nevertheless, it is clear from Laclau's own arguments that such a recognition is decisive for the formation of a democratic politics. Indeed, according to Laclau the only approach that is compatible with "a true democratic politics" is the following:

> It wholly accepts the plural and fragmented nature of contemporary societies but, instead of remaining in this particularistic moment, it tries to inscribe this plurality in equivalential logics which make possible the construction of new public spheres. Difference and particularisms are the necessary starting point, but out of it, it is possible to open the way to a relative universalization of values which can be the basis for a popular hegemony. This universalization and its open character certainly condemns all identity to an unavoidable hybridization, but hybridization does not necessarily mean decline through the loss of identity: it can also mean empowering existing identities through the opening of new possibilities. Only a conservative identity, closed on itself, could experience hybridization as a loss. But this democratico-hegemonic possibility has to recognize the constitutive contextualized/decontextualized terrain of its constitution and take full advantage of the political possibilities that this undecidability opens.[56]

Laclau can here be seen to describe the formation of a hegemony that does not rely on a radical investment. The "relative universalization" of a democratic hegemony does not lay claim to incarnate the fullness of absolute universality. If the democratic identity proceeded from such a sense of fullness, it would have to experience hybridization as a loss and could not see it as a chance for new alliances and political transformation. Democratic politics, then, presupposes that the impossibility of fullness is experienced as the *possibility* of both the identity one wants to maintain and the change one wants to bring about.

Laclau makes a similar point elsewhere by arguing that democratic politics hinges on the "symbolization of impossibility *as such* as a positive value":

> This point is important; although positivization is unavoidable, nothing prevents this positivization from symbolizing impossibility as such, rather than concealing it through the illusion of taking us beyond it. . . . The possibility of this weakened type of naturalization is important for democratic politics,

which involves the institutionalization of its own openness and, in that sense, the injunction to identify with its ultimate impossibility.[57]

This is certainly an important point, but it is incompatible with the theory of radical investment. According to the theory of radical investment, the positive content that symbolizes the common denominator of society can only become an object of attachment by being identified as the incarnation of fullness. If this is correct, a hegemonic formation can never mobilize support by symbolizing impossibility as such but necessarily engages us in "the illusion of taking us beyond it." As Laclau puts it elsewhere, a hegemonic practice will always "make of a certain particular content the very name of the fullness."[58] Moreover, according to his conception of desire it is the investment in the idea of fullness that allows political actors "to engage themselves in a more militant way and with an ethical density that other people lack."[59] One is thus led to wonder how Laclau himself can ever make the radical investment that is supposedly required for his political engagements. To make a radical investment, I have to believe that the object of my engagement incarnates the fullness of society, whereas Laclau devotes all his writings to repudiating the belief that anything can incarnate the fullness of society.

The structural contradiction in Laclau's theory should now be apparent. On the one hand, he maintains that political engagement requires a radical investment that identifies the object of engagement with the idea of fullness. On the other hand, the democratic society that Laclau advocates actually precludes such a radical investment. To make a radical investment in the foundations of a society, one cannot believe that these foundations are contingent and finite, whereas democracy explicitly presents its foundations as contingent and finite. As Laclau puts it: "the only democratic society is one which permanently shows the contingency of its own foundations."[60]

Furthermore, while Laclau claims that we all desire an absolute fullness, it is evident from his own texts that he does not think that absolute fullness is desirable. A clear example is his discussion of emancipation. The classical notion of emancipation presupposes that the goal of emancipation is to eliminate violence and antagonisms in favor of a totally free society. Insofar as Laclau assumes that we are driven by a desire for fullness, he remains bound to this traditional notion of emancipation. For example, he claims that the aim of political demands is "not actually their *concretely* specified targets: these are only the contingent occasion of achieving (in a partial way) something that utterly transcends them: the fullness of society."[61] At the same time, Laclau himself provides the resources to deconstruct this traditional notion of emancipation. A persistent argument in his work asserts that violence and antagonisms are not something one can aim to eliminate in favor of freedom. On the contrary, violence and antagonisms are the very condition of a free society:

> Let us suppose that we move to the opposite hypothesis, the one contained in the classical notion of emancipation—that is a society from which violence and antagonisms have been *entirely* eliminated. In this society, we can only enjoy the Spinozian freedom of being conscious of necessity. This is a first paradox of a free community: that which constitutes its condition of impossibility (violence) constitutes at the same time its condition of possibility. Particular forms of oppression can be eliminated, but freedom only exists in so far as the achievement of a total freedom is an ever receding horizon. A totally free and a totally determined society would be, as I have argued elsewhere, exactly the same.[62]

Laclau here stops short of deconstructing the idea of freedom by retaining total freedom as a *horizon* toward which we strive. However, the logic of his own argument shows that total freedom cannot even be a horizon, since it is neither thinkable nor desirable. Thus, in another text Laclau argues that a totally free society is not only unachievable but *undesirable*, since it would cancel out freedom:

> I would argue that the contamination of emancipation by power is not an unavoidable empirical imperfection to which we have to accommodate, but involves a higher human ideal than a universality representing a totally reconciled human essence, because a fully reconciled society, a transparent society, would be entirely free in the sense of self-determination, but that full realization of freedom would be equivalent to the death of freedom, for all possibility of dissent would have been eliminated from it. Social division, antagonism and its necessary consequence—power—are the true conditions of a freedom which does not eliminate particularity.[63]

Although the same logic recurs in a number of Laclau's texts, it never leads him to question the concept of desire that is based on a lack of fullness. Despite the demonstration that complete freedom is the death of freedom, that total autonomy is total determination, and that total fullness is total emptiness, Laclau maintains that absolute fullness constitutes the desired horizon of emancipatory struggle. As we have seen, he thereby fails to account for how the struggle for democracy is possible. To desire democracy cannot be to desire an ideal fullness, since even the ideal state of democracy is temporal and alterable. The desire for democracy presupposes that we are not driven toward an ideal fullness but toward *living on* as finite beings.

Let me be very clear here to avoid any misunderstanding. I am not proposing an opposition between a "good" democratic desire for survival and a "bad" totalitarian desire for fullness. Rather, I argue that the desire for fullness *has never been operative* in a political struggle or anything else. The desire for totalitarianism cannot be a desire for absolute fullness, since in a state of absolute fullness there would be no time for totalitarianism. For the same reason, the difference between democracy and totalitarianism is not that the former "affirms" finitude whereas the latter does not. As I have argued, the affirmation of temporal finitude is unconditional because everyone is engaged by it *without exception*. Consequently, even the most totalitarian regime presupposes an affirmation of the finitude of its own hegemonic body. If it did not affirm the finitude of its own body, it would never feel threatened and exercise repressive power against perceived enemies, since it would never care about what happened to the finite body. My point here is not to deny the differences between democracy and totalitarianism or the urgency of deciding between them; I am only stressing that these matters cannot be settled on the basis of an opposition between a desire that is inherently democratic and a desire that is inherently totalitarian. To maintain such an opposition would be to depoliticize the difference between democracy and totalitarianism. There would be a criterion for decision making that is not liable to political manipulation and hence exempt from the need for political scrutiny. The hyperpolitical point is rather that every desire is essentially corruptible and cannot be immune from becoming totalitarian.

The logic of radical atheism can thus be seen to have two major consequences for the thinking of the political. First, the logic of radical atheism deconstructs every form of sovereignty, including the sovereignty of any given form of democracy. Hence, my insistence on the necessity of "negotiation" throughout this book should not be seen as an a priori concession to the established norms of democratic debate. Rather, my argument is that there is nothing but negotiation for structural reasons, so every act is a form of negotiation. Blowing yourself up on the street is a form of negotiation just as much as debating in a parliament is a form of negotiation.

Why? Because there is negotiation as soon as a power is not sovereign but has to relate itself to other powers that restrict its sovereignty. And since there cannot even in principle be a wholly sovereign power (such a power would cancel itself out since there would be nothing in relation to which it could exercise its power), there is nothing but negotiation. One effect of this argument is that it provides a theoretical explanation of how it is possible that Western democratic regimes, even when they respect the formal liberal rules, can be much more violent than the allegedly "terrorist" acts they oppose.

Such politicization, however, cannot rely on either a sovereign subject that makes incontestable decisions or on any transcendent rule for which decisions one should make. I am certainly not denying the urgency and necessity of making prescriptions (they are an irreducible part of any ethics or politics), but I am arguing that no prescriptions can be derived from the logic of deconstruction.[64] The logic of deconstruction shows why no prescription can have a transcendent status; rather, every prescription is subject to a constitutive undecidability. There is nothing that inherently ensures that it is better to criticize more rather than less, to be more terroristic rather than less, or vice versa. Rather, the relation between given prescriptions and the making of decisions must be reinvented from time to time. I want to emphasize that the *must* here is not normative; it does not designate how decisions *should* be made but how decisions *are* made, whatever you do. There cannot be any decisions that are entirely programmed by a rule or a norm, since decisions can only be made through the unpredictable coming of time. The same goes for the institution and maintenance of rules and norms themselves; they can only be instituted and maintained through the unpredictable coming of time and are thus never reducible to a program.

The first consequence of a radically atheist thinking of politics, then, is that it gives access to a hyperpolitical logic that spells out that nothing is unscathed or unquestionable. The second consequence is that the logic of radical atheism transforms the most fundamental assumptions about what is desirable. Political philosophy has traditionally determined corruption as an evil that supervenes on something that precedes it or as a lamentable fact of life that ought to be overcome in an ideal future. In contrast, Derrida maintains that the essential corruptibility of autoimmunity is not a privation but the condition for even the highest good or the most ideal justice. In his formulation, "the possibility of evil, or of perjury, must be intrinsic to the good or to justice for either to be possible."[65] As I have argued, this logic follows from a radically atheist conception of desire, where justice and the good are essentially matters of mortal survival. Mortal survival opens the chance for everything that is desired *and* the threat of everything that is feared, since without mortal survival there can be nothing at all. Mortal survival is thus a necessary but not sufficient requirement for justice and goodness. The affirmation of survival is the condition for any ability to respond to suffering, but this does not mean that the affirmation of survival is simply in the service of life. It is rather the source of all passion for life *and* the source of all resentment for life. Without the affirmation of survival there would be no compassion and love (since one would not be committed to anything), but there would also be no suffering and hate (since one would not be threatened by anything).

Emancipatory struggle has therefore never been driven by a desire for absolute fullness but presupposes the unconditional affirmation of survival. Without the affirmation of survival one would never care for a better future and be compelled to make decisions about what is more or less violent. The urgency of such decisions is not mitigated by the fact that the fate of violence cannot finally be decided. On the contrary, the undecidable coming of time is what makes the question of violence urgent, since it exposes us to violence in the first place. This argument confirms the need for emancipatory narratives at the same time as it transforms the understanding of the desire that informs these narratives. Emancipatory politics does not aspire to a *telos* of absolute liberation, but must always negotiate an irreducible discrimination. Whatever future one desires is both inherently violent (since it can only come at the expense of other futures) and is itself exposed to violence (since it may be negated by the coming of other futures).

The drive for survival thus occupies the same structural position in my account as the drive for fullness in Laclau's account. Laclau argues that the drive for fullness informs both democratic and totalitarian struggles, whereas I argue that the drive for survival informs both democratic and totalitarian struggles. The difference is that the drive for survival allows us to account for how it is possible to desire democracy, while also accounting for why this desire is essentially corruptible and inherently violent. If one desires democracy, one cannot desire a state of being that is exempt from time. To desire democracy is by definition to desire something temporal, since democracy must remain open to its own alteration in order to be democratic. Again, this does not mean that the desire for democracy necessarily is more virtuous than other desires but that it spells out the violent affirmation of survival that is operative in every desire. This logic of radical atheism enables us to assess the problems of politics and the challenges of democracy in a new light. It cannot, however, finally teach us how to live or how to act. There is no cure for the condition of autoimmunity and every promise of change—every promise of a better future—only pledges to what is mortal.

Notes

Introduction

1. My use of the term "radical" bears some explanation. Derrida himself has expressed reservations about the verb "to radicalize" insofar as it implies a movement toward a unitary root or ground (see *Specters of Marx*, 184n9/152n1). My use of the term "radical," however, does not point to a unitary root or ground but seeks to demonstrate that the root uproots itself and the ground undermines itself. Radical atheism goes to the "root" of the religious conception of desire in order to show that it is divided against itself.

2. See also *Rogues*, where Derrida recalls the importance of the theme of spacing for his work from the 1960s onward and objects to the idea that there would have been a "turn" in his thinking (38–39/63–64). Throughout this book double page references refer to the English translation first, followed by page references to the original edition.

3. For a more detailed discussion of the distinction between negative and positive infinity see Chapter 1 and, in particular, Chapter 3.

4. See "How to Avoid Speaking," 7–9/540–43; and *Sauf le Nom*, 68/79–80. See also *Writing and Difference*, 116/170–71.

5. Hart, *The Trespass of the Sign*, 104, 201. Subsequent page references are given in the text.

6. Hart, "Religion," 56.

7. See in particular Marion's essay "In the Name," which is an explicit response to Derrida's writings on negative theology and develops Marion's earlier remarks on the subject in *The Idol and Distance* and *God Without Being*. My page references in the text refer to "In the Name."

8. See, for example, the following passage: "God cannot be seen, not only because nothing finite can bear his glory without perishing, but above all because

a God that could be conceptually comprehended would no longer bear the title 'God.' . . . Every thing in the world gains by being known—but God, who is not of the world, gains by not being known conceptually. The idolatry of the concept is the same as that of the gaze: imagining oneself to have attained God and to be capable of maintaining him under our gaze, like a thing in the world" (Marion, "In the Name," 34).

9. Marion, *The Idol and Distance*, 141/185.

10. See Derrida, *Writing and Difference*, 337n37/398n1.

11. Derrida, *Speech and Phenomena*, 54/60–61.

12. See, for example, *Writing and Difference*, 326n29/275n2. See also Derrida's remark that the deconstruction of the divine *logos* should not be construed as a "'return to finitude'" in accordance with the motif of "'the death of God'" (*Of Grammatology*, 68/99). Insofar as finitude is understood as the privation of fullness, "*différance* is also something other than finitude" (ibid.). Geoffrey Bennington has previously called attention to this remark (see his *Derridabase*, 115–16). My argument is that it presents a version of what I analyze as Derrida's radical atheism. A traditional atheism construes finitude as a lack of being that we desire to transcend, whereas radical atheism argues that finitude is the condition for everything that can be desired. For the same reason, radical atheism is not a critique that simply denounces the religious tradition. Rather, the logic of radical atheism allows one to read the religious tradition against itself from within.

13. For a further development of this argument concerning desire in relation to negative theology (in particular the writings of Meister Eckhart and Pseudo-Dionysius) see Chapter 4, where I also take issue with the accounts of the relation between negative theology and deconstruction proposed by John Caputo and Hent de Vries.

14. For Derrida's account of inheritance see, in particular, *Specters of Marx*, 16/40; and *For What Tomorrow*, 3–6/15–18.

Chapter 1

1. Derrida, *Rogues*, 33/57–58.

2. See, for example, *Rogues*, 109/154–55; "Autoimmunity: Real and Symbolic Suicides," 187–88n7; and *Politics of Friendship*, 76/94.

3. Cf. the section on the principle of noncontradiction further on in the *Metaphysics*, where Aristotle writes that "the same thing cannot in one and the same time be and not be" (1061b–62a).

4. Derrida, *Of Grammatology*, 166/236–37.

5. In a review of Richard Beardsworth's *Derrida and the Political*, Bennington has objected to the idea that deconstruction should be regarded as a thinking

of time. While I largely agree with Bennington's appraisal of Beardsworth, I take issue with his argument regarding Derrida's notion of time. Referring to Derrida's essay "Ousia and Grammè," Bennington claims that "there can be no non-metaphysical concept of time" (*Interrupting Derrida*, 173) since the concept of time is an "irreducibly metaphysical concept," which "relies on the centering of the present, and the determination of past and future as mere modifications of it" (ibid., 175). This is a one-sided presentation of Derrida's argument in "Ousia and Grammè." Derrida argues that the metaphysical concept of time itself contains the resources to deconstruct the metaphysical determination of being as presence. Indeed, Derrida holds that "these resources are mandatory from the moment when the sign 'time' . . . begins to function in a discourse. It is on the basis of this formal necessity that one must reflect upon the conditions for a discourse exceeding metaphysics" (60–61/70). Consequently, Derrida proposes a "*formal rule* for anyone wishing to *read* the texts of the history of metaphysics" (62/72). This formal rule consists in following the "play of submission and subtraction" (62/72) in the treatment of time in the history of metaphysics. On the one hand, time is *submitted* to the metaphysical determination of being as presence. On the other hand, time is *subtracted* from the metaphysical determination of being as presence, since the constitution of time undermines the idea of a presence in itself. For example, in his *Philosophy of Nature* Hegel points out that time is "that being which, inasmuch as it *is*, is not, and inasmuch as it is *not*, is" (§ 258). Time contradicts the metaphysical determination of what *is* because it can never be in itself but is always "coming-to-be and passing away" (§ 258). In opposition to this relentless division of time, Hegel holds out "the true Present," which he identifies not with time but with eternity (§ 259).

Following the play of submission and subtraction in the metaphysical treatment of time, Derrida maintains that one cannot deconstruct the metaphysics of presence by *opposing* another concept of time to the concept of time as succession. Such an operation would repeat the fundamental move of metaphysics, which consists in opposing a fundamental presence to the succession of time. Rather, Derrida argues that one must think the succession of time via "the hidden passageway that makes the problem of presence communicate with the problem of the written trace" (34/37). The point is precisely that the structure of the written trace—as I will seek to demonstrate in detail—allows one to think the succession of time without grounding it in a primordial presence. The structure of the trace entails a coimplication of time and space, so it is untenable to appeal to a "time" that is exempt from space. Rather, time must be thought as *spacing* before any opposition between time and space. As Derrida points out in "Ousia and Grammè": "Time is that which is thought on the basis of Being as presence, and if something—which bears a relation to time, but is not time—is to be thought beyond the determination of Being as presence, it cannot be a question of something that still could be called *time*" (60/69). This passage may seem to confirm Bennington's reading, but, again, it is only one side of Derrida's argument. On the one hand, time needs to be given a different name insofar as it has been submitted to the metaphysical determination of being as presence. On the other hand, the very treatment of time in the history of metaphysics has always been forced to subtract time from the determination of being as presence, since the being of time is incompatible with the being of presence. Cf. here Derrida's apparently contradictory statements in *Speech and Phenomena*. First, Derrida asserts that "what is called time would need to be given a different name—for 'time' has always designated a movement thought on the basis of the present, and can mean nothing else" (68/77; trans. mod.). Second, he asserts that time "cannot be thought on the basis of the present and the self-presence of a present being" (86/96; trans. mod.). These apparently contradictory assertions become compatible if we read them with regard to the play of submission and subtraction in the metaphysical treatment of time. While time has been submitted to the logic of identity that determines being as presence, time has also been subtracted from the determination of being as presence, since time cannot be thought in terms of a self-identical being. As Derrida points out in *Speech and Phenomena*, "the word 'time' itself, as it has always been understood in the history of metaphysics, is a metaphor which *at the same time* indicates and dissimulates the 'movement' of this auto-affection" (85/95). The autoaffection in question concerns the most elementary succession from one now to another. The word "time" dissimulates the implications of this autoaffection insofar as it is submitted to the idea of a self-identical presence. But the word "time" also indicates the implications of this autoaffection, since even the most elementary succession must be subtracted from the idea of a self-identical presence. As we will see, the succession of time divides the being of presence in advance and accounts for why time must be thought as spacing.

6. For the same reason, Derrida's notion of originary synthesis revises the concept of origin itself. If the synthesis is originary, there cannot ever have been a simple element or an absolute beginning.

7. See Derrida, *Margins of Philosophy*, 55/63.

8. See, for example, *For What Tomorrow*, where Derrida states that there can be no life without the structure of the trace (21/43); and *Acts of Literature*, where he refers to "the limitless generality of *différance*" (71). In the course of this book I will analyze numerous versions and aspects of these arguments in his work. Derrida specifically employs the term "ultra-transcendental" in a section of the *Grammatology* where he elaborates his notion of the originary trace. As Derrida points out, the notion of an originary trace is "in fact contradictory and not acceptable within the logic of identity" (61/90). The thinking of the trace requires a different logic of identity, which employs the metaphysical notion of origin

against itself. If the trace is originary, the very concept of origin is contradicted from within, since the trace is divided from its first inception and cannot ever be given in itself. The originary trace is thus another name for the ultratranscendental condition of spacing, since it spells out "that the origin did not even disappear, that it was never constituted except reciprocally by a nonorigin, the trace, which thus becomes the origin of the origin" (61/90). Derrida recalls his use of the term "ultratranscendental" in a number of texts (e.g., *Negotiations*, 354; and *Rogues*, 174n14/207n1). More often, he uses the term "quasi-transcendental," while indicating that the two terms can be used interchangeably. Thus, in the course of a discussion at Oxford University in 1999, Derrida states that "I am an ultra-transcendentalist or a quasi-transcendentalist" (*Arguing with Derrida*, 107; cf. the remark on 108 that *life is différance*). I prefer to use the term "ultratranscendental" for strategic reasons, since it reinforces the radical status that Derrida grants the spacing of time and since it answers more directly to the term "the unconditional" that is prominent in *Rogues*.

9. For a recent example of how Derrida's work is read in accordance with the structure of the Kantian Idea, see Daniel W. Smith, "Deleuze and Derrida, Immanence and Transcendence: Two Directions in Recent French Thought." The tendency to assimilate Derrida's arguments to the structure of the Kantian Idea has a long history in the reception of his work, which has been admirably analyzed by Bennington in *Derridabase, Legislations, Interrupting Derrida*, and *Other Analyses*. As Bennington rightly observes, "a very common misconstrual of what Derrida is doing involves normalizing it on just the model of the Kantian Idea it is, I am sure, tending to disrupt" (*Other Analyses*, 77); see also chapter 13 of Bennington's *Interrupting Derrida* for an excellent critique of the Idea structure in Marian Hobson's reading of Derrida. Despite his insightful critiques of Kantian misreadings of Derrida, however, Bennington does not go far enough in his dissociation of Derrida's thinking from the Kantian Idea. Bennington holds that Derrida's notion of democracy "cannot really still be thought within the terms of the regulative Idea" because it is "*perpetually* a promise, never fulfilled" (*Interrupting Derrida*, 33). This formulation is misleading, since it suggests that there is a promised fulfillment of democracy that remains out of reach. Thus, Bennington falls back on the model of reading Derrida that he himself has criticized. For example, while noting that the improvisation of something absolutely new is impossible, Bennington claims that

> the attempt at such an improvisation, necessarily failing, leaves a trace or a mark that can be seen as a *promise* of such an inaugurality. We may not ever be able to *perform* something radically inventive but, in a movement of thought that brings Derrida interestingly close to the Kant of the Ideas of Reason and of the Sublime (and close too, thereby, to the later Lyotard), we can in some sense *think* and even *call for* something radically inventive. Derrida's reformulation of this structure is to say that we are

thereby *promising* such a thing, and that is supposed to capture the sense in which the *possible* (or at least in some formal sense thinkable, i.e. the absolutely new or idiomatic) is nonetheless *impossible.* (*Other Analyses,* 172)

Bennington's argument is a sophisticated version of the misreading I address in this chapter. Following the logic of deconstruction, the absolute is not *possible* to think while being *impossible* to realize in the world. Rather, even on the most formal level of thought the absolute is impossible, and this impossibility is not a negative failure to achieve the ideal. For the same reason, the promise does not promise a fulfillment that remains out of reach. On the contrary, the promise is always a promise of temporal finitude and must therefore remain open to the possibility of nonfulfillment in its very fulfillment. This impossibility of absolute fulfillment is not a lack of fulfillment but the possibility of any fulfillment that can be desired. See my analysis of the structure of the promise in Chapter 4.

10. See Derrida, *Rogues,* 142, 174n14/197, 207n1.

11. Cf. Kant's remark further on in the *Critique of Pure Reason:* "the synthesis of the manifold parts of space, through which we apprehend it, is nevertheless successive, and thus occurs in time" (B 349).

12. Derrida's reference to "electronic card indexes and reading machines" as technological novelties is of course clearly marked by the date of its writing (1967). Today the examples of technological inscriptions would be far more advanced, but this would not alter Derrida's argument.

13. See *Rogues,* xiv, 135, 142–44/13, 188–89, 196–98.

14. See Chapter 3, where I take issue with the "ethical" readings of Derrida proposed by Robert Bernasconi, Drucilla Cornell, and Simon Critchley. See also Chapter 4, where I criticize the readings proposed by John Caputo and Richard Kearney.

15. Derrida, *Learning to Live Finally,* 51–52/54–55. Subsequent page references are given in the text.

16. Cf. Derrida's remark in his essay "Et Cetera": "yes and no, then! Otherwise, and without the no, a yes would never be possible" (301).

17. See Derrida's analysis of the relation between affirmation and memory in "Ulysses Gramophone," 276/89–90; and in *Mémoires,* 20/42.

18. Derrida, "Nietzsche and the Machine," 247–48.

19. Derrida, "Hostipitality," 362, cf. 363–364. Already in 1984, Henry Staten provided a powerful account of the conceptual logic of deconstruction in terms of the law of contamination: "The point of departure of deconstruction from philosophy is thus quite subtle. The value and necessity of pure concepts and categories are not denied, but they are no longer the last word. We no longer simply note and then set aside the factual or empirical contamination of our unities, but see that they are impure always and in principle, and pursue the implications of this essential impurity" (*Wittgenstein and Derrida,* 19). Thus, Staten

cogently argues that Derrida's thinking should be understood in relation to the philosophical notion of form. If pure form traditionally has been conceived as an indivisible unity, Staten maintains that for Derrida the pure form of self-identity is inhabited by a "constitutive outside" (*Wittgenstein and Derrida*, 15–19, 23) that makes it essentially open to contamination. With a memorable phrase, Staten describes the structure of the trace as "the pure form of essential impurity" (*Wittgenstein and Derrida*, 53).

20. See, in particular, Derrida, *Given Time*, chapter 1.

21. The most influential misreading of Derrida's notion of "the impossible" has been developed by John Caputo, with whom I take issue at length in Chapter 4. For Caputo's reading of the gift, which I also address in Chapter 4, see his *The Prayers and Tears of Jacques Derrida*, 160–229.

22. See, for example, *Negotiations*, 360–62; and *Rogues*, 84/123. I address these passages in Chapter 4, in the course of elucidating Derrida's complex logic of the impossible.

23. See Derrida, *Given Time*, 29–30/45–47.

24. For Derrida's articulation of the necessary link between the gift and time see *Given Time*, 27–28/43–45. See also Derrida's claim further on in the same book: "the gift only gives to the extent that it *gives time*. . . . *There where there is gift, there is time*. What it gives, the gift, is time" (41/59–60).

25. For the passage in question see *Given Time*, 40/59.

26. Derrida, *Given Time*, 54/76. Subsequent page references are given in the text.

27. See also *The Gift of Death*, where Derrida maintains that whatever is given is a matter of mortal survival, which is incompatible with immortality:

If something radically impossible is to be conceived of—and everything derives its sense from this impossibility—it is indeed dying *for the other* in the sense of dying *in place of* the other. I can give the other everything except immortality, except this *dying for her* to the extent of dying in place of her and so freeing her from her own death. I can die for the other in a situation where my death gives him a little longer to live, I can save someone by throwing myself in the water or fire in order to temporarily snatch him from the jaws of death, I can give her my heart in the literal or figurative sense in order to assure her a certain longevity. But I cannot die in her place, I cannot give her my life in exchange for her death. Only a mortal can give, as we said earlier. That should now be adjusted to read: and that mortal can only give to what is mortal since he can give everything except immortality, everything except salvation as immortality. (43/47)

28. For examples of influential misreadings of Derrida's notion of justice see my discussion of Critchley in Chapter 3 and Caputo in Chapter 4.

29. Derrida, "Force of Law," 255/58. Subsequent page references are given in the text.

30. See Derrida's argument that "there is no justice except to the degree that some event is possible which, as event, exceeds calculation, rules, programs, anticipations and so forth" ("Force of Law," 257/61).

31. See *Specters of Marx*, where Derrida spells out that the undeconstructible condition of justice is the disjointure of time, which he also describes as "the de-totalizing condition of justice," since it inscribes the possibility of corruption, evil, and mischief (*Un-Fug*) at the heart of justice itself. The undeconstructible condition of justice is thus "a condition that is itself *in deconstruction* and remains, and must remain (that is the injunction) in the disjointure of the *Un-Fug*" (28/56).

32. See Kant's remark that "nothing happens" in eternity, since whatever happens belongs to time ("The End of All Things," 222).

33. The main source in Derrida for the conception of infinite finitude is Hegel rather than Kant, in particular the discussion of negative and positive infinity in Hegel's *Science of Logic*. See my analysis in Chapter 3.

34. For a more general discussion of Derrida's essay see Peter Fenves's excellent introduction to his edited collection *Raising the Tone of Philosophy*.

35. Cf. Derrida's statement in the same text: "'Come' is *only* derivable, absolutely derivable, but only from the other, from nothing that may be an origin . . . from nothing not already derivable and arrivable without *rive* [bank, shore]" (166–67/95).

36. The argument here—that each death is the end of the world—is elaborated twenty years later in *Chaque fois unique, la fin du monde* and in the simultaneously published *Béliers*. I discuss the argument and its implications in Chapter 4.

37. See Derrida's suggestive commentary on Maurice Blanchot's elliptical sentence "Dead—immortal" (*Mort—immortel*). In Derrida's reading the sentence signifies that one is "dead *because* immortal, dead *insofar as* immortal (an immortal does not live) . . . for once dead one no longer dies and, according to all possible modes, one has become immortal . . . an immortal is someone who is dead" (*Demeure*, 67/86). Derrida goes on to emphasize that "the 'dead—immortal' did not in the least signify eternity. The immortality of death is anything save the eternity of the present" (69/89). Rather, that immortality is the same as death means that life can only be given through the infinite finitude of survival. "The abidance [*demeurance*] that we will discuss does not *remain* like the permanence of an eternity. It is time itself" (69/89).

Chapter 2

1. The most important study in this regard is *La voix et le phénomène*, translated as *Speech and Phenomena* and abbreviated as *SP* in the text. Derrida's other

studies of Husserl include *Edmund Husserl's Origin of Geometry*; and Derrida's remarkable master's thesis, *Le problème de la genèse dans la philosophie de Husserl*. Furthermore, *Writing and Difference* (abbreviated as *WD*) features one essay on Husserl and *Margins of Philosophy* another. See also Derrida's commentary on Husserl in the chapter "Linguistics and Grammatology," in *Of Grammatology* (abbreviated as *OG*); in the essay "Violence and Metaphysics," from *Writing and Difference*; and in *On Touching*. For an early but still valuable account of Derrida's relation to Husserl, see Henry Staten's excellent book *Wittgenstein and Derrida*.

2. Husserl's most important writings on the phenomenology of internal time-consciousness have been gathered in the tenth volume of *Husserliana*, entitled *Zur Phänomenologie des inneren Zeitbewußtseins, 1893–1917*. Hereafter abbreviated as *Hua* 10. Page references refer only to the German edition, since these page numbers are also continually marked in the margins of the English edition.

3. See Zahavi's acclaimed and indeed admirable study *Self-Awareness and Alterity*. Bernet's central book, *La vie du sujet*, gathers a large number of texts written between the 1970s and the 1990s. See also Bernet's articles "Is the Present Ever Present? Phenomenology and the Metaphysics of Presence"; and "An Intentionality Without Subject or Object?" Daniel Birnbaum's *The Hospitality of Presence* further develops Bernet's perspective on Husserl's theory of subjectivity.

4. *Hua* 10:192. See also ibid., 22–23; and the first book of Husserl's *Ideen* (*Hua* 3:93).

5. See *Hua* 10:332, 342, 355.

6. For an account of how Husserl came to posit this level of consciousness see Brough, "The Emergence of an Absolute Consciousness in Husserl's Early Writings on Time-Consciousness."

7. *Hua* 10:119; see also Appendix 12, 126–27.

8. See *Hua* 10:112, 127, 285–89, and § 36, 37, 38, 39.

9. See, for example, Bernet, "Is the Present Ever Present?" 108–12; and Birnbaum, *The Hospitality of Presence*, 131–35.

10. See Derrida's analysis in *Speech and Phenomena*, 60–66/67–74; and in *Le problème de la genèse dans la philosophie de Husserl*, 127–28, 168–69.

11. See *Hua* 10:284, 343–44, as well as § 37, 38, 39.

12. See Merleau-Ponty, *Phenomenology of Perception*, in particular 424–26/484–87; and Ricoeur, *Temps et Récit*, vol. 3. See also Bernet's essay "La présence du passé," in *La vie du sujet*, 215–41.

13. See Ricoeur, *Temps et Récit*, 3:46–47; Zahavi, *Self-Awareness and Alterity*, 85–87, 89–90; Birnbaum, *The Hospitality of Presence*, 176–80; Brough, "Husserl and the Deconstruction of Time," 516–17; Cobb-Stevens, "Derrida and Husserl on the Status of Retention," 370–74.

14. See *Hua* 10:112, 127, 333–34, 371.

15. See James, *The Principles of Psychology*, as well as *The Works of William James*, 13. For a trenchant critique of James's theory see Shaun Gallagher, *The Inordinance of Time*, 17–31.

16. For Husserl's discussion of this analogy see, for example, the fifth of his *Cartesian Meditations*; and § 54 in *The Crisis of European Sciences and Transcendental Phenomenology*. In chapter 6 of *Edmund Husserl's Origin of Geometry*, Derrida briefly calls attention to the analogy and precipitates his argument that it has critical implications for Husserl's conception of presence, an argument that is developed in *Speech and Phenomena*.

17. In his book *Derrida and Husserl: The Basic Problem of Phenomenology*, Leonard Lawlor has rightly emphasized the importance of Husserl's notion of *Vergegenwärtigung* for Derrida's thinking. However, Lawlor does not engage the critiques that Husserl scholars have directed against Derrida's reading of *Vergegenwärtigung* and does not pursue the issue with regard to Husserl's phenomenology of time beyond Derrida's own remarks on the subject. Lawlor aptly points to the importance of the distinction between form and content in Husserl's phenomenology of internal time-consciousness (*Derrida and Husserl*, 185), but he does not develop the distinction, which is crucial to the critique that Husserl scholars have directed against Derrida's reading. In order to engage these critiques—and to demonstrate the necessity of *Vergegenwärtigung* on the deepest level of transcendental phenomenology—one must proceed to the level of "the absolute flow" in Husserl's account of internal time-consciousness, which is what I seek to do in this chapter.

18. See Ricoeur, *Temps et Récit*, 3:46–47; Zahavi, *Self-Awareness and Alterity*, 85–87, 89–90; Birnbaum, *The Hospitality of Presence*, 170, 176–80, 184; Brough, "Husserl and the Deconstruction of Time," 529; Cobb-Stevens, "Derrida and Husserl on the Status of Retention," 370–74.

19. See Henrich's influential essay "Fichtes ursprüngliche Einsicht"; and Henry's *L'essence de la manifestation* and *Phénoménologie matérielle*. Henrich and Henry are consistent in the sense that only an absolutely self-generating instance could put an end to the regress of reflection, by grounding its dyadic structure in a monadic unity. Following the same logic, Husserl emphasizes that consciousness must be "*consciousness* in each of its phases" (*Hua* 10: Appendix 9, 119); that is, it must be self-aware without delay if we are to avoid an infinite regress.

20. Henry's *L'essence de la manifestation* appeared in 1963, four years before Derrida's *La voix et le phénomène*, which can be seen as an implicit polemic against Henry. A comparative study of the two books would in any case reveal a systematic disagreement between Henry and Derrida that is instructive for understanding their respective positions.

21. See Gasché, *The Tain of the Mirror*, 225–39. See also *Of Grammatology*, 165–66/235–37, and *Speech and Phenomena*, 82/92.

22. Ibid., 236.

23. See Bernet, "An Intentionality Without Subject or Object?"; and Bernet, *La vie du sujet*, 297–327.

24. It is here instructive to compare Husserl's theory of time with Merleau-Ponty's chapter "Temporality" in his *Phenomenology of Perception*. Like Husserl, Merleau-Ponty argues that there must be an ultimate consciousness that is given *in itself*—namely, without being divided by time—since we would otherwise be launched onto an infinite regress (422/483). While Merleau-Ponty maintains that this ultimate consciousness should not be understood as an "eternal subject," he nevertheless designates it as a fundamental presence in which the self coincides with itself (424/485). What Merleau-Ponty posits is thus a pure autoaffection, where "the affecting agent and the affected recipient are one" (426/487). At the same time, however, Merleau-Ponty himself admits that the structure of autoaffection necessarily involves at least two instances and that "the word consciousness has no meaning independently of this duality" (426/488). As we will see in detail, this conflict between the metaphysical demand for an originary unity and the minimal dyad of temporal autoaffection haunts Husserl's phenomenology of time as well.

25. *Hua* 10:83 (trans. mod.). See *Hua* 10:381–82 for the other manuscript version.

26. See Zahavi, *Self-Awareness and Alterity*, 73.

27. See Bernet, "Is the Present Ever Present?" 107–11.

28. See Birnbaum, *The Hospitality of Presence*, 127. Subsequent page references are given in the text.

29. Zahavi, *Self-Awareness and Alterity*, 135.

30. See Derrida's description of "temporalization as the opening of the present to *another* absolute present. This being outside itself of time is its *spacing*: an *arche-stage*. This stage, as the relation of one present to another present *as such*, that is, as non-derived re-presentation . . . produces the structure of the sign in general as 'reference,' as being-for-something (*für etwas sein*), and radically forbids its reduction. There is no constituting subjectivity. The very concept of constitution itself must be deconstructed" (*SP*, 84–85/94; trans. mod.). See also Derrida's argument concerning how "the possibility of re-petition in its most general form, the trace in its most universal sense, is a possibility that not only must inhabit the pure actuality of the now but constitute it through the very movement of *différance* that it introduces" (*SP*, 67/75; trans. mod.).

31. See *Of Grammatology*, where Derrida points out that "the double movement of retention and protention" is not limited to "the possibilities of the 'intentional consciousness'" but rather answers to an arche-writing that is at work on every level of life (84/125).

32. See the section "Of Transcendental Violence" in Derrida's essay "Violence and Metaphysics," from *Writing and Difference*.

33. Derrida, *Of Grammatology*, 110/162; see also 106, 112, 135/156, 164–65, 195.

34. See, for example, chapters 5 and 6 of *Speech and Phenomena*; and *Positions*, where Derrida reinforces that for him alterity and spacing are "absolutely indissociable" (81, 94, 106–7n42/107, 130, 108–9n31). See also *Rogues*, where he recalls his persistent argument that alterity must be understood in terms of spacing and maintains that there has been no ethical or political "turn" in his thinking (38–39/63–64). I will seek to consolidate this claim in the next chapter.

Chapter 3

1. To be sure, Derrida himself refers to Levinas (along with a number of others: Nietzsche, Freud, Heidegger, contemporary biology) when he accounts for his choice of the term "trace" in *Of Grammatology*. But as Derrida points out, his implied reference to these discourses does not mean that he endorses them. Moreover, Derrida goes on to explain that his use of the term designates the "arche-phenomenon of 'memory,'" which must be thought before the opposition of nature and culture, animality and humanity." The trace is thus inextricable from "*différance* as temporalization" and from the finitude of life in general. See *Of Grammatology*, 70–71/102–4.

2. See the essay "Enigma and Phenomenon," which further reinforces that for Levinas the "absolute past" answers to what traditionally has been designated as absolute presence, namely the One. It is pivotal to note that when Levinas says that the One has never been present, he uses the term "presence" as synonymous with a time of disintegration. Exempting the One from disjointed presence thus becomes a way of saving it from the contamination of finitude: "He who has passed beyond has never been a presence. He preceded all presence and exceeded every contemporaneity in a time which is not . . . a disintegration and disappearance of finite beings, but the original antecedence of God relative to a world which cannot accommodate him, the immemorial past which has never presented itself . . . but is the One, which every philosophy would like to express, beyond being" (*Basic Philosophical Writings*, 77).

3. See the chapter "Rhetoric and Injustice" in section 1 of *Totality and Infinity*, as well as "Reason and the Face" in section 3. See also Derrida's comments on Levinas's metaphysics of "expression" and "living speech" (*WD*, 101–3/149–52) and on Levinas's idea of a pure language without rhetoric (147–48/218–20).

4. See Levinas, *Otherwise Than Being or Beyond Essence*, 143–45, 199/183–85.

5. For a succinct summary of the main traits of the ethicotheoretical decision of metaphysics see Derrida, *Limited Inc*, 93/173–74.

6. Derrida outlines his thinking of essential corruptibility in *Limited Inc*

(77–79/146–49). In later work it is reiterated as an essential pervertibility; see, for example, *Adieu*, 34–35/68–69; and *Of Hospitality*, 53, 55, 65, 79/51, 53, 61, 75.

7. For Derrida's brief remarks on lesser violence see *Writing and Difference*, 313n21, 117, 130/136n1, 172, 191.

8. Cf. Derrida's claim that *time is violence*: "In the last analysis, if one wishes to determine violence as the necessity that the other not appear as what it is, that it not be respected except in, for, and by the same, that it be dissimulated by the same in the very freeing of its phenomenon, then time is violence" (*WD*, 195/133).

9. Derrida develops this double argument in the section "Of Transcendental Violence" in "Violence and Metaphysics."

10. See, for example, *Mémoires*, where Derrida spells out "the other *as other*, that is, as mortal for a mortal" (39/57).

11. See, for example, *Humanisme de l'autre homme*, where Levinas maintains that "Egoism" is "Evil" (81). Levinas's denunciation of egoism should be contrasted with Derrida's affirmation of a constitutive narcissism: "I believe that without a movement of narcissistic reappropriation, the relation to the other would be absolutely destroyed, it would be destroyed in advance. The relation to the other—even if it remains asymmetrical, open, without possible reappropriation—must trace a movement of reappropriation in the image of oneself for love to be possible, for example. Love is narcissistic" (*Points . . .* , 199). While Derrida does not explicitly engage Levinas in this remark, it exemplifies a recurrent schema in his readings of Levinas. What Levinas deplores as a contamination of the proper relation to the other (in this case, self-love) is for Derrida the possibility of any relation to the other. To eliminate contamination is thus to eliminate the relation to the other in advance. This answers to Derrida's general argument that pure nonviolence is pure violence.

12. Cf. Chalier, who observes that Levinas's philosophy "requires that the subject knows how to distinguish between the brutal heteronomy of the tyrant" and the ethical heteronomy of the other (Chalier, *What Ought I to Do?* 62, 78–79).

13. Derrida does not develop this remark, but we can establish its pertinence by considering Hegel's account of time in his *Philosophy of Nature*. Here, Hegel states that "negativity, thus posited for itself, is Time" (§ 257). The temporal can never be given in itself but is always "coming-to-be and passing away" (§ 258). This inherent negativity of time entails that time is incompatible with the determination of being as presence in itself: "it is that being which, inasmuch as it *is*, is not, and inasmuch as it is *not*, is" (§ 258). It is therefore crucial for Hegel that the Notion is "neither within time, nor something temporal" (§ 258). To be dialectical, the power of time must be subjected to the power of the Notion, which negates the negativity of time in the movement of sublation. Inversely, to think time as irreducible is to think a negativity that cannot be sublated: "infinite time,

when it is still conceived as time, not as sublated time, is also to be distinguished from eternity. It is not this time but another time, and again another time, and so on . . . if thought cannot resolve the finite into the eternal" (§ 247).

14. See Derrida's claims that "*infinite différance is finite*" (*SP*, 102/114) and that "finitude becomes infinitude, according to a non-Hegelian identity" (*Dissemination*, 253/285). These formulations are notorious for their opacity, but following the logic I develop under the heading of infinite finitude, we can account for Derrida's apparent paradoxes. On the one hand, the movement of *différance* is infinite, since the tracing of time is the condition for anything to be and thus operates indefinitely. On the other hand, the movement of *différance* is finite, since the tracing of time itself is absolutely destructible and thus may be extinguished, in which case everything would be extinguished. The logic of this argument can be further clarified if we relate it to a central argument in Hegel's discussion of finitude. In *Science of Logic* Hegel points out that "no philosophy or opinion, or understanding, will let itself be tied to the standpoint that the finite is absolute; the very opposite is expressly present in the assertion of the finite; the finite is limited, transitory, it is *only* finite, not imperishable; this is directly implied in its determination and expression. But the point is, whether in thinking of the finite one holds fast to the *being* of finitude and lets the *transitoriness* continue to be, or whether the *transitoriness* and the *ceasing-to-be cease to be*" (130). This passage succinctly delineates the difference between the dialectical and the deconstructive understanding of finitude. For Hegel the negation of time—the "ceasing-to-be" that is intrinsic to all finite beings—is overcome by the negation of the negation, the "ceasing to be of the ceasing-to-be." For Derrida, on the contrary, finitude is infinitely finite and can never be sublated in a positive infinity. The ceasing to be of the ceasing-to-be would not bring about consummation; it would rather eliminate the condition for anything to be.

15. See Rodolphe Gasché's essay "Structural Infinity," which provides a valuable account of Hegel's and Derrida's respective conceptions of infinity. Gasché rightly emphasizes that for Derrida positive infinity (and thus totalization) is impossible for "structural" reasons and not because of empirical limitations. Gasché, however, does not address the link between the impossibility of totalization and the constitution of time, which Derrida makes explicit in "Violence and Metaphysics." For Derrida the movement of temporalization is not an effect of the empirical but is the "ultratranscendental" condition for the infinite finitude of being in general. Thus, the constitutive movement of temporalization is the reason *why* totalization is impossible for structural (necessary) and not empirical (contingent) reasons.

16. See Beardsworth, *Derrida and the Political*, 137.

17. See, for example, Cornell and Critchley (*The Ethics of Deconstruction*), both of whom refer to Bernasconi in their attempts to find an "ethical mo-

ment" in deconstruction and to mitigate the critique of Levinas in "Violence and Metaphysics." See also Jill Robbins, who relies on Bernasconi and Critchley for her claim that "the alterities with which Derrida's work is concerned may be shown to have an ethical force" and that "it is possible to make explicit in Derrida's work the ethical—in Levinas's sense of the word—significance that invests it, the ethical demand to which it responds" (*Altered Reading*, 29–30).

18. For a trenchant reading of *Adieu* along these lines see Bennington's chapter "Deconstruction and Ethics" in his *Interrupting Derrida*.

19. See Levinas, *Otherwise Than Being or Beyond Essence*, 157–60/200–204.

20. For an insightful critique of Cornell in a different context, see chapter 3 of Vicki Kirby's remarkable book *Telling Flesh*.

21. For example, in "Justice Without Ethics?" Bernasconi holds that what Derrida calls "justice" answers to what Levinas calls "the ethical." I take issue with this conception, which has been further developed by Critchley, in the following section of this chapter.

22. See, for example, Critchley's assertion that Derrida affirms "the primacy of an ethics of hospitality, whilst leaving open the sphere of the political as a realm of risk and danger" (*Ethics-Politics-Subjectivity*, 275). On Critchley's account, this is Derrida's argument in *Adieu*. As we have seen, however, *Adieu* elucidates the constitutive violence of an arche-betrayal or arche-perjury, which undermines Levinas's distinction between ethics and politics. The arche-necessity of discriminating between innumerable others is also a persistent theme throughout *Politics of Friendship*.

23. See *Ethics-Politics-Subjectivity*, where Critchley attempts to legitimize his reading by maintaining that Derrida employs "[Levinas's] conception of justice to illuminate his own account" (99, 151). But, in fact, Derrida warns against such a reading in the very passage that Critchley refers to: "since I would have other difficult questions about Levinas's difficult discourse, I cannot be content to borrow a conceptual trait without risking confusions or analogies. And so I will go no further in this direction" ("Force of Law," 250/49). The point, then, is that we cannot base an analogy between Levinas and Derrida on the simple fact that they both speak of justice as a relation to the other. Rather, an expression such as "the other" does not have any inherent meaning, which is why we must follow the precise articulation and syntax of the arguments in question. If we do that, I argue, it turns out that Levinas's and Derrida's respective notions of "the other" are incompatible.

24. See *Of Hospitality*, where Derrida maintains that unconditional hospitality is not a regulative Idea, which would be unattainable because of the limitations of finitude. Rather, unconditional hospitality is impossible for conceptual, structural reasons and thus "barred" by internal contradictions, as Derrida puts it (149/131).

25. As Derrida puts it in *Adieu*: "this possible hospitality to the worst is necessary so that good hospitality can have a chance, the chance of letting the other come" (35/69). This should be linked to what Derrida in *Of Hospitality* calls "the incalculable timing of hospitality" (127/113), which opens the chance of beneficial or devastating contretemps. Because of this undecidable, nonethical opening, any "ethics of hospitality" is "limited and contradictory *a priori*" (65/63; see also ibid., 55, 81, 125/53, 75, 111).

26. For Derrida's distinction between hospitality of invitation and hospitality of visitation see in particular his "Hostipitality," 360–62; "Autoimmunity: Real and Symbolic Suicides," 128–30; "As If It Were Possible, 'Within Such Limits,'" 400–401n8/296–97n1; and *For What Tomorrow*, 59–61/101–4.

Chapter 4

1. Augustine, *Confessions*, book 4, chapter 6. Subsequent references to the *Confessions* are given in the text, cited by book number and chapter number respectively.

2. Derrida, *Mémoires*, 29/49. Subsequent page references are given in the text.

3. For a deconstructive analysis of the treatment of time in book 11 of Augustine's *Confessions* see the chapter "Tidens distentio: Augustinus," in Martin Hägglund, *Kronofobi*. For incisive commentary on Augustine and mourning see also Henry Staten's *Wittgenstein and Derrida*, 136–39, and his magnificent *Eros in Mourning*, 6–8.

4. This collection of texts first appeared in English in 2001 under the title *The Work of Mourning*, edited and with an excellent introduction by Pascale-Anne Brault and Michael Naas. In 2003 an expanded French edition appeared under the title *Chaque fois unique, la fin du monde*. I refer to the title of the French edition because it contains a preface by Derrida that is not available in the English edition. Except for the quotation from this preface, page references in the text refer to the English edition first, followed by page references to the French edition.

5. See Kant, *Religion Within the Limits of Reason Alone*, 32.

6. Derrida, in *Arguing with Derrida*, ed. Simon Glendinning, 54.

7. See in particular Augustine's *On Free Choice of the Will*, 1.16.

8. In addition to *The Prayers and Tears of Jacques Derrida*, see Caputo's books *Against Ethics*; *Deconstruction in a Nutshell*; and *On Religion*. Caputo has also contributed essays to the volumes on Derrida and religion that he has coedited; see *God, the Gift, and Postmodernism*; *Questioning God*; and *Augustine and Postmodernism*. The two volumes dedicated to Caputo's work are *Religion With/ Out Religion*, ed. James H. Olthuis, and *A Passion for the Impossible*, ed. Mark

Dooley. For additional studies of Derrida that defer to Caputo see Hugh Rayment-Pickard, *Impossible God*; Theodore W. Jennings, *Reading Derrida/Thinking
Paul*; Owen Ware, "Impossible Passions"; and James K. A. Smith, *Jacques Derrida*.

  9. Caputo, *The Prayers and Tears of Jacques Derrida*, 3. All page references to
Caputo given in the main text refer to this book.

  10. Eckhart, "Detachment," in *The Best of Meister Eckhart*, 88. Subsequent
page references are given in the text.

  11. See Eckhart, Sermon 25, in *Meister Eckhart: A Modern Translation*,
212–17.

  12. For this definition of God see Eckhart, Sermon 21, in *Meister Eckhart:
Teacher and Preacher*, 281.

  13. See Eckhart, "Counsels on Discernment," in *Meister Eckhart: Sermons and
Treatises*, 2:253. See also Eckhart's remark that "one must discard the form and
unite with the formless essence, for God's spiritual comfort is intangible and is
only offered to those who despise all mortal consolations" ("Detachment," in
The Best of Meister Eckhart, 97).

  14. See Eckhart, Sermon 28, in *Meister Eckhart: A Modern Translation*, 231. Cf.
the argument in Eckhart's treatise "The Kingdom of God":

> It sounds strange to say that the soul must lose her God, yet I affirm that in a way it is
> more necessary to perfection that the soul lose God than that she lose creatures. Every-
> thing must go. The soul must subsist in absolute nothingness. It is the full intention of
> God that the soul shall lose her God, for as long as the soul possesses God, is aware of
> God, knows God, she is aloof from God. God desires to annihilate himself in the soul
> in order that the soul may lose herself. For that God is God he gets from creatures.
> When the soul became a creature she obtained a God. When she lets slip her creature-
> hood, God remains to himself that he is, and the soul honors God most in being quit
> of God and leaving him to himself. (Eckhart, *Meister Eckhart*, ed. Pfeiffer, 274)

  15. See Pseudo-Dionysius, *The Celestial Hierarchy*, in *Pseudo-Dionysius: The
Complete Works*, 151–52.

  16. Caputo quotes the passage in *On Religion*, 7, and repeatedly alludes to it
in *The Prayers and Tears of Jacques Derrida*.

  17. Derrida, *Rogues*, 84/123. The same formulation can be found in "Autoimmunity: Real and Symbolic Suicides," 134.

  18. Derrida, "As If It Were Possible, 'Within Such Limits,'" 361/308. Subsequent page references are given in the text.

  19. Derrida, "Autoimmunity: Real and Symbolic Suicides," 120.

  20. See Derrida, *Specters of Marx*, 28/56; as well as my analysis in Chapter 1.

  21. See *The Prayers and Tears of Jacques Derrida*, where Caputo writes that "in
the kingdom of God, where God rules, God will give us just enough of what we
need today, and not so much as to burden us with wealth or with seeking wealth"

(224). According to Caputo, "the kingdom is now, today," so we should stop worrying about tomorrow: "Have the madness not to ask what you shall eat or drink or wear, not to ask where your next meal is coming from, not to seek job security, medical insurance, or guaranteed housing. . . . Stop thinking about tomorrow. Let tomorrow worry about itself" (224). To be sure, Caputo holds that there is "time" in the kingdom of God, but it is a time that cancels out the past and the future in the absolute instance of "today." Hence, it is no time at all. See also Caputo's later essay on the kingdom of God:

> The coming of the kingdom lays anxiety to rest, for the rule of God, which is in the midst of us, sustains us. Rather than something futural, this is a *presential* time, a time of presencing, which lets today be today. . . . Forget what is owed to you in the past; forget what you owe to the future; tear up the chain of time and take today as a gift, let us say a free gift, a free as opposed to a bound time, an open or released time. In it, something new and freeing has begun now which is now with us and frees us from the past and future. (Caputo, "Reason, History, and a Little Madness," 99, 101)

22. See Kearney's influential book *The God Who May Be*, and his essay "Desire of God." I quote from the essay, but the same arguments can be found in chapter 4 of *The God Who May Be*. A collection of essays has recently been devoted to Kearney's work: see Manoussakis, *After God*.

23. See Caputo in *The Prayers and Tears of Jacques Derrida*: "Like prophetic religion, deconstruction awaits the coming of the just one" (118).

24. Caputo, "Discussion with Richard Kearney," 131.

25. Derrida, "Perhaps or Maybe," 9. Subsequent page references are given in the text.

26. Derrida, "Hospitality, Justice, and Responsibility," 80. See also Derrida, *Memoirs of the Blind*.

27. Caputo, *Against Ethics*, 91.

28. The *salut* figures in five texts that were all first published in 1996: *Monolingualism of the Other*; "Faith and Knowledge"; "'Dead Man Running'"; "How to Name"; and "Avances." It recurs in a number of subsequent texts, such as *On Touching*; *H. C. for Life*; and *Chaque fois unique, la fin du monde*.

29. Derrida, "'Dead Man Running,'" 258/168. Subsequent page references are given in the text.

30. Derrida, "How to Name," 218/203. Subsequent page references are given in the text.

31. Hence, I take issue with John Llewelyn's account of the messianic in his *Appositions of Jacques Derrida and Emmanuel Levinas*. Llewelyn provides a paraphrase of Levinas's notion of messianic triumph but does not raise any critical questions and, moreover, suggests an affinity with Derrida's notion of the messianic, without pursuing a specific discussion of the issues involved (229–30).

Apparently, Llewelyn thinks that the suggested affinity is convincing enough to close his entire book. My argument is, on the contrary, that the question of "the messianic" exemplifies the general incompatibility of Levinas's and Derrida's respective thinking, which I analyzed in Chapter 3.

32. Derrida, *A Taste for the Secret*, 20. Subsequent page references are given in the text.

33. Caputo, *The Prayers and Tears of Jacques Derrida*, xxviii. Subsequent page references are given in the text.

34. Caputo, *Deconstruction in a Nutshell*, 159. Subsequent page references are given in the text.

35. See, for example, *The Prayers and Tears of Jacques Derrida*, xxi, 205; and Caputo, *On Religion*, 114.

36. Derrida, *Specters of Marx*, 167/266.

37. Derrida, "Faith and Knowledge," 56/30.

38. Derrida, "Nietzsche and the Machine," 255.

39. Derrida's brief remarks on the concept of "resurrection" can also be seen to adhere to such a radical atheism. On the one hand, Derrida refutes every religious notion of resurrection, since each death is an irrevocable end of the world that excludes resurrection (see *Chaque fois unique*, 11). On the other hand, he opens the possibility of reading the desire for resurrection against itself. On such a reading, the desire for resurrection does not stem from a desire for "an immortal body or a glorious body" but rather from the desire for mortal survival that "engages us to a vulnerable body, one that may be forgotten again" (see "Language Is Never Owned," 107).

40. Derrida, *The Other Heading*, 78/76.

41. Derrida, "As If It Were Possible, 'Within Such Limits,'" 362/308–9. Subsequent page references are given in the text.

42. Derrida, "Avances," 38.

43. Derrida, "Nietzsche and the Machine," 255. See also "A Certain Impossible Possibility of Saying the Event," 458–59.

44. Derrida, *Memoires*, 150/143.

45. Caputo, *The Prayers and Tears of Jacques Derrida*, 147.

46. See my analysis of Derrida's notion of the apocalyptic in Chapter 1.

47. Derrida, "The Animal That Therefore I Am (More to Follow)," 386–87/36.

48. Derrida, *Writing and Difference*, 108/160. See also "How to Avoid Speaking," where Derrida recalls his definition of the trace or *différance* as an infinite finitude, which entails that "the distinction between a finite and an infinite cause of the trace" is "secondary" and "itself an effect of trace or *différance*" (29/561). See also Derrida's remark on the general necessity of the tracing of time ("How to Avoid Speaking," 12/545).

49. De Vries, *Philosophy and the Turn to Religion*, 434. Unless otherwise indicated all page references to de Vries refer to this book.

50. The context of Derrida's statement is a discussion of *khōra* as a name for "that spacing which, not allowing itself to be dominated by any theological, ontological, or anthropological instance . . . does not even announce itself as 'beyond being' in accordance with a path of negation, a *via negativa*." The spacing of *khōra* is "radically heterogeneous to the safe and sound, to the holy and the sacred," and is neither "the Good, nor God." On the contrary, it "will always resist them, will always have been (and no future anterior, even, will have been able to reappropriate, inflect or reflect a *chora* without faith or law) the very place of an infinite resistance" ("Faith and Knowledge," 57–58/34–35). De Vries does not address any of these claims when he quotes the passage in question. See de Vries, *Philosophy and the Turn to Religion*, 110.

51. Gasché, "God, for Example," 170. For de Vries's objections to Gasché, see *Philosophy and the Turn to Religion*, 90, 355–57.

52. See also de Vries's remarks that "the figure, the desire, and promise of 'God'" is "the best exemplary instance of the structure of the trace" (93) and that "'God' may well be the most proper name for this trace itself" (355).

53. Derrida, "'Others Are Secret Because They Are Other,'" 159/393–94. See also *Writing and Difference*, 230/339.

54. See de Vries's *Religion and Violence*, where he claims that "what is undeconstructable, for Derrida, is not finitude" but rather "the fact that the historicity of finite existence remains tainted by a certain religiosity (theologemes and the rites of 'positive' religion)" (200). Contrary to de Vries's claim, theologemes and the rites of religion are *deconstructible* because the spacing of time—and thus radical finitude—is undeconstructible.

55. Apophatic theology is another name for negative theology and characteristically makes negative assertions about God (emphasizing what He is not). It is distinguished from kataphatic theology, which makes positive assertions about God.

56. De Vries's privileging of the name of God is even more apparent in his book *Minimal Theologies*, where he defines the premise for a minimal theology as follows: "The word *God* would thus signal itself *nowhere* and *everywhere*: almost nothing, it is at the same time the very heart of—at least all linguistic—meaning. But this meaning absolves itself from whatever *criteria* one would want to measure it against, whether semantically, epistemologically, normatively, pragmatically, or aesthetically. And this insight is not only the fruit of a modernist sensibility but lies at the very heart of the Scriptures" (590). De Vries seeks to align Derrida with such a minimal theology, but he can do so only by conflating Derrida with Levinas. As Peter Gilgen has pointed out, "perhaps the most insistent line of argumentation in *Minimal Theologies* consists of a leveling of the

profound differences between Levinas and Derrida" (99). Thus, de Vries maintains that the fundamental traits of minimal theology are to be found in "Levinas's philosophy of the trace of the absolutely other, especially as systematized—formalized, and, as it were, generalized, even radicalized and dramatized—in the studies Derrida has devoted to this author" (*Minimal Theologies*, 24). Again, de Vries does not provide an analysis of what Derrida means by the trace. As I demonstrated in Chapter 3, Levinas's and Derrida's respective notions of the trace are incompatible. For Levinas the trace is the trace of the positive infinity of God. For Derrida, on the contrary, the trace is the trace of the infinite finitude of time from which nothing is exempt.

57. Derrida, "The Animal That Therefore I Am (More to Follow)," 389/39.

58. See Caputo, *On Religion*, 3, 24–31.

59. See Caputo, *The Prayers and Tears of Jacques Derrida*, xxii, chapter 6, and "Conclusion."

60. For an insightful analysis of the relation to the mother in Augustine and Derrida, see the chapter on *Circumfession* in David Farrell Krell's excellent book, *The Purest of Bastards*, 175–99.

61. Derrida explicitly maintains that "I quite rightly pass for an atheist" (*Circumfession*, 155/146). Caputo tries to come to terms with this statement by claiming that Derrida's "passion for God rightly passes for an atheism about a certain Hellenistic God . . . that very finite Hellenistic creature called God" (*The Prayers and Tears of Jacques Derrida*, 334, 336). Derrida's passion for God would rather be in alliance with what Caputo calls a "Jewish Augustinianism" (333). This proposed alliance is quite untenable. While Caputo takes the title of his book from the prayers and tears in *Circumfession*, he never assesses that Derrida's prayers and tears stem from precisely the desire for mortal life that Augustine condemns after his religious conversion. Derrida himself reinforces that *Circumfession* is a "non-Christian deconstruction" of Augustine and that "it is not a Jewish deconstruction" ("Response to Catherine Malabou," 142). See also Derrida's remark that "I am being as non-Jewish as possible, as atheistic as possible" ("Confessions and 'Circumfession': A Roundtable with Jacques Derrida," 37). When asked to clarify his avowed atheism in the same roundtable, Derrida points out that his position with regard to atheism "depends on what the name God names" (38). My argument is that once we trace how Derrida employs the name "God," we can see how he adheres to a radical atheism. Contrary to Caputo's claim, it is not a matter of rejecting a finite creature called God but of rejecting any other God than a finite creature. In *Circumfession* Derrida glosses his God as "the other me, the other in me, the atheist God" (216/201) and emphasizes that "God goes to earth to death in me" (272/252). Derrida's passion for an impossible God is thus not a passion for a God for whom everything is possible. On the contrary, it is a passion for a mortal other. As Derrida writes in *Mémoires*: "The impossible here

is the other, such as he comes to us: as a mortal, to us mortals. And whom we love as such, affirming this to be good" (32/52).

62. For Derrida's account of this rule see *Circumfession* (35/37); and his "Response to Catherine Malabou" (139).

63. Derrida quotes one version of this question (*cur confitemur Deo scienti*: "Why we confess to God, when he knows [everything about us]") on the opening page of *Circumfession* (3/7). As Derrida points out, this formulation of the question is not literally Augustine's. It is rather a chapter title given in the 1649 French translation of the *Confessions* by Robert Arnauld d'Andilly, which was the first translation in which Derrida read the *Confessions* (see *Circumfession*, 8/11–12). For Augustine's treatment of the question see in particular *Confessions* 11.1. Derrida quotes passages from this section of the *Confessions* further on in *Circumfession* (75–76/74–75).

64. See Derrida's analysis of testimony as a making of truth in *Demeure*: "As a promise to *make truth*, according to Augustine's expression, where the witness must be irreplaceably alone, where the witness alone is capable of dying his own death, testimony always goes hand in hand with at least the *possibility* of fiction, perjury, and lie. Were this possibility to be eliminated, no testimony would be possible any longer; it could no longer have the meaning of testimony" (27/28). See also Derrida's comment on his making of truth in *Circumfession*: "I was not relying on making the truth; I was not relying on the truth that was made. I was just trying to demonstrate that this originality of making the truth was, of course, open to perjury, to invention, and to lying" ("Response to Catherine Malabou," 140).

65. Cf. Derrida's argument in *Demeure*: "Every one of us can say at every instant: really, I don't remember what I felt; I can't describe what I felt at that moment, it's impossible, and I can't analyze it in any case. What was me is no longer me," which entails that "I" cannot "answer for what this other me—more other than any other—did, or even thought or felt because of the troubling vertiginousness that calls into the chasm of that instant and especially because what separates the two egological identities is nothing less than death itself, that is to say, everything, an infinite world. The two die but he is dead, I survive, he survived, I am dead" (66/85).

66. For Derrida's analysis of the temporality of testimony see in particular *Demeure*, 33, 40–41/36–37, 46–48.

67. Cf. Derrida's declaration in *Circumfession*:

it remains to be understood of time, and of the time of writing, i.e., the inheritance of the last will of which nothing has yet been said, I'm sure of that, that touches the nerve of that for which one writes when one does not believe in one's own survival nor in the survival of anything at all, when one writes for the present but a present that is *made*, you hear, in the sense in which SA wants to *make* truth, only out of the return upon itself of that refused, *denied,* survival, refusals and denials attested by the writing itself, the last will of each word, where my writing enjoys this self-privation, exulting in giving itself as a present, before witnesses, the mortality that inheritance primarily means. . . . (284–85/262–63)

68. For Derrida's analysis of the temporality of the date see his essay "Schibboleth: For Paul Celan," which can be read usefully alongside *Circumfession,* where the inscription and anniversary return of dates is a major motif. I have elsewhere developed Derrida's analysis of the date as a model for reading the temporality of writing in general and the temporality of poetic address in particular. See Hägglund, *Kronofobi,* chapter 1.

69. Derrida, "'This Strange Institution Called Literature,'" in *Acts of Literature,* 34. Subsequent page references are given in the text.

70. See Derrida, "'Dialanguages,'" 143–52/153–61. Subsequent page references are given in the text.

71. See Derrida's brief but suggestive remark in *A Taste for the Secret:* "I don't believe there can be full enjoyment [*jouissance*]. If it were full it would not be enjoyment" (88–89).

72. See Derrida's play on *garder* in his essay "Aphorism Countertime," where he writes, "Un gage peut toujours s'inverser qui garde la mort" (422/524). Nicholas Royle aptly translates this sentence as "A pledge which keeps (off) death can always invert itself."

73. See *Learning to Live Finally,* where Derrida emphasizes that he cannot learn how to live insofar as learning to live means "learning to die, learning to take into account, so as to accept, absolute mortality" (24). The movement of survival that makes it *possible* to learn how to live—by giving us time to live in the first place—is rather what makes it *impossible* to learn how to die, since the movement of survival is a resistance to and not an acceptance of absolute death. As Derrida points out: "learning to live is always narcissistic. One wants to live as much as possible, to save oneself, to persevere" (30). Learning to live is thus impossible as such, since it consists in struggling against the death it is supposed to learn to accept. Like everyone else, Derrida is at war with himself, in an autoimmune battle that he cannot finally master or come to terms with: "I am at war with myself . . . and I say contradictory things that are, we might say, in a real tension; they are what construct me, make me live, and will make me die. I sometimes see this war as terrifying and difficult to bear, but at the same time I know that it is life. I will find peace only in eternal rest. Thus, I cannot say that I assume this contradiction, but I know that it is what keeps me alive, and makes me ask precisely the question you recalled earlier: 'how does one learn to live?'" (49). See also an earlier interview with Derrida, where he objects to the idea of an art of dying:

I do not think that there is an *ars moriendi*. . . . If there is death, if death happens, it will defeat any kind of art of dying. What I describe as the modality of the maybe does not imply that we teach ourselves or deliberately choose the maybe, it is not a matter of choice. We try all the time to resist the perhaps, to protect ourselves against the absolutely unpredictable coming. . . . What I try to describe under the strange word perhaps is not an art of living, an ethics, it is an affection, we are exposed to the perhaps. And we have to take into account the fact that, however prepared, protecting, resisting we may be, we remain exposed to what is coming. ("Perhaps or Maybe," 6)

74. In an earlier passage in *Circumfession* Derrida writes: "I'm having a great time, I will have had such a great time, but it costs a crazy price" (141/134). There may always be a crazy price to pay for the given time, since anything can befall him even when he has the greatest time. Like everyone else, Derrida cannot know what will happen to him but is rather "drawing nonknowledge from the future of what happens" (142/135). As I have argued throughout this book, such nonknowledge does not stem from a cognitive limitation but from the unpredictable coming of time as the condition for anything to happen. Derrida maintains that he does not "love nonknowledge for itself" (141/135)—it is rather the source of both hope and fear—but without it nothing would be desirable: "this nonknowledge is the only interesting thing, the best condition for having a great time like a lunatic, that's the happening I oppose or reveal to G.'s absolute theologic program, not that I love nonknowledge for itself" (141/134–35).

75. See the similar formulation in Derrida's text in memory of Louis Marin: "He is no more, he whom we see in images or in recollection, he of whom we speak, whom we cite, whom we try to let speak—he is no more, he is no longer here, no longer there. *And nothing can begin to dissipate the terrifying and chilling light of this certainty.* As if respect for this certainty were still a debt, the last one, owed to the friend" (*The Work of Mourning*, 159–60/198; my emphasis).

Chapter 5

1. Derrida, *Specters of Marx*, 87/144; see my analysis in Chapters 3 and 4.

2. As Derrida writes, "if there is a deconstruction of all presumption to a determining certainty of a present justice, it itself operates on the basis of an 'idea of justice' that is infinite, infinite because irreducible, irreducible because owed to the other . . . because it has *come*, because it is *coming* [*parce qu'elle est* venue] the coming of the other as always other singularity" ("Force of Law," 254/55). The idea of justice is thus indissociable from the negative infinity of time: "Justice remains *to come*, it remains *by coming* [*la justice reste à venir*], it *has* to come [*elle a à venir*], it *is* to-come, the to-come [*elle* est *à venir*], it deploys the very dimension of events irreducibly to come. It will always have it, this à-venir, and will always have had it" ("Force of Law," 256/60).

3. See "Force of Law," where Derrida argues that it is the undecidable time of justice that opens for "the transformation, the recasting or refounding [*la refondation*] of law and politics" (257/61). The undecidable time of justice is "the chance of the event and the condition of history," but for the same reason "it can always be reappropriated by the most perverse calculations" (257/61), since there is no guarantee that the transformation of the law is for the better.

4. In his sophisticated and nuanced essay "Derrida's Democracy to Come," Matthias Fritsch has further developed Beardsworth's notion of lesser violence. Fritsch rightly argues against the idea that unconditional openness to the future can be stipulated as a normative ideal, since there is no guarantee that "reduction of violence is, in all contexts, achieved by unconditional hospitality and openness to the future to come" (587). Rather, Fritsch argues that "political invention must be open to decide against openness: surely, there are singular situations where openness to the other is inadvisable, where a reduction of violence is to be expected not from unconditional hospitality but from (further) conditions, demands, and normative expectations placed on the other" (588). Nevertheless, Fritsch himself goes on to argue for another version of normative openness to the future. According to Fritsch, "the failure to recognize ineluctable aporias, can, and often does, lead to a violence that can be reduced by the ethical demand for unconditional hospitality. Given the (quasi-transcendental) impossibility of closing political identities and structures once and for all, the attempt to do so may be expected to generate unnecessary violence" (589). Thus, while Fritsch is well aware that ultimate closure is just as impossible as ultimate openness, he nonetheless maintains an opposition between attempts to close down the future and attempts to keep it open. To be sure, Derrida himself sometimes gives in to a similar logic. For example, in "Politics and Friendship" Derrida tries to draw a distinction between democratic and nondemocratic systems by arguing that the latter "are above all systems that *close* and *close themselves off* from this coming of the other. . . . In the end and beyond all the classical critiques of fascist, Nazi and totalitarian violence in general, one can say that these are systems that close the 'to come' and that close themselves into the presentation of the presentable" (182). Likewise, in "Autoimmunity: Real and Symbolic Suicides" Derrida marshals the view that what is unacceptable in the terrorism he ascribes to "'the Bin Laden effect'" is "above all, the fact that such actions and such discourse *open onto no future and, in my view, have no future*" (113). These passages clearly imply an opposition between "good" systems or actions that are open to the future and "bad" systems or actions that close down the future. Such an opposition, however, is untenable given the logic of deconstruction. The openness to the future is unconditional in the sense that *everything* (including every system or action) necessarily is open to the future, but it is not unconditional in the sense of a normative ideal. The mistake is thus to assume that one can derive a normative

affirmation of the future from the unconditional "yes" to the coming of the future. Fritsch is more incisive on this issue than other of Derrida's commentators, but he nevertheless holds on to the idea that for Derrida "the affirmation of a radically open future—a future that undermines metaphysical foundations— entails its own intrinsic normativity" ("Derrida's Democracy to Come," 574). My argument is, on the contrary, that there is no such intrinsic normativity in deconstruction. Despite occasional inconsistencies, Derrida himself underscores that no norms or rules can be derived from the constitutive condition of undecidability. In every system there is openness to the future, but there is no guarantee that it is better to be *more* open rather than *less* open to the future.

5. Derrida, *Rogues*, 37/62. Subsequent page references are given in the text.

6. See Derrida's analysis in ibid., 48–49, 52/74–75, 79–80.

7. "By definition, there is no given criterion, no assured rule, no incontestable unit of calculation, no trustworthy and natural mediating schema to regulate this calculation of the incalculable and this common or universal measure of the incommensurable" (ibid., 53/81).

8. Ibid., 36/61.

9. See also "Autoimmunity: Real and Symbolic Suicides," where Derrida claims that democracy answers to what *there is* in general and links it to the impossibility of being in itself that is the condition of temporality (120).

10. See Schmitt, *The Concept of the Political*, 26–27.

11. See the "Vorwort" in Carl Schmitt, *Der Begriff des Politischen: Text von 1932 mit einem Vorwort und drei Corollarien*. This preface is not available in the English translation, which is based on the 1932 rather than the 1963 edition.

12. Schmitt, *The Concept of the Political*, 27.

13. See also Derrida's account of the relation between law and justice in *Rogues*: "Justice can never be reduced to law, to calculative reason, to lawful distribution, to the norms and rules that condition law, as evidenced by its history and its ongoing transformation" (149/205–6). The reason why justice cannot be reduced to law is because it is exceeded by those it excludes and by the unpredictable coming of time. Derrida abbreviates this spatial and temporal excess as "the relationship to the incalculable singularity of the other. It is there that justice exceeds law but at the same time motivates the movement, history, and becoming of juridical rationality, indeed the relationship between law and reason, as well as everything that, in modernity, will have linked the history of law to the history of critical reason. The heterogeneity between justice and law does not exclude but, on the contrary, calls for their inseparability: there can be no justice without an appeal to juridical determinations and to the force of law; and there can be no becoming, no transformation, history, or perfectibility of law without an appeal to a justice that will nonetheless always exceed it" (*Rogues*, 150/207–8).

14. Derrida, *For What Tomorrow*, 92/153.

15. For Derrida's delineation of this double approach to the problem of sovereignty see ibid., 92/152–53; "Provocations: Forewords," in *Without Alibi*, xix; and *Rogues*, 158/216–17.

16. Derrida, *Rogues*, xiv/13, 109/154.

17. For Derrida's discussion of the passive decision as the condition of the event see in particular *Politics of Friendship*, 67–69/86–88; and *Rogues*, 152/210. See also "Force of Law," 255/58.

18. Cf. Derrida's account in his "Remarks on Deconstruction and Pragmatism":

> All that a deconstructive point of view tries to show, is that since convention, institutions and consensus are stabilizations (sometimes stabilizations of great duration, sometimes micro-stabilizations), this means that they are stabilizations of something essentially unstable and chaotic. Thus, it becomes necessary to stabilize precisely because stability is not natural; it is because there is instability that stabilization becomes necessary; it is because there is chaos that there is a need for stability. Now, this chaos and instability, which is fundamental, founding and irreducible, is at once naturally the worst against which we struggle with laws, rules, conventions, politics and provisional hegemony, but at the same time, it is a chance, a chance to change, to destabilize. If there were continual stability, there would be no need for politics, and it is to the extent that stability is not natural, essential, or substantial, that politics exists. (83–84)

A page further on Derrida links the same logic to the notion of "hyperpoliticization" (85).

19. For Laclau's discussions of undecidability see in particular *New Reflections on the Revolution of Our Time*, 30–31; "Deconstruction, Pragmatism, Hegemony," 47–48; and *Emancipation(s)*, 77–79, 119.

20. Laclau, *New Reflections on the Revolution of Our Time*, 31.

21. The thought of essential corruptibility and the necessity of perilous transactions can be seen to inform all of Derrida's reflections on political responsibility. In *For What Tomorrow* he maintains that "the risk must be reevaluated at every moment, in shifting contexts giving rise to exchanges that are in each case original" (22/45). Political decisions therefore proceed "by gradations rather than by clearly defined oppositions of the type: I am this *or* that. No, I am this *and* that; and I am this rather than that, according to the situations and the urgencies at hand" (22/45; see also 76/126–27). Derrida's own political interventions also clearly acknowledge the perilous transaction between positions and the essential corruptibility of values. For example, when he takes on the debate between those who advocate liberal drug policies and those who advocate restrictive drug policies, he makes the following remark, which is characteristic of the deconstructive reason he exercises in political debates:

Depending on the circumstances (tirelessly analyzed, whether macroscopically or microscopically) the discourse of "interdiction" can be justified *just as well or just as badly* as the liberal discourse. Repressive practice (in all its brutal or sophisticated, punitive or re-educational forms) can be justified just as well or just as badly as permissive practice (with all its ruses). Since it is impossible to justify absolutely either the one or the other of these practices, one can never absolutely condemn them. In an emergency, this can only lead to equivocations, negotiations, and unstable compromises. And in any given, progressively evolving situation, these will need to be guided by a concern for the singularity of each individual experience and by a socio-political analysis that is at once as broadly and as finely tuned as possible. I say this not to avoid the question, any more than I do to argue for relativism or opportunism; rather, I would simply describe the state of affairs in which such decisions have to be made. (Derrida, "The Rhetoric of Drugs," 239/252)

22. Laclau, *Emancipation(s)*, 78.

23. Critchley, *Ethics-Politics-Subjectivity*, 111.

24. Laclau himself has explicitly argued against the Levinasian position that Critchley advocates. Laclau's most forceful arguments against the Levinasian position are articulated in *Emancipation(s)*, 77–78. Critchley has never responded to these arguments. The one time he refers to them he simply notes, "Needless to say, I do not agree," without providing any counterarguments or even an account of Laclau's arguments. See Critchley, "Is There a Normative Deficit in the Theory of Hegemony?" 117. For Laclau's refusal to ground his thinking of radical democracy in a primordial ethics see also his essay "Deconstruction, Pragmatism, Hegemony," 58, 66–67.

25. Critchley, *Ethics-Politics-Subjectivity*, 112. The same question is posed by Critchley in his later essay "Is There a Normative Deficit in the Theory of Hegemony?" 116.

26. Critchley, "Is There a Normative Deficit in the Theory of Hegemony?" 121.

27. Laclau, "Glimpsing the Future," 291.

28. Ibid., 295.

29. See the following essays by Laclau: "Can Immanence Explain Social Struggles?" (on Hardt and Negri); "Bare Life or Social Indeterminacy" (on Agamben); "An Ethics of Militant Engagement" (on Badiou); "Community and Its Paradoxes" and "Deconstruction, Pragmatism, Hegemony" (on Rorty).

30. Laclau, "Can Immanence Explain Social Struggles?" 6 (my emphasis).

31. Ibid., 8.

32. Ibid.

33. Laclau and Mouffe, *Hegemony and Socialist Strategy*, xii. Subsequent page references are given in the text.

34. Laclau and Mouffe borrow the phrase "democratic revolution" from Alexis

de Tocqueville's *Democracy in America*. For Tocqueville, democracy is defined by the fact that "the noble" can no longer simply assume "the privileges which he believed to be legitimate" and the serf no longer "looks upon his own inferiority as a consequence of the immutable order of nature" (8–9).

35. Laclau, *On Populist Reason*, 125.

36. Laclau, "The Signifiers of Democracy," 232.

37. Laclau, "Constructing Universality," 302.

38. Laclau, "Glimpsing the Future," 287. See also his "Ethics, Normativity, and the Heteronomy of the Law"; and *On Populist Reason*, 115–16.

39. Laclau, "On the Names of God," 260–61.

40. For Lacan's notion of the Thing see in particular *Seminar VII*.

41. For Lacan's remarks on the drive see in particular *Seminar XI* and *Seminar XX*. For instructive commentary on Lacan's notion of the drive see Alenka Zupančič, *Ethics of the Real*; and Joan Copjec, *Imagine There's No Woman*.

42. Copjec, *Imagine There's No Woman*, 38.

43. Ibid., 60. See also Copjec's formulation that "the jouissance of the drive, of the organ of the libido, *replaces* the jouissance attributed to the primordial union, the blissful state of the body without organs" (64; my emphasis). Zupančič also points out that the ontological lack of being is the common denominator for both desire and the drive; see Zupančič, *Ethics of the Real*, 242.

44. Laclau, *On Populist Reason*, 115.

45. Ibid., 116.

46. Laclau, "Glimpsing the Future," 315–16. In the same essay Laclau also maintains that "I do not think that the status of psychoanalytic categories is regional (ontic) but ontological" (315) and that "I see psychoanalysis as the only valid road to explain the drives behind [hegemonic] construction—I see it, indeed, as the most fruitful approach to the understanding of human reality" (326).

47. Laclau, *Emancipation(s)*, 72. For variations of the same example see *New Reflections on the Revolution of Our Time*, 66; *The Making of Political Identities*, 3; *Emancipation(s)*, 44; "On the Names of God," 262; "An Ethics of Militant Engagement," 133; "Glimpsing the Future," 284; and *On Populist Reason*, 96.

48. Laclau, *On Populist Reason*, 96–97.

49. See Laclau, "Ethics, Normativity, and the Heteronomy of the Law."

50. Laclau, *New Reflections on the Revolution of Our Time*, 83.

51. Laclau, *Emancipation(s)*, 122; see also 16–17; and *New Reflections on the Revolution of Our Time*, 4, 35–36.

52. Laclau, *Emancipation(s)*, 122–23.

53. Laclau, "Theory, Democracy, and the Left," 17.

54. Laclau, *On Populist Reason*, 226.

55. Laclau, "Ethics, Normativity, and the Heteronomy of the Law," 182.

56. Laclau, *Emancipation(s)*, 65.

57. Laclau, "Structure, History and the Political," 199.

58. Laclau, "On the Names of God," 264.

59. Laclau, "Ethics, Normativity, and the Heteronomy of the Law," 180. See also Laclau's assertion that "only if I live an action as incarnating an impossible fullness transcending it does the investment become an *ethical* investment" ("Identity and Hegemony," 84). See also "On the Names of God," 258, 264–65.

60. Laclau, "Identity and Hegemony," 86.

61. Ibid., 84.

62. Laclau, *Emancipation(s)*, 116; see also 114–15.

63. Laclau, "Structure, History and the Political," 208.

64. As Derrida himself points out in *Rogues*, after having delineated his thinking of the constitutive spacing of time: "No politics, no ethics, and no law can be, as it were, *deduced* from this thought. To be sure, nothing can be *done* [*faire*] with it" (xv/14–15).

65. Derrida, "A Certain Impossible Possibility of Saying the Event," 460.

Works Cited

Aristotle. *Metaphysics*. Trans. W. D. Ross. In *The Basic Works of Aristotle*, ed. R. McKeon. New York: Modern Library, 2001.

———. *Physics*. Trans. R. Waterfield. Oxford: Oxford University Press, 1996.

Augustine. *The City of God*. Trans. M. Dods. New York: Modern Library, 1994.

———. *Confessiones*. Loeb edition. Cambridge, MA: Harvard University Press, 1912.

———. *Confessions*. Trans. Rex Warner. New York: New American Library, 1963.

———. *On Free Choice of the Will*. Trans. T. Williams. Indianapolis, IN: Hackett, 1993.

Beardsworth, Richard. *Derrida and the Political*. London: Routledge, 1996.

Bennington, Geoffrey. *Derridabase*. In *Jacques Derrida*. Chicago: University of Chicago Press, 1993.

———. *Interrupting Derrida*. London: Routledge, 2000.

———. *Legislations: The Politics of Deconstruction*. London: Verso, 1994.

———. *Other Analyses: Reading Philosophy*. http://bennington.zsoft.co.uk/index.html#OtherAnalyses. Bennington Books, 2004.

Bernasconi, Robert. "Deconstruction and the Possibility of Ethics." In *Deconstruction and Philosophy: The Texts of Jacques Derrida*, ed. J. Sallis. Chicago: University of Chicago Press, 1987.

———. "Justice Without Ethics?" *PLI: Warwick Journal of Philosophy* 6 (summer 1997): 58–69.

———. "The Trace of Levinas in Derrida" [1985]. In *Derrida and Différance*, ed. D. Wood and R. Bernasconi. Evanston, IL: Northwestern University Press, 1988.

Bernet, Rudolf. "An Intentionality Without Subject or Object?" *Man and World* 27 (1994): 231–55.

————. "Is the Present Ever Present? Phenomenology and the Metaphysics of Presence." *Research in Phenomenology* 12 (1982): 85–112.

————. *La vie du sujet: Recherches sur l'interprétation de Husserl dans la phénoménologie.* Paris: PUF, 1994.

Birnbaum, Daniel. *The Hospitality of Presence: Problems of Otherness in Husserl's Phenomenology.* Stockholm: Almqvist and Wiksell International, 1998.

Brough, John B. "The Emergence of an Absolute Consciousness in Husserl's Early Writings on Time-Consciousness." *Man and World* 3 (1972): 298–326.

————. "Husserl and the Deconstruction of Time." *Review of Metaphysics* 46 (1993): 503–36.

Butler, Judith, Ernesto Laclau, and Slavoj Žižek. *Contingency, Hegemony, Universality: Contemporary Dialogues on the Left.* London: Verso, 2000.

Caputo, John D. *Against Ethics.* Bloomington: Indiana University Press, 1993.

————. *Deconstruction in a Nutshell.* New York: Fordham University Press, 1997.

————. "Discussion with Richard Kearney." In Caputo and Scanlon, *God, the Gift, and Postmodernism.*

————. *On Religion.* London: Routledge, 2001.

————. *The Prayers and Tears of Jacques Derrida: Religion Without Religion.* Bloomington: Indiana University Press, 1997.

————. "Reason, History, and a Little Madness." In *Questioning Ethics*, ed. R. Kearney and M. Dooley. London: Routledge, 1999.

Caputo, John D., Mark Dooley, and Michael J. Scanlon, eds. *Questioning God.* Bloomington: Indiana University Press, 2001.

Caputo, John D., and Michael J. Scanlon, eds. *Augustine and Postmodernism: Confessions and Circumfession.* Bloomington: Indiana University Press, 2005.

————. *God, the Gift, and Postmodernism.* Bloomington: Indiana University Press, 1999.

Cobb-Stevens, Richard. "Derrida and Husserl on the Status of Retention." In *Analecta Husserliana* 19. Dordrecht: Reidel, 1985, 367–81.

Copjec, Joan. *Imagine There's No Woman: Ethics and Sublimation.* Cambridge, MA: MIT Press, 2003.

Chalier, Catherine. *What Ought I to Do? Morality in Kant and Levinas.* Trans. J. M. Todd. Ithaca, NY: Cornell University Press, 2002.

Cornell, Drucilla. *The Philosophy of the Limit.* New York: Routledge, 1992.

Critchley, Simon. *Ethics-Politics-Subjectivity: Essays on Derrida, Levinas and Contemporary French Thought.* London: Verso, 1999.

————. "Is There a Normative Deficit in the Theory of Hegemony?" In *Laclau: A Critical Reader*, ed. S. Critchley and O. Marchart. London: Routledge, 2004.

————. *The Ethics of Deconstruction: Derrida and Levinas* [1992]. Expanded 2nd ed. Edinburgh: Edinburgh University Press, 1999.

Derrida, Jacques. *Acts of Literature.* Ed. D. Attridge. London: Routledge, 1992.

————. *Adieu to Emmanuel Levinas.* Trans. M. Naas and P.-A. Brault. Stanford, CA: Stanford University Press, 1999. Trans. of *Adieu à Emmanuel Lévinas.* Paris: Galilée, 1997.

————. "The Animal That Therefore I Am (More to Follow)." Trans. D. Wills. *Critical Inquiry* 28, no. 2 (winter 2002): 369–418. Trans. of "L'animal que donc je suis (à suivre)." In *L'animal que donc je suis.* Paris: Galilée, 2006.

————. "Aphorism Countertime." Trans. N. Royle. In *Acts of Literature*, ed. D. Attridge. Trans. of "L'aphorisme à contretemps." In *Psyché: Inventions de l'autre.* Paris: Galilée, 1987.

————. *Archive Fever.* Trans. E. Prenowitz. Chicago: University of Chicago Press, 1995. Trans. of *Mal d'archive.* Paris: Galilée, 1995.

————. *Arguing with Derrida.* Ed. S. Glendinning. Oxford: Blackwell, 2001.

————. "As If It Were Possible, 'Within Such Limits.'" Trans. B. Elwood and E. Rottenberg. In *Negotiations: Interventions and Interviews, 1971–2001*, ed. E. Rottenberg. Stanford, CA: Stanford University Press, 2002. Trans. of "Comme si c'était possible, 'within such limits.'" In *Papier machine.* Paris: Galilée, 2001.

————. *A Taste for the Secret.* Trans. G. Donis. Cambridge, UK: Polity Press, 2001.

————. "Autoimmunity: Real and Symbolic Suicides." Trans. P.-A. Brault and M. Naas. In *Philosophy in a Time of Terror*, ed. G. Borradori. Chicago: University of Chicago Press, 2003.

————. "Avances." In Serge Marcel, *Le tombeau du dieu artisan.* Paris: Minuit, 1995.

————. *Béliers.* Paris: Galilée, 2003.

————. "A Certain Impossible Possibility of Saying the Event." Trans. G. Walker. *Critical Inquiry* 33, no. 2 (winter 2007): 441–61.

————. *Chaque fois unique, la fin du monde.* Ed. P.-A. Brault and M. Naas. Paris: Galilée, 2003.

————. *Circumfession.* Trans. G. Bennington. In *Jacques Derrida.* Chicago: University of Chicago Press, 1993. Trans. of *Circonfession.* In *Jacques Derrida.* Paris: Seuil, 1991.

————. "Confessions and 'Circumfession': A Roundtable with Jacques Derrida." In Caputo and Scanlon, *Augustine and Postmodernism.*

————. "'Dead Man Running': Salut, Salut." Trans. E. Rottenberg. In *Negotiations: Interventions and Interviews, 1971–2001*, ed. E. Rottenberg. Stanford, CA: Stanford University Press, 2002. Trans. of "'Il courait mort': salut, salut." In *Papier machine.* Paris: Galilée, 2001.

————. *Demeure: Fiction and Testimony.* In *The Instant of My Death.* Trans. E. Rottenberg. Stanford, CA: Stanford University Press, 2000. Trans. of *Demeure: Maurice Blanchot.* Paris: Galilée, 1998.

————. "'Dialanguages.'" Trans. P. Kamuf. In *Points . . . Interviews, 1974–1994,* ed. E. Weber. Stanford, CA: Stanford University Press, 1995. Trans. of "Dialangues." In *Points de suspension: Entretiens,* ed. E. Weber. Paris: Galilée, 1992.

————. *Dissemination.* Trans. Barbara Johnson. Chicago: University of Chicago Press, 1981. Trans. of *La dissemination.* Paris: Seuil, 1972.

————. *Edmund Husserl's Origin of Geometry: An Introduction.* Trans. John P. Leavey Jr. Lincoln: University of Nebraska Press, 1978 [1962].

————. "Et Cetera." Trans. G. Bennington. In *Deconstructions: A User's Guide,* ed. N. Royle. New York: Palgrave, 2000.

————. "Faith and Knowledge." Trans. S. Weber. In *Acts of Religion,* ed. G. Anidjar. London: Routledge, 2002. Trans. of "Foi et savoir." In *Foi et savoir: Suivi de le siècle et le pardon.* Paris: Seuil, 2000.

————. "Force of Law: The 'Mystical Foundation of Authority.'" Trans. M. Quaintance. In *Acts of Religion,* ed. G. Anidjar. London: Routledge, 2002. Trans. of *Force de loi: Le "Fondement mystique de l'autorité."* Paris: Galilée, 1994.

————. *For What Tomorrow.* Trans. J. Fort. Stanford, CA: Stanford University Press, 2004. Trans. of *De quoi demain.* Paris: Fayard and Galilée, 2001.

————. *The Gift of Death.* Trans. D. Wills. Chicago: University of Chicago Press, 1995. Trans. of "Donner la mort." In *L'éthique du don,* ed. J.-M. Rabaté and M. Wetzel. Paris: Transition, 1992.

————. *Given Time.* Trans. P. Kamuf. Chicago: University of Chicago Press, 1992. Trans. of *Donner le temps.* Paris: Galilée, 1991.

————. *H. C. for Life.* Trans. L. Milesi and S. Herbrechter. Stanford, CA: Stanford University Press, 2006.

————. "Hospitality, Justice, and Responsibility." In *Questioning Ethics,* ed. R. Kearney and M. Dooley. London: Routledge, 1999.

————. "Hostipitality." Trans. G. Anidjar. In *Acts of Religion,* ed. G. Anidjar. London: Routledge, 2002.

————. "How to Avoid Speaking: Denials." Trans. K. Frieden. In *Languages of the Unsayable: The Play of Negativity in Literature and Literary Theory,* ed. S. Budick and W. Iser. New York: Columbia University Press, 1989. Trans. of "Comment ne pas parler: Denegations." In *Psyché: Inventions de l'autre.* Paris Galilée, 1987.

————. "How to Name." In Michel Deguy, *Recumbents.* Trans. W. Baldridge. Middletown, CT: Wesleyan University Press, 2005. Trans. of "Comment nommer." In *Le poète que je cherche à être: Cahiers Michel Deguy*, ed. Y. Charnet. Paris: Belin, 1996.

———. "Language Is Never Owned." Trans. T. Dutoit and P. Romanski. In *Sovereignties in Question*, ed. T. Dutoit and O. Pasanen. New York: Fordham University Press, 2005.

———. *Learning to Live Finally*. Trans. P.-A. Brault and M. Naas. Hoboken, NJ: Melville House, 2007. Trans. of *Apprendre à vivre enfin*. Paris: Galilée, 2005.

———. *Le problème de la genèse dans la philosophie de Husserl*. Paris: PUF, 1990.

———. *Limited Inc.* Trans. S. Weber. Evanston, IL: Northwestern University Press, 1988. Trans. of *Limited Inc*. Paris: Galilée, 1990.

———. *Margins of Philosophy*. Trans. A. Bass. Chicago: University of Chicago Press, 1982. Trans. of *Marges de la philosophie*. Paris: Minuit, 1972.

———. *Mémoires: For Paul de Man*. Trans. C. Lindsay, J. Culler, and E. Cadava. New York: Columbia University Press, 1986. Trans. of *Mémoires pour Paul de Man*. Paris: Galilée, 1988.

———. *Memoirs of the Blind: The Self-Portrait and Other Ruins*. Trans. P.-A. Brault and M. Naas. Chicago: University of Chicago Press, 1993.

———. *Monolingualism of the Other; or, The Prosthesis of Origin*. Trans. P. Mensah. Stanford, CA: Stanford University Press, 1998. Trans. of *Le monolinguisme de l'autre: Ou la prothèse d'origine*. Paris: Galilée, 1996.

———. *Negotiations: Interventions and Interviews, 1971–2001*. Ed. and trans. E. Rottenberg. Stanford, CA: Stanford University Press, 2002.

———. "Nietzsche and the Machine." Trans. R. Beardsworth. In *Negotiations: Interventions and Interviews, 1971–2001*, ed. E. Rottenberg. Stanford, CA: Stanford University Press, 2002.

———. "No Apocalypse, Not Now (Full Speed Ahead, Seven Missiles, Seven Missives)." Trans. C. Porter and P. Lewis. *Diacritics* 14, no. 2 (1984): 20–31. Trans. of "No apocalypse, not now (à toute vitesse, sept missiles, sept missives)." In *Psyché: Inventions de l'autre*. Paris Galilée, 1987.

———. *Of Grammatology*. Trans. G. Spivak. Baltimore: Johns Hopkins University Press, 1976. Trans. of *De la grammatologie*. Paris: Minuit, 1967.

———. *Of Hospitality*. Trans. R. Bowlby. Stanford, CA: Stanford University Press, 2000. Trans. of *De l'hospitalité*. Paris: Calmann-Lévy, 1997.

———. "On a Newly Arisen Apocalyptic Tone in Philosophy." Trans. P. Fenves. In *Raising the Tone of Philosophy*, ed. P. Fenves. Baltimore: Johns Hopkins University Press, 1993. Trans. of *D'un ton apocalyptique adopté naguère en philosophie*. Paris: Galilée, 1983.

———. *On Touching: Jean-Luc Nancy*. Trans. C. Irizarry. Stanford, CA: Stanford University Press, 2005. Trans. of *Le toucher: Jean-Luc Nancy*. Paris: Galilée, 2000.

———. *The Other Heading*. Trans. P.-A. Brault and M. Naas. Bloomington: Indiana University Press, 1992. Trans. of *L'autre cap*. Paris: Minuit, 1991.

———. "'Others Are Secret Because They Are Other.'" Trans. R. Bowlby. In *Paper Machine*. Stanford, CA: Stanford University Press, 2005. Trans. of "'Autrui est secret parce qu'il est autre.'" In *Papier machine*. Paris: Galilée, 2001.

———. "Ousia and Grammè." Trans. A. Bass. In *Margins of Philosophy*. Chicago: University of Chicago Press, 1982. Trans. of "Ousia et Grammè." In *Marges de la philosophie*. Paris: Minuit, 1972.

———. "Perhaps or Maybe: Jacques Derrida in Conversation with Alexander Garcia Düttman." *PLI: Warwick Journal of Philosophy* 6 (summer 1997): 1–18.

———. *Points . . . Interviews, 1974–1994*. Ed. E. Weber. Trans. P. Kamuf and others. Stanford, CA: Stanford University Press, 1995. Trans. of *Points de suspension: Entretiens*. Ed. E. Weber. Paris: Galilée, 1992.

———. "Politics and Friendship." Trans. R. Harvey. In *Negotiations: Interventions and Interviews, 1971–2001*. Ed. E. Rottenberg. Stanford, CA: Stanford University Press, 2002.

———. *Politics of Friendship*. Trans. G. Collins. London: Verso, 1997. Trans. of *Politiques de l'amitié*. Paris: Galilée, 1994.

———. *Positions*. Trans. A. Bass. Chicago: University of Chicago Press, 1981. Trans. of *Positions*. Paris: Minuit, 1972.

———. *The Post Card*. Trans. A. Bass. Chicago: University of Chicago Press, 1987. Trans. of *La carte postale*. Paris: Flammarion, 1980.

———. "Remarks on Deconstruction and Pragmatism." Trans. S. Critchley. In *Deconstruction and Pragmatism*, ed. C. Mouffe. London: Routledge, 1996.

———. *Resistances of Psychoanalysis*. Trans. P.-A. Brault and M. Naas. Stanford, CA: Stanford University Press, 1998. Trans. of *Résistances de la psychanalyse*. Paris: Galilée, 1996.

———. "Response to Catherine Malabou." In Caputo and Scanlon, *Augustine and Postmodernism*.

———. "The Rhetoric of Drugs." Trans. M. Israel. In *Points . . . Interviews, 1974–1994*, ed. E. Weber. Stanford, CA: Stanford University Press, 1995. Trans. of "Rhétorique de la drogue." In *Points de suspension: Entretiens*, ed. E. Weber. Paris: Galilée, 1992.

———. *Rogues: Two Essays on Reason*. Trans. P.-A. Brault and M. Naas. Stanford, CA: Stanford University Press, 2005. Trans. of *Voyous: Deux essais sur la raison*. Paris: Galilée, 2003.

———. *Sauf le nom (Post-Scriptum)*. Trans. T. Dutoit. In *On the Name*, ed. T. Dutoit. Stanford, CA: Stanford University Press, 1995. Trans. of *Sauf le nom*. Paris: Galilée, 1993.

———. "Schibboleth: For Paul Celan." Trans. T. Dutoit. In *Sovereignties in*

Question, ed. T. Dutoit and O. Pasanen. New York: Fordham University Press, 2005. Trans. of *Schibboleth: Pour Paul Celan*. Paris: Galilée, 1986.

———. *Specters of Marx*. Trans. P. Kamuf. London: Routledge, 1994. Trans. of *Spectres de Marx*. Paris: Galilée, 1993.

———. *Speech and Phenomena*. Trans. D. B. Allison. Evanston, IL: Northwestern University Press, 1973. Trans. of *La voix et le phénomène*. Paris: PUF, 1967.

———. "Ulysses Gramophone." Trans. T. Kendall. In *Acts of Literature*, ed. D. Attridge. London: Routledge, 1992. Trans. of "Ulysse Gramophone." In *Ulysse gramophone: Deux mots pour Joyce*. Paris: Galilée, 1987.

———. "Violence and Metaphysics." Trans. A. Bass. In *Writing and Difference*. London: Routledge, 1978. Trans. of "Violence et métaphysique." In *L'écriture et la différence*. Paris: Seuil, 1967.

———. *Without Alibi*. Ed. and trans. P. Kamuf. Stanford, CA: Stanford University Press, 2002.

———. *The Work of Mourning*. Ed., trans., and with an introduction by P.-A. Brault and M. Naas. Chicago: University of Chicago Press, 2001.

———. *Writing and Difference*. Trans. A. Bass. London: Routledge, 1978. Trans. of *L'écriture et la différence*. Paris: Seuil, 1967.

de Vries, Hent. *Minimal Theologies: Critiques of Secular Reason in Adorno and Levinas*. Baltimore: Johns Hopkins University Press, 2005.

———. *Philosophy and the Turn to Religion*. Baltimore: Johns Hopkins University Press, 1999.

———. *Religion and Violence: Philosophical Perspectives from Kant to Derrida*. Baltimore: Johns Hopkins University Press, 2002.

Dooley, Mark, ed. *A Passion for the Impossible: John D. Caputo in Focus*. Albany: SUNY Press, 2003.

Eckhart, Meister. *The Best of Meister Eckhart*. Ed. H. Backhouse. New York: Crossroad, 1993.

———. *Meister Eckhart*. Ed. F. Pfeiffer. Trans. C. de B. Evans. London: Watkins, 1924.

———. *Meister Eckhart: Sermons and Treatises*. Vol. 2. Trans. M. O. Walshe. London: Watkins, 1981.

———. *Meister Eckhart: A Modern Translation*. Ed. R. B. Blakney. New York: Harper, 1957.

———. *Meister Eckhart: Teacher and Preacher*. Ed. B. McGinn. New York: Paulist Press, 1986.

Fenves, Peter. *Raising the Tone of Philosophy*. Ed. P. Fenves. Baltimore: Johns Hopkins University Press. 1993.

Fritsch, Matthias. "Derrida's Democracy to Come." In *Constellations* 9, no. 4 (2002): 574–97.

Gallagher, Shaun. *The Inordinance of Time*. Evanston, IL: Northwestern University Press, 1998.

Gasché, Rodolphe. "God, for Example." In *Inventions of Difference: On Jacques Derrida*. Cambridge, MA: Harvard University Press, 1994.

——. "Structural Infinity." In *Inventions of Difference: On Jacques Derrida*. Cambridge, MA: Harvard University Press, 1994.

——. *The Tain of the Mirror: Derrida and the Philosophy of Reflection*. Cambridge, MA: Harvard University Press, 1986.

Gilgen, Peter. "The Deconversion of Hent de Vries." *Journal for Cultural and Religious Theory (JCRT)* 7, no. 1 (winter 2005): 83–102.

Hägglund, Martin. *Kronofobi: Essäer om tid och ändlighet*. Stockholm/Stehag: Brutus Östlings Bokförlag Symposion, 2002.

Hart, Kevin: "Religion." In *Understanding Derrida*, ed. J. Reynolds and J. Roffe. New York: Continuum, 2004.

——. *The Trespass of the Sign: Deconstruction, Theology, and Philosophy*. 2nd ed. New York: Fordham University Press, 2000.

Hegel, G. W. F. *Philosophy of Nature (Encyclopaedia Part Two)*. Trans. A. V. Miller. Oxford: Clarendon Press, 1970.

——. *Science of Logic*. Trans. A. V. Miller. Amherst, NY: Prometheus Books, 1999.

Henrich, Dieter. "Fichtes ursprüngliche Einsicht." In *Subjektivität und Metaphysik: Festschrift für Wolfgang Cramer*, ed. D. Henrich and H. Wagner. Frankfurt am Main: Klostermann, 1966.

Henry, Michel. *L'essence de la manifestation*. Paris: PUF, 1963.

——. *Phénoménologie matérielle*. Paris: PUF, 1990.

Husserl, Edmund. *Cartesian Meditations: An Introduction to Phenomenology*. Trans. D. Cairns. The Hague: Martinus Nijhoff, 1960. Trans. of *Cartesianische Meditationen*. In *Husserliana* 1. Ed. S. Strasser. The Hague: Martinus Nijhoff, 1950.

——. *Ideen zu einer reinen Phänomenologie und phänomenologischen Philosophie I*. In *Husserliana* 3, ed. K. Schumann. The Hague: Martinus Nijhoff, 1976.

——. *On the Phenomenology of the Consciousness of Internal Time (1893–1917)*. Trans. J. B. Brough. Dordrecht: Kluwer Academic Publishers, 1991. Trans. of *Zur Phänomenologie des inneren Zeitbewußtseins, 1893–1917*. In *Husserliana* 10, ed. R. Boehm. The Hague: Martinus Nijhoff, 1966.

——. *The Crisis of European Sciences and Transcendental Phenomenology*. Trans. D. Carr. Evanston, IL: Northwestern University Press, 1970.

James, William. *The Principles of Psychology*. 1890. New York: Dover, 1950.

——. *The Works of William James: Essays in Radical Empiricism*. Ed. R. B. Perry. 1912. Cambridge, MA: Harvard University Press, 1976.

Jennings, Theodore W. *Reading Derrida/Thinking Paul: On Justice.* Stanford, CA: Stanford University Press, 2005.

Kant, Immanuel. *Critique of Pure Reason.* Ed. and trans. Paul Guyer and Allen W. Wood. Cambridge, UK: Cambridge University Press, 1998.

―――. "The End of All Things." In *Religion and Rational Theology*, ed. and trans. Allen W. Wood and George di Giovanni. Cambridge, UK: Cambridge University Press, 1996.

―――. *Religion Within the Limits of Reason Alone.* Trans. T. M. Greene and H. H. Hudson. New York: Harper, 1960.

Kearney, Richard. "Desire of God." In Caputo and Scanlon, *God, the Gift, and Postmodernism.*

―――. *The God Who May Be: A Hermeneutics of Religion.* Bloomington: Indiana University Press, 2001.

Kirby, Vicki. *Telling Flesh: The Substance of the Corporeal.* London: Routledge, 1997.

Krell, David Farrell. *The Purest of Bastards: Works of Mourning, Art, and Affirmation in the Thought of Jacques Derrida.* University Park: Pennsylvania State University Press, 2000.

Lacan, Jacques. *Seminar II: The Ego in Freud's Theory and in the Technique of Psychoanalysis.* Ed. J.-A. Miller. Trans. S. Tomaselli. New York: Norton, 1988.

―――. *Seminar VII: The Ethics of Psychoanalysis.* Ed. J.-A. Miller. Trans. D. Porter. London: Routledge, 1992.

―――. *Seminar XI: The Four Fundamental Concepts of Psychoanalysis.* Ed. J.-A. Miller. Trans. A. Sheridan. New York: Norton, 1998.

―――. *Seminar XX: Encore, On Feminine Sexuality, The Limits of Love and Knowledge.* Ed. J.-A. Miller. Trans. B. Fink. New York: Norton, 1998.

Laclau, Ernesto. "Bare Life or Social Indeterminacy?" In *Sovereignty and Life: Essays on the Work of Giorgio Agamben.* Stanford, CA: Stanford University Press, forthcoming.

―――. "Can Immanence Explain Social Struggles?" *Diacritics* 31, no. 4 (winter 2001): 3–10.

―――. "Community and Its Paradoxes." In Laclau, *Emancipation(s).*

―――. "Constructing Universality." In Butler, Laclau, and Žižek, *Contingency, Hegemony, Universality.*

―――. "Deconstruction, Pragmatism, Hegemony." In *Deconstruction and Pragmatism*, ed. C. Mouffe. London: Routledge, 1996.

―――. *Emancipation(s).* London: Verso, 1996.

―――. "Ethics, Normativity, and the Heteronomy of the Law." In *Law, Justice, and Power: Between Reason and Will*, ed. S. Cheng. Stanford, CA: Stanford University Press, 2004.

———. "An Ethics of Militant Engagement." In *Think Again: Alan Badiou and the Future of Philosophy*, ed. P. Hallward. New York: Continuum, 2004.

———. "Glimpsing the Future: A Reply." In *Laclau: A Critical Reader*, ed. S. Critchley and O. Marchart. London: Routledge, 2004.

———. "Identity and Hegemony." In Butler, Laclau, and Žižek, *Contingency, Hegemony, Universality*.

———, ed. *The Making of Political Identities*. London: Verso, 1994.

———. *New Reflections on the Revolution of Our Time*. London: Verso, 1990.

———. *On Populist Reason*. London: Verso, 2005.

———. "On the Names of God." In *The 8 Technologies of Otherness*, ed. S. Golding. London: Routledge, 1997.

———. "The Signifiers of Democracy." In *Democracy and Possessive Individualism*, ed. H. Carens. New York: SUNY Press, 1993.

———. "Structure, History and the Political." In Butler, Laclau, and Žižek, *Contingency, Hegemony, Universality*.

———. "Theory, Democracy, and the Left: An Interview with Ernesto Laclau." *Umbr(a): A Journal of the Unconscious* (2001): 7–27.

Laclau, Ernesto, and Chantal Mouffe. *Hegemony and Socialist Strategy: Towards a Radical Democratic Politics*. 2nd ed. London: Verso, 2001.

Lawlor, Leonard. *Derrida and Husserl: The Basic Problem of Phenomenology*. Bloomington: Indiana University Press, 2002.

Levinas, Emmanuel. *Basic Philosophical Writings*. Ed. A. T. Peperzak, S. Critchley, and R. Bernasconi. Bloomington: Indiana University Press, 1996.

———. *Humanisme de l'autre homme*. Montpellier: Fata Morgana, 1972.

———. *Otherwise Than Being or Beyond Essence*. Trans. A. Lingis. Pittsburgh: Duquesne University Press, 1998. Trans. of *Autrement qu'être ou au-delà de l'essence*. The Hague: Martinus Nijhoff, 1974.

———. *Totality and Infinity: An Essay on Exteriority*. Trans. A. Lingis. Pittsburgh: Duquesne University Press, 1969. Trans. of *Totalité et infini: Essai sur l'extériorité*. The Hague: Martinus Nijhoff, 1961.

———. "The Trace of the Other." Trans. A. Lingis. In *Deconstruction in Context*, ed. M. C. Taylor. Chicago: University of Chicago Press, 1986.

Llewelyn, John. *Appositions of Jacques Derrida and Emmanuel Levinas*. Bloomington: Indiana University Press, 2002.

Marion, Jean-Luc. *God Without Being*. Trans. Thomas A. Carlson. Chicago: University of Chicago Press, 1991. Trans. of *Dieu sans l'être*. Paris: Fayard, 1982.

———. *The Idol and Distance*. Trans. Thomas A. Carlson. New York: Fordham University Press, 2001. Trans. of *L'Idole et la distance*. Paris: Grasset, 1991.

———. "In the Name: How to Avoid Speaking of 'Negative Theology.'" In Caputo and Scanlon, *God, the Gift, and Postmodernism*.

Manoussakis, John Panteleimon, ed. *After God: Richard Kearney and the Religious Turn in Continental Philosophy.* New York: Fordham University Press, 2005.

Merleau-Ponty, Maurice. *Phenomenology of Perception.* Trans. C. Smith. London: Routledge, 1962. Trans. of *Phénoménologie de la perception.* Paris: Gallimard, 1945.

Olthuis, James H., ed. *Religion With/Out Religion: The Prayers and Tears of John D. Caputo.* London: Routledge, 2002.

Pseudo-Dionysius. *Pseudo-Dionysius: The Complete Works.* Trans. C. Luibhéid. New York: Paulist Press, 1987.

Rayment-Pickard, Hugh. *Impossible God: Derrida's Theology.* Burlington, VT: Ashgate, 2003.

Ricoeur, Paul. *Temps et récit.* Vol. 3, *Le temps raconté.* Paris: Seuil, 1985.

Robbins, Jill. *Altered Reading: Levinas and Literature.* Chicago: University of Chicago Press, 1999.

Schmitt, Carl. *The Concept of the Political.* Trans. George Schwab. Chicago: University of Chicago Press, 1996.

———. *Political Theology.* Trans. George Schwab. Cambridge, MA: MIT Press, 1985.

———. "Vorwort." In *Der Begriff des Politischen: Text von 1932 mit einem Vorwort und drei Corollarien.* Berlin: Duncker und Humblot, 1963.

Smith, Daniel W. "Deleuze and Derrida, Immanence and Transcendence: Two Directions in Recent French Thought." In *Between Deleuze and Derrida,* ed. Paul Patton and John Protevi. New York: Continuum, 2003.

Smith, James K. A. *Jacques Derrida: Live Theory.* New York: Continuum, 2005.

Staten, Henry. *Eros in Mourning: Homer to Lacan.* Baltimore: Johns Hopkins University Press, 1995.

———. *Wittgenstein and Derrida.* Lincoln: University of Nebraska Press, 1984.

Tocqueville, Alexis de. *Democracy in America.* Ed. P. Bradley. Trans. H. Reeve. New York: Vintage, 1990.

Ware, Owen. "Impossible Passions: Derrida and Negative Theology." *Philosophy Today* 49, no. 2 (summer 2005): 171–83.

Zahavi, Dan. *Self-Awareness and Alterity: A Phenomenological Investigation.* Evanston, IL: Northwestern University Press, 1999.

Zupančič, Alenka. *Ethics of the Real: Kant, Lacan.* London: Verso, 2000.

Index

Absolute immunity, 8–9, 30–32, 43, 118–19, 121, 123, 127, 129, 132, 145. See also unscathed

Absolutely other, 79–80, 85–87, 89–90, 93–94, 227n56. See also infinitely other, wholly other

Affirmation, 2, 33–35, 49, 96–97, 129–30, 139, 161, 164–66, 202, 204–5, 231–32n4

Agamben, Giorgio, 187, 234n29

Alterity/the other, 31, 43, 64, 74–76, 79–81, 84–100, 102–5, 110, 112, 115, 124–29, 144–45, 162, 165, 176, 184, 187, 219n11, 221n23

Apocalypse, 45–47

Apperception, 10, 23–24, 27, 58

Arche-writing, 49, 51–53, 71–73, 75, 143–44. See also différance, spacing, trace/trace structure of time

Aristotle, 14, 16, 112, 208n3

Atheism, 1–2, 8–9, 48–49, 111–12, 116–17, 119, 121, 130, 132, 136, 139, 142–43, 146, 151, 153–54, 163, 191, 197, 202–3, 205, 207n1, 208n12, 225n39, 227n61. See also logic of radical atheism

Augustine, 8, 107–9, 112–14, 146–48, 150, 153–54, 163

Autoaffection, 63, 65–67, 70–71, 73–74, 88, 108, 184, 210n52, 217n24. See also heteroaffection

Autoimmunity, 8–9, 13–15, 19, 30–32, 42, 48, 118–19, 127, 141, 160, 174, 177, 183, 195–96, 203, 205

Badiou, Alain, 187, 234n29

Beardsworth, Richard, 94, 170, 208–10n5, 231–32n4

Bennington, Geoffrey, 147, 152–55, 208n12, 208–10n5, 211–12n9, 220n14, 221n18

Bernasconi, Robert, 10, 76, 95–96, 98, 100, 212n,14m 220–21n17, 221n21

Bernet, Rudolf, 10, 52, 55, 67, 69, 215n3, n9, n12, 217n23, n27

Birnbaum, Daniel, 69

Blanchot, Maurice, 214n37

Brault, Pascale-Anne, 222n4

Brough, J. B., 215n6, n13, 216n18

Caputo, John, 116–17, 120–24, 127–28, 134–35, 140–41, 146, 213n21, 227n61

Chance/threat, 2, 31–33, 35–36, 39, 82, 84, 91, 121, 136, 140, 149, 158, 161, 164, 176, 177, 204. See also worst/best

Chora (*kh<mac>ora*), 226n50. See also spacing

Cobb-Stevens, Richard, 215n13, 216n18

Confession, 8, 11, 146, 148–49, 153.
Contamination, 35–37, 212n19, 219n11
Copjec, Joan, 192–93, 235n41–43
Cornell, Drucilla, 10, 76, 100, 212n14,
    220n17, 221n20
Critchley, Simon, 10, 76, 96–98, 101–2,
    186–87, 212n14, 213n28, 221n22–23,
    234n24

Death, 1–2, 14, 47–48, 107–8, 110–11,
    118–19, 129–31, 138, 147–52, 159–63,
    214n37, 229n73. See also fear of
    death, survival
"Death of God," 7–8, 208n12
Decision, 40–42, 81–83, 97, 105, 124–25,
    166, 181–85, 203–4. See also passive
    decision, undecidability
Democracy, 11, 13–14, 19, 171–77, 184,
    186–87, 190–91, 194–96, 200, 202,
    204–5, 211n9, 234–35n34
Derrida, Jacques, passim. Works
    by: Acts of Literature, 156, 210n8,
    229n69; Adieu to Emmanuel
    Levinas, 98–99, 219n6, 221n18,
    n22, 222n25; "The Animal That
    Therefore I am (More to Follow),"
    142, 145, 225n47, 227n57; "Aphorism
    Countertime," 229n72; Archive
    Fever, 141–42; Arguing with Derrida,
    113, 211n8, 222n6; "As If It Were
    Possible, 'Within Such Limits,'"
    121, 137, 222n26, 223n18, 225n41;
    A Taste for the Secret, 164, 225n32,
    229n71; "Autoimmunity: Real and
    Symbolic Suicides," 121–22, 208n2,
    223n17, n19, 232n9; "Avances." 138,
    224n28, 225n42; Béliers, 214n36; "A
    Certain Impossible Possibility of
    Saying the Event," 203–4, 225n43,
    236n65; Chaque fois unique, la fin
    du monde, 110–11, 214n36, 222n4,
    224n28, 225n39; Circumfession, 11,
    146–56, 159–61; "Confessions and
    'Circumfession': A Roundtable with
    Jacques Derrida," 227n61; "'Dead

Man Running': Salut, Salut," 128–29,
    224n28, n29; Demeure, 214n37,
    228n64, n65, n66; "Dialanguages,"
    156–59, 229n70; Dissemination, 51,
    220n14; Edmund Husserl's Origin of
    Geometry, 215n1, 216n6; "Et Cetera,"
    212n16; "Faith and Knowledge," 8,
    85, 100–1, 120–21, 127, 136, 143–44,
    224n28, 225n37, 226n50; "Force of
    Law," 41–42, 111, 169, 213n29, 214n30,
    221n23, 230n2, 231n3, 233n17; For
    What Tomorrow . . . , 183, 208n14,
    210n8, 222n26, 233n14–15, n21;
    The Gift of Death, 94–95, 213n27;
    Given Time, 36–39, 213n24; H.
    C. for Life, 224n28; "Hospitaliy,
    Justice, and Responsibility," 224n26;
    "Hostipitality," 36, 212n19, 222n26;
    "How to Avoid Speaking: Denials,"
    4, 207n4, 225n48; "How to Name,"
    130–32, 224n28, 224n30; "Language
    Is Never Owned," 225n39; Learning
    to Live Finally, 33–34, 212n15,
    229n73; Le problème de la genèse
    dans la philosophie de Husserl,
    215n1, n10; Limited Inc, 177–78,
    218n,5, n6; Margins of Philosophy,
    3, 17–18, 210n7, 215n1; Mémoires
    for Paul de Man, 50, 107–10, 138,
    161–63, 212n17, 219n10, 222n2,
    225n44, 228–29n61; Memoirs of the
    Blind, 224n26; Monolingualism of
    the Other, 224n28; "Nietzsche and
    the Machine," 35–36, 136, 212n18,
    225n38, n43; "No Apocalypse, Not
    Now," 46–47; Of Grammatology,
    4, 26–30, 75, 80–81, 208n12, n14,
    215n1, 216n21, 217n31, 218n33, n1; Of
    Hospitality, 103–4, 219n6, 221n24,
    222n25; "On a Newly Arisen
    Apocalyptic Tone in Philosophy,"
    46, 214n34; On Touching: Jean-Luc
    Nancy, 2, 9, 215n1, 224n28; The Other
    Heading, 137, 225n40; "'Others Are
    Secret Because They Are Other',"

144, 226n53; "Ousia and Grammè,"
16, 18, 20, 209–10n5; "Perhaps or
Maybe." 125–26, 224n25, 229–30n73;
Points . . . Interviews 1974–1994,
219n11; "Politics and Friendship,"
231n4; *Politics of Friendship*, 89,
107, 112, 114–116, 122, 126, 136, 142,
178–82, 184, 208n2, 221n22, 233n17;
Positions, 218n34; *The Post Card*, 156;
"Remarks on Deconstruction and
Pragmatism," 233n18; *Resistances
of Psychoanalysis*, 25; "Response
to Catherine Malabou," 227n61,
228n62, n64; "The Rhetoric of
Drugs," 233–34n21; *Rogues*, 13, 15,
24–25, 29–31, 104–5, 121, 126–28,
142, 172–77, 182–85, 195–96, 207n2,
208n1, n2, 211n8, 212n10, n13, 213n22,
218n34, 223n17, 232n5, n13, 233n15,
n16, n17, 236n64; *Sauf le Nom*, 4,
124, 143–44, 207n4; "Schibboleth:
For Paul Celan," 229n68; *Specters
of Marx*, 14, 43, 77–78, 82, 84,
101–3, 123, 132–141, 166–69, 207n1,
208n14, 214n31, 223n20, 225n36,
230n1; *Speech and Phenomena*, 8, 15,
71–72, 208n11, 210n5, 214n1, 215n10,
216n16, n20, n21, 217n30, 218n34;
"Ulysses Gramophone," 35–36,
212n17; "Violence and Metaphysics,"
76, 83–87, 90, 92–95, 215n1, 218n32,
219n9, 220n15; *Without Alibi*, 233n15;
The Work of Mourning, 110–11, 222n4,
230n75; *Writing and Difference*, 6,
19–20, 48, 73, 76, 80, 207n4, 208n10,
n12, 215n1, 218n32, 219n7, 225n48,
226n53
Descartes, Rene, 86–87, 95
Desire, 1–2, 9, 11, 28, 30, 32–34, 37–39,
43, 48, 104, 107–23, 126, 128–30, 132,
136, 139–41, 146–48, 150–52, 155–60,
162–65, 169–71, 191–205
Destructibility, 47, 111, 162, 196
Detachment, 117–19
De Vries, Hent, 143–45, 226n54,
226–27n56

Diachrony, 91–92
Dictatorship, 117
Différance, 2–4, 16–19, 25–28, 38, 67,
70, 93, 95, 144, 177–78, 208n12,
210–11n8, 217n30, 218n1, 220n14,
225n48. See also arche-writing,
infinite finitude, spacing, trace/trace
structure of time
Discrimination, 78, 82, 84, 88, 94–95,
98–99, 101, 105, 123, 140, 166, 175,
204
Disjointure, 77–78, 82, 102, 105, 214n31
Double bind, 14, 32, 34, 79, 107–8, 110,
115, 121–22, 136, 149, 158–59, 161

Eckhart, Meister, 117–19, 223n13–14
Economy, 37–39, 48
Economy of violence, 82–84, 170–71,
174, 176, 183
Emancipation, 11, 78, 190, 200–1, 204
End of the world, 45–47, 110–11,
214n36, 225n39
Equality, 172–77, 189, 196
Eschatology, 120, 134
Essential corruptibility, 81, 85, 97,
105–6, 177, 179, 184–85, 202–4,
218n6, 233n21
Ethics/the ethical, 10, 31, 75–77, 79–82,
84–85, 88–90, 94, 96–105, 126,
133, 165, 183–87, 222n25. See also
nonethical opening of ethics
Event, 16–17, 29–31, 40–42, 45–46,
72, 97, 105, 123, 125–27, 153–55, 158,
183–84
Extended presence, 60–61

Faith, 120, 126–27
Fear of death, 2, 34, 91, 107, 114, 122,
149–51, 159, 165
Fenves, Peter, 214n34
Finitude, 1–4, 19–21, 30–34, 36, 41,
46–47, 73, 86, 92–95, 110–11, 118–19,
140–45, 159, 161–62, 164–66, 168,
197, 202, 208n12, 220n14. See also
mortality

Freedom, 172–74, 176, 194, 196–97, 201
Friendship, 40, 89, 107–10, 112, 114–16, 125–26, 163, 179–81
Fritsch, Matthias, 231–32n4

Gallagher, Shaun, 226n15
Gasché, Rodolphe, 67, 144, 216n21, 220n15, 226n51
Genesis, 142–43
Gilgen, Peter, 226n56
God, 1, 3–8, 11, 20–22, 28, 30, 48, 79–80, 85, 87, 92, 93, 99, 108–9, 111–14, 117–24, 128, 136, 140, 142–48, 150–51, 153–55, 163, 218n2, 227n6
Good and evil, 8–9, 43–44, 104, 112–16, 119, 124–28, 203–4. See also radical evil
Good beyond being, 79, 84–86, 88, 92, 95, 133
Gift, 36–39, 120–23

Hauntology, 82, 84, 140. See also spectrality
Hägglund, Martin, 222n3, 229n68
Hardt, Michael, 187, 234n29
Hart, Kevin, 4–6, 207n5–6
Hegel, G.W.F., 92–93, 209n5, 219n13–15
Heidegger, Martin, 144–45, 218n1
Henrich, Dieter, 66, 216n19
Henry, Michel, 66, 216n19–20
Heteroaffection, 66–67, 71, 74–75, 184
History/historicity, 27–28, 86–87, 95
Horizon, 201
Hospitality, 19, 36, 39, 101, 103–6, 126, 222n25, 231–32n4
Husserl, Edmund, 10, 15, 18–19, 25, 52–75
Hyperpolitical, 181–84, 187, 202–3, 233n18

"I love you," 114–15
Immortality, 1–2, 7–8, 21, 28, 30, 33–34, 43–44, 48–49, 111, 120, 130–31, 136, 138, 147, 151, 163, 213n27, 214n37

Impossibility/possibility, impossible/possible, 18, 25, 37–38, 81, 90, 94, 120–23, 140–41, 158, 162, 169, 171, 195, 199, 212n9, 213n27, 227–28n61
Infinite finitude, 3–4, 46, 93, 95, 97, 110, 131, 143–45, 168, 220n14–15, 225n48, 227n56
Infinite justice, 168–69
Infinite perfectibility, 169, 195
Infinite regress, 23, 25, 56–58, 62, 67–69, 216n19, 217n24
Infinite responsibility, 94–95, 168
Infinitely other, 93–94, 110. See also absolutely other, wholly other
Infinity, 3–4, 44–46, 49, 86–87, 92–95, 133, 143, 166–69, 195, 220n14–15. See also infinite finitude
Inheritance, 12

James, William, 61–63
Jennings, T. W., 223n8
Justice, 19, 39–43, 77–78, 82–84, 101–2, 105–6, 120–24, 138–42, 166–70, 182–83, 194, 198, 203–4. See also law

Kant, Immanuel, 10, 19–30, 38, 40, 43–45, 47–48, 58, 93, 112–13, 195–96, 211–12n9. See also Kantian Idea/regulative Idea, transcendental aesthetic, transcendental dialectic
Kantian Idea/regulative Idea, 10, 19, 30, 37–40, 43, 48, 101, 112, 169, 195–96, 211–12n9, 221n24
Kearney, Richard, 11, 123–25, 127–28, Kingdom of God, 120–23, 140, 223–24n21
Kirby, Vicki, 221n20
Krell, David Farrell, 227n60

Lacan, Jacques, 11, 192–93
Lack, 1, 9, 32, 34, 37, 48, 126, 132, 156–58, 164, 169, 191–95, 197, 201, 208
Laclau, Ernesto, 11, 184–205

Law, 40–42, 83, 101, 123, 141, 172, 174, 182–83. See also justice
Lawlor, Leonard, 216n17
Levinas, Emmanuel, 10, 76–102, 133, 186, 226–27n56
Lesser violence, 82–84, 170–71, 231–32n4
Life, 1–2, 8–9, 14, 18–19, 27–30, 33–36, 39, 43, 46–49, 73, 79, 107–10, 114, 120–23, 129–31, 140–42, 154–56, 159–61, 164–65, 175, 195, 204, 210–11n8. See also survival
Llewelyn, John, 224–25n31
Logic of deconstruction, 4–5, 9–10, 15, 29–30, 43, 46, 77–79, 93, 99–101, 118, 171, 203, 212n9, 231–32n4. See also essential corruptibility, impossibility/possibility
Logic of noncontradiction, 14–18, 20–22, 24–25, 29–30, 52, 70, 72, 210n8
Logic of radical atheism, 1–2, 10–12, 112, 116, 136, 202–3, 205, 208n12
Love of ruins, 111

Marion, Jean-Luc, 5–8, 207–8n7–9
Merleau-Ponty, Maurice, 61, 217n24
Messianic, 120, 132–39, 224–25n31
Metaphysics of presence, 5–6, 20, 54–55, 57, 59, 67, 81, 127, 209n5
Mortality, 1–2, 7–8, 32–34, 39, 48, 91, 107–12, 114–15, 129–30, 138, 145, 147, 150–51, 160, 162–63, 212n27, 229n73. See also finitude
Mouffe, Chantal, 188–89
Mourning, 47, 107–12, 121–22, 148–51, 161–63

Naas, Michael, 222n4
Narcissism, 155, 219n11
Negative theology, 3–8, 116–120, 143, 145
Negotiation, 100–1, 103, 105, 171, 177, 202–3
Negri, Antonio, 187, 234n29

Nonethical opening of ethics, 75, 85, 88, 97, 99, 102, 105, 222n25
Normativity, 31, 83, 104–5, 171, 184, 196, 203, 231–32n4. See also prescription

Omniscience, 153–55
Openness to the other, 31, 43, 105, 187, 231–32n4
Origin of the world, 111. See also end of the world

Peace, 43, 75–76, 78, 81–82, 84, 86, 92, 99–100, 106, 132–36, 140–41, 147, 170, 174
Perjury, 99–100, 127, 154, 204
Phenomenological reduction, 53–54
Politics/the political, 11, 78, 83–84, 96–102, 105, 171–72, 177–82, 184–88, 190, 199, 202–5. See also hyperpolitical, ultrapolitical
Passive decision, 184, 233n17
Plato, 51, 79, 86, 95
Plotinus, 79
Prescription, 31, 82, 90, 105, 203. See also normativity
Promise, 40, 97, 132–39, 205
Protention, 60–61, 65, 70–71, 73, 217n31
Pseudo-Dionysius, 4–7, 119, 144–45

Quasitranscendental, 211n8. See also ultratranscendental

"Radical," 207n1
Radical evil, 112–16, 119, 125–27. See also good and evil
Rayment-Pickard, Hugh, 223n8
Reason, 10, 22, 24–26, 43, 166, 185, 233–34n21. See also logic of deconstruction, logic of noncontradiction
Renvoi (spatial and temporal), 174–77
Re-presentation (*Vergegenwärtigung*), 64–66, 68, 71, 74–75, 216n17
Responsibility, 88–89, 94–95, 101, 106, 165–68, 183, 233n21.

Resurrection, 225n39. See also salvation
Retention, 60–63, 65–68, 70–71, 73,
    217n31
Ricoeur, Paul, 10, 52, 61, 215n12–13,
    216n18
Robbins, Jill, 221n17
Rorty, Richard, 187, 234n29
Royle, Nicholas, 229n72

Salut, 128–32, 136. See also resurrection,
    salvation
Salvation, 128–32, 136, 213n27. See also
    resurrection
Schmitt, Carl, 178–83
Self-awareness, 63, 65, 67, 70–71, 73
Shakespeare, William, 77
Sincerity, 80–81
Smith, Daniel W., 211n9
Smith, James K.A., 223n8
Sovereignty, 5, 20, 24–25, 29–30, 142,
    177, 180–84, 188–89, 191, 202–3
Spacing (becoming-space of time and
    becoming-time of space), 2–3, 6, 10,
    18–19, 25, 27–29, 35, 38, 69, 71–73,
    75, 80, 84–85, 88, 115, 121, 143–44,
    172, 174–77, 209–10n5, 211n8,
    217n30, 226n50, 236n64. See also
    arche-writing, différance, trace/trace
    structure of time
Spectrality, 82, 140, 179. See also
    hauntology
Staten, Henry, 212–13n19, 215n1, 222n3
Succession, 1, 16, 18, 22–23, 26, 44, 56,
    58, 62, 69, 109, 158, 209–10n5
Suicide, 165
Survival, 1–2, 11, 34, 39, 46–49, 108,
    111, 121–22, 129–31, 136–42, 145–46,
    148–52, 155–56, 159–60, 162–68, 170,
    197, 202, 204–5
Synthesis, 10, 17–18, 22–24, 26–27, 56,
    58, 71, 73, 210n6, 212n11. See also
    trace/trace structure of time

Testimony, 154–55

Time/temporality, 1–3, 10, 14–49, 52–75,
    78–79, 82, 86, 88, 91–93, 102–6,
    108–9, 114–15, 117–18, 121–23, 126–45,
    153–60, 164–72, 174–75, 177, 183–87,
    195, 202–5, 209–10n5
Time-consciousness, 10, 17, 22–23,
    26–27, 55–57, 61–75
Totality, 30, 86–87, 93, 95, 99
Totalitarianism, 13, 190, 198, 202
Transcendental aesthetic, 10, 24–28
Transcendental dialectic, 10, 24–25,
    29–30, 38
Trace/trace structure of time, 1–2, 4,
    9, 18–19, 27–28, 30, 46–47, 49, 51,
    66, 71–73, 79–80, 88, 91–92, 96, 129,
    141, 143–44, 152, 156, 160, 164, 167,
    177, 209n5, 210–11n8, 217n30, 228n1,
    225n48, 227n56. See also arche-
    writing, différance, infinite finitude,
    spacing
Ultratranscendental, 10, 19, 26–29,
    31–32, 38, 46, 73, 211n8, 220n15

Ultrapolitical, 182. See also
    hyperpolitical
Unconditional/the unconditional, 2, 10,
    19, 25, 29–30, 33–34, 38–40, 42–43,
    48–49, 97, 101, 103–5, 124, 129, 139,
    164–65, 183–84, 202, 204, 211n8,
    231–32n4
Undecidability/undecidable, 39–40–42,
    77, 81, 83–84, 88, 90, 96–97, 102–3,
    105–6, 114–15, 125, 127, 132, 134, 136,
    142, 165–66, 171–72, 176, 182–83,
    185–87, 190–91, 195, 203–4, 222n25,
    231n3, 232n4. See also decision,
    passive decision
Undeconstructible, 40, 42, 105, 123,
    143–44, 214n31, 226n54.
Unscathed, 8–9, 127–28, 162, 165, 203.
    See also absolute immunity

Violence, 10–11, 32, 40, 42–43, 75–78, 81–86, 88–91, 95–97, 99–101, 104–6, 116, 123, 135, 141–42, 162, 165–66, 170–71, 174–77, 182–83, 190, 196, 201, 203–5, 219n11, 231–32n4. See also lesser violence

Ware, Owen, 223n8

Worst/best, 9, 32–33, 36, 46, 99, 118–19, 123, 128, 140. See also chance/threat
Wholly other, 87, 94, 144–45. See also absolutely other, infinitely other

Zahavi, Dan, 10, 52, 55, 60–61, 68–70, 215n3, n13, 216n18, 217n26, n29
Zupancic, Alenka, 235n41, n43

MERIDIAN

Crossing Aesthetics

Cornelia Vismann, *Files: Law and Media Technology*

Anne-Lise François, *Open Secrets: The Literature of Uncounted Experience*

Jean-Luc Nancy, *The Discourse of the Syncope: Logodaedalus*

Carol Jacobs, *Skirting the Ethical: Sophocles, Plato, Hamann, Sebald, Campion*

Cornelius Castoriadis, *Figures of the Thinkable*

Jacques Derrida, *Psyche: Inventions of the Other*, 2 volumes, edited by Peggy Kamuf and Elizabeth Rottenberg

Mark Sanders, *Ambiguities of Witnessing: Literature and Law in the Time of a Truth Commission*

Sarah Kofman, *The Sarah Kofman Reader*, edited by Thomas Albrecht, with Georgia Albert and Elizabeth Rottenberg

Hannah Arendt, *Reflections on Literature and Culture*, edited by Susannah Young-ah Gottlieb

Alan Bass, *Interpretation and Difference: The Strangeness of Care*

Jacques Derrida, *H. C. for Life, That Is to Say . . .*

Ernst Bloch, *Traces*

Elizabeth Rottenberg, *Inheriting the Future: Legacies of Kant, Freud, and Flaubert*

David Michael Kleinberg-Levin, *Gestures of Ethical Life*

Jacques Derrida, *On Touching—Jean-Luc Nancy*

Jacques Derrida, *Rogues: Two Essays on Reason*

Peggy Kamuf, *Book of Addresses*

Giorgio Agamben, *The Time that Remains: A Commentary on the Letter to the Romans*

Jean-Luc Nancy, *Multiple Arts: The Muses II*

Alain Badiou, *Handbook of Inaesthetics*

Jacques Derrida, *Eyes of the University: Right to Philosophy 2*

Maurice Blanchot, *Lautréamont and Sade*

Giorgio Agamben, *The Open: Man and Animal*

Jean Genet, *The Declared Enemy*

Shosana Felman, *Writing and Madness: (Literature/Philosophy/Psychoanalysis)*

Jean Genet, *Fragments of the Artwork*

Shoshana Felman, *The Scandal of the Speaking Body: Don Juan with J. L. Austin, or Seduction in Two Languages*

Peter Szondi, *Celan Studies*

Neil Hertz, *George Eliot's Pulse*

Maurice Blanchot, *The Book to Come*

Susannah Young-ah Gottlieb, *Regions of Sorrow: Anxiety and Messianism in Hannah Arendt and W. H. Auden*

Jacques Derrida, *Without Alibi*, edited by Peggy Kamuf

Cornelius Castoriadis, *On Plato's 'Statesman'*

Jacques Derrida, *Who's Afraid of Philosophy? Right to Philosophy 1*

Peter Szondi, *An Essay on the Tragic*

Peter Fenves, *Arresting Language: From Leibniz to Benjamin*

Jill Robbins, ed. *Is It Righteous to Be? Interviews with Emmanuel Levinas*

Louis Marin, *Of Representation*

Daniel Payot, *The Architect and the Philosopher*

J. Hillis Miller, *Speech Acts in Literature*

Maurice Blanchot, *Faux pas*

Jean-Luc Nancy, *Being Singular Plural*

Maurice Blanchot / Jacques Derrida, *The Instant of My Death / Demeure:
    Fiction and Testimony*

Niklas Luhmann, *Art as a Social System*

Emmanual Levinas, *God, Death, and Time*

Ernst Bloch, *The Spirit of Utopia*

Giorgio Agamben, *Potentialities: Collected Essays in Philosophy*

Ellen S. Burt, *Poetry's Appeal: French Nineteenth-Century Lyric and the Political
    Space*

Jacques Derrida, *Adieu to Emmanuel Levinas*

Werner Hamacher, *Premises: Essays on Philosophy and Literature
    from Kant to Celan*

Aris Fioretos, *The Gray Book*

Deborah Esch, *In the Event: Reading Journalism, Reading Theory*

Winfried Menninghaus, *In Praise of Nonsense: Kant and Bluebeard*

Giorgio Agamben, *The Man Without Content*

Giorgio Agamben, *The End of the Poem: Studies in Poetics*

Theodor W. Adorno, *Sound Figures*

Louis Marin, *Sublime Poussin*

Philippe Lacoue-Labarthe, *Poetry as Experience*

Ernst Bloch, *Literary Essays*

Jacques Derrida, *Resistances of Psychoanalysis*

Marc Froment-Meurice, *That Is to Say: Heidegger's Poetics*

Francis Ponge, *Soap*

Philippe Lacoue-Labarthe, *Typography: Mimesis, Philosophy, Politics*

Giorgio Agamben, *Homo Sacer: Sovereign Power and Bare Life*

Emmanuel Levinas, *Of God Who Comes to Mind*

Bernard Stiegler, *Technics and Time, 1: The Fault of Epimetheus*

Werner Hamacher, *pleroma—Reading in Hegel*

Serge Leclaire, *Psychoanalyzing: On the Order of the Unconscious and the Practice of the Letter*

Serge Leclaire, *A Child Is Being Killed: On Primary Narcissism and the Death Drive*

Sigmund Freud, *Writings on Art and Literature*

Cornelius Castoriadis, *World in Fragments: Writings on Politics, Society, Psychoanalysis, and the Imagination*

Thomas Keenan, *Fables of Responsibility: Aberrations and Predicaments in Ethics and Politics*

Emmanuel Levinas, *Proper Names*

Alexander García Düttmann, *At Odds with AIDS: Thinking and Talking About a Virus*

Maurice Blanchot, *Friendship*

Jean-Luc Nancy, *The Muses*

Massimo Cacciari, *Posthumous People: Vienna at the Turning Point*

David E. Wellbery, *The Specular Moment: Goethe's Early Lyric and the Beginnings of Romanticism*

Edmond Jabès, *The Little Book of Unsuspected Subversion*

Hans-Jost Frey, *Studies in Poetic Discourse: Mallarmé, Baudelaire, Rimbaud, Hölderlin*

Pierre Bourdieu, *The Rules of Art: Genesis and Structure of the Literary Field*

Nicolas Abraham, *Rhythms: On the Work, Translation, and Psychoanalysis*

Jacques Derrida, *On the Name*

David Wills, *Prosthesis*

Maurice Blanchot, *The Work of Fire*

Jacques Derrida, *Points . . . : Interviews, 1974–1994*

J. Hillis Miller, *Topographies*

Philippe Lacoue-Labarthe, *Musica Ficta (Figures of Wagner)*

Jacques Derrida, *Aporias*

Emmanuel Levinas, *Outside the Subject*

Jean-François Lyotard, *Lessons on the Analytic of the Sublime*

Peter Fenves, *"Chatter": Language and History in Kierkegaard*

Jean-Luc Nancy, *The Experience of Freedom*

Jean-Joseph Goux, *Oedipus, Philosopher*

Haun Saussy, *The Problem of a Chinese Aesthetic*

Jean-Luc Nancy, *The Birth to Presence*